Financial Systems and Economic Crises

Sebastian-Ilie Dragoe and Camelia Oprean-Stan

# Financial Systems and Economic Crises

## The Main Determinants of Financial Instability

PETER LANG

**Bibliographic Information published by the Deutsche Nationalbibliothek**

The Deutsche Nationalbibliothek lists this publication in the Deutsche Nationalbibliografie; detailed bibliographic data is available online at http://dnb.d-nb.de.

**Library of Congress Cataloging-in-Publication Data**

A CIP catalog record for this book has been applied for at the Library of Congress.

ISBN 978-3-631-87694-7 (Print)
E-ISBN 978-3-631-87947-4 (E-PDF)
E-ISBN 978-3-631-87948-1 (EPUB)
10.3726/b19738



Peter Lang – Berlin · Bruxelles · Lausanne · New York · Oxford



This publication has been peer reviewed.

www.peterlang.com

# Preface

Rational expectations, maximizing utility, "cleaning up" markets, and equilibrium are all concepts and models in current macroeconomics. The equilibrium idea has always won out over leverage, giving the impression that major disruptive events can't happen or that when they do they can be rapidly controlled to restore normalcy. Because of this belief, economists assume that no matter how far the economy deviates from normal, it will always return to equilibrium, either with intervention (Keynesian) or without intervention (libertarians). The equilibrium framework will always understate the hazards, focusing instead on achieving a specific ideal growth rate while neglecting the process and the debt that was/will be generated to achieve it.

According to the rational anticipations theory, economic agents form expectations about the future evolution of prices as a result of their unpredictable evolution and, thus, any systematic state intervention in the economy is irrelevant because economic agents will predict both the evolution of prices and possible government policies and so fiscal and monetary policies will only have an impact on prices and not on economic growth or employment. The rational expectations hypothesis further states that market players use data appropriately, are familiar with economic theory literature, and do not commit systematic errors.

The condition of macroeconomics has deteriorated in the past seven decades, and most macroeconomic models ignore debt levels and flows. What's more, prior to the Great Recession, all macroeconomists explained economics solely by observing trends. There were no significant deviations from the expected trend. The authors of this book believe that in addition to exception of wars and pandemics, finance is another source of crises; furthermore, especially when the economy's sensitivity to the financial system is reduced, there will be only modest negative economic growth but no true recessions as defined by the National Bureau of Economic Research.

Even if entrepreneurs have all the information and can accurately forecast future events, they will not hide from the repercussions of credit growth but will take advantage of the opportunity to profit from freshly created money (Huerta de Soto, 2006). Only under post-Keynesian and Austrian theories are businessmen duped by bankers' joy.

Furthermore, there are no banks or money production in macroeconomic models; instead, there is just an intermediation from agents with a low propensity for consumption or impatience to those with a larger propensity for consumption or patience. Only in the event of a liquidity trap does debt become significant. When you exclude the foreign investment or foreign debt component and look at the world as a whole, the overall level of debt has no bearing on aggregate net value – one person's obligation is another person's asset. As a result, debt level only matters if debt distribution matters and if highly indebted players face different restrictions than players with little debt (Krugman & Eggertsson, 2011). The misperception of Paul Krugman and other orthodox economists is that commercial banks do not function as intermediate financial resources; rather, banks produce money, implying more purchasing power. Even more crucial is the debt level, given the high debt service ratio, which places a severe load on the economy, as well as the fact that in a fragile financial climate, tiny changes can generate large impulses and an economy does not require powerful shocks to enter a recession.

What was particularly similar between the post–Great Depression and the post–Great Recession periods was that both were preceded by large accumulations of debt and greater debt deleverage. In this context, nevertheless, the debt-deflation theory proposed by Fisher (1933) was not understood by the academic environment. Fisher's idea was less influential in academic circles because of the counterargument that deflation by debt represents only a redistribution of money from one group (borrowers) to another (creditors). Pure redistributions, it has been proposed, should not have major macroeconomic consequences in the absence of uncomfortably big variations in marginal propensities for consumption between groups (Bernanke, 2000, p. 24). Whereas Bernanke does not agree with these intellectuals who believe that debt-induced deflation is merely a transfer of wealth, he also misunderstands Fisher's thesis since he sees debt not as the source of crises but, rather, as a means of propagation. Random shocks, according to him and other macroeconomists, generate recessions by preventing enterprises and families from borrowing or refinancing due to the loss of collateral.

In the current state of stagnation (secular stagnation), academics, economic decision-makers, and economic agents' knowledge of the importance of the finance sector has become a prerequisite for the implementation of long-term economic and monetary policies. The aim to provide solutions enabling the creation of cohesive policies in order to create long-term prosperity is thus the motive of the authors for adopting the topic addressed.

This book explains the various aspects of the main determinants of financial instability that are less discussed and clarified in specialized literature as well as emphasizes that the financial system is the source of the crisis and not just a means of propagating it as most mainstream economists claim.

# Table of Contents

# List of Abbreviations

| | |
|---|---|
| 10Y-2Y | 10 years Treasury rates constant maturity – 2-year Treasury rates |
| 10Y-3M | 10 years Treasury rates constant maturity – 3 months Treasury rates |
| 10Y-3MO | 10 years Treasury rates constant maturity – 3 months Treasury rates |
| 2Y-FF | 2 years Treasury rates – Federal Funds rate |
| AAA_FF | Seasoned AAA Corporate Bond Yield – Fed Funds |
| ADF | Augmented Dickey-Fuller |
| ADS Index | Aruoba–Diebold–Scotti Index |
| AIC | Akaike criterion |
| BEA | Bureau of Economic Analysis |
| CFNAI | Chicago Fed National Activity Index |
| COMMERCIAL_PAPER_BR | Commercial paper minus bill rate spread |
| GS5_FF | 5 years Treasury rates constant maturity – Federal Funds rate |
| GS7_FF | 7 years Treasury rates constant maturity – Federal Funds rate |
| GSEs | Government-sponsored enterprises |
| HOUSING_STARTS | Privately owned housing starts: 1-unit structures |
| HQC | Hannan–Quinn criterion |
| IMF | International Monetary Fund |
| LASSO | Least absolute shrinkage and selection operator |
| M0 | Monetary base |
| MAD | Mean absolute deviation |
| MARGIN_DEBIT | Margin debit change in report to the average of the last 12 months |
| MONTHLY_SUPPLY_H | Monthly supply of houses |
| MORTGAGE30US_F | 30-year fixed-rate mortgage average – Federal Funds rate |
| NBER | National Bureau of Economic Research |
| PCE | Price consumer expenditure |

| | |
|---|---|
| PERMITS | Private housing units authorized by building permits |
| PMI_50 | Purchase Managers' Index |
| ROW | Rest of the world |
| S10Y_3M | 10 years Treasury rates constant maturity – 3 months Treasury rates |
| S10Y_FF | 10 years Treasury rates constant maturity – Federal Funds rate |
| SIC | Schwartz criterion |
| SPV | Special purpose vehicle |
| SSRr | Restricted sum of squared residuals |
| SSRu | Unrestricted sum of squared residuals |
| STD | Standard deviation |
| U.S. | United States |
| VaR | Value-at-risk |
| VAR | Vector autoregression |
| ZLB | Zero lower bound |

# Introduction

The major goal of this book is to show that all economic crises (except those caused by pandemics, wars, and supply shocks) originate from negative fluctuations and disturbances in the finance sector. Such a view is crucial not just for understanding the role of finance in the economic cycle but also for predicting recessions. The Holy Grail of macroeconomics has always been the recession forecasting. The ability to predict recession is crucial not only for governments and the financial industry (more specifically, central banks) to ensure employment and quality of life but also for investors to hedge their investments and large businesses to adapt their production and inventories.

In order to achieve the main goal, the following secondary objectives were set: examination and testing of the financial-monetary economy's fundamentals; a series of econometric research to demonstrate the significance of money and finance in the actual economy; from a historical perspective, examining the impact of the financial system on economic crises; constructing an argument against equilibrium theory; studying the most important recession predictors and demonstrating that almost all recessions have financial foundations; a study of the primary causes of financial instability; investigate possible methods for guaranteeing financial stability and a resilient financial system; presenting an econometric model for predicting recessions based mostly on financial data and demonstrating that such a model may have predicted the Great Recession; after the Great Recession, predicting the next recession in the United States; an examination of Romania's recession lag; and an examination of how the Coronavirus recession differs from other recessions.

This study tests hypotheses and applies analytical tools and procedures that are often employed in the study of the financial-monetary economy and financial instability. Several econometric research and analyses have been conducted that show the importance of money and finance in the actual economy. Secondary data could be obtained in databases released by important organizations such as the World Bank, the International Monetary Fund, the National Bureau of Economic Research, Eurostat, and the Bureau of Economic Analysis, among others. They are analyzed with well-known econometric tools and used in the financial area, such as EViews. The findings of this research are provided in the book as studies, analyses, and recommendations and are summarized in the major chapter conclusions.

The book can give academics and policymakers important and practical insights since the presumed impact of this study on literature and practice is underscored by the following key original contributions and results which demonstrate that, because negative shifts in the financial system precede recessions, financial variables can report a crisis much earlier than real variables, as early as two months before a potential crisis; that financial variables can better predict recessions and industrial performance indicators can better predict negative GDP fluctuations; and that is possible indeed to develop a model that can predict recessions and negative GDP fluctuations.

There are a few terms and phrases that will be used more frequently in this study and are explained in the sections that follow.

The nonfinancial sector is referred to as the "real economy." For example, the phrase "credit for the real economy" actually means "credit to nonfinancial sectors" (e.g., households, businesses, and government).

The entire value of final products and services generated at the national level over a period of time (typically quarterly or annually) is reflected in the gross domestic product (GDP).

The nominal GDP is adjusted with the GDP deflator to produce real GDP. Economic growth is measured in terms of real GDP.

Potential GDP reflects the economy's productive capacity by reflecting the "full employment" GDP, which is the amount of GDP that can be achieved when the economy uses a high resource rate and follows a stable inflation path. A mix of factor inputs – labor, capital, and total factor productivity – is used to calculate potential GDP (Moisa, Necula, & Bobeica, 2010). To begin with, GDP is regressed on labor and capital with constant substitution elasticity. The Solow residual is the resultant residual, which is supposed to reflect technical developments. To extract the technical trends, the residual is filtered. After that, the efficiency-level trend is incorporated into the regression. This tool is used by policymakers to assess output gaps and evaluate which instruments can be utilized and to what extent, in order to bring actual GDP closer to potential GDP.

The liquidity trap defined by Krugman is a situation in which monetary policy loses control because the nominal interest rate is 0 or near-0% and monetary policy is unable to encourage investment and consumption since cash and bonds are perfect substitutes (Krugman, 1998).

"Sick recoveries that die in their infancy" and "depressions that feed on themselves and leave a hard and seemingly immovable core of unemployment" are described as "secular stagnation" (Hansen, 1939). He attributed this to the aging population, technological development, and a lack of demand.

# 1 The Radiography of the Financial System, with a Focus on the United States

**Abstract:** This chapter discusses how the financial system works, what the Federal Reserve's key tools are, how it can influence monetary aggregates, and how finance affects real GDP. It focuses on presenting an overview of the current U.S. financial system and its evolution since 1959 (the start of Federal Reserve database for monetary aggregates). The first subchapter presents general aspects of the financial system. The second subchapter presents a discussion on the series of empirical tests conducted to get a clear view of the relationships involving economic activity and financial variables. But before that, the focus of the research is on the most relevant coordinates of the financial-monetary economy. Also provided at the end of the second subchapter is an argument against the long-run neutrality and superneutrality which uses Austrian theory arguments, correlations between money supply, monetary base and GDP deflator, and calculations of money elasticity of real output. In the next subchapter, we provide an analysis of the developments in the U.S. financial system. There are proxies created to assess credit stock that flows into GDP, and not into speculations, and which test the stability of velocities in order to find out whether Fed can target nominal GDP with credit aggregates. The malleability of the banking system in the United States is tested using a time-series model predictive of the interconnectedness of the various entities operating in the financial system and checking how both banks and nonbanks respond to shocks in monetary policy. It is also investigated whether Federal Reserve had a bigger role than supply chain innovations in determining the Great Moderation. The last part of the subchapter analyzes the dynamic lead-lag patterns between short- and long-term interest rates. The findings could help us understand why inverted yield curve occurs since it is believed that long-term interest rates may be affected by short-term interest rates in normal times.

**Keywords:** financial system, financial-monetary economy, monetary base, money multiplier theory

## 1.1. The different aspects of the financial system in general

The financial system includes loan and depository markets (banks), as well as money, bond, stock, mortgage, foreign exchange, derivative, and crypto asset markets.

The purpose of money market is to invest excess cash and earn a higher rate of return than retaining funds in cash or in a bank current account. The money market instruments are: treasury bills, repurchase agreements, commercial paper, banker's acceptances, certificates of deposit, and eurodollars. The mortgage market is a market for long-term loans in which real estate is used as collateral. Because the sale of mortgages in secondary markets is difficult and the default risk is unknown, the United States developed a market for securitized mortgages.

As described by Directive (EU) 2018/843, the crypto assets market is made up of the demand and supply of virtual currencies. Cryptocurrencies function as electronic payment systems that allow parties to conduct transactions without the use of a financial intermediary. Miners are rewarded with newly minted crypto assets for recording transactions.

National financial systems are frequently divided into two types: banking-based financial systems and market-based financial systems. Romanian, German, and Japanese financial systems are more inclined toward bank funding, whereas the United States and United Kingdom are more market-oriented. The bank-based system is built on relationships and collateral, whereas market financing is based on faith in contracts (Ergungor, 2004). According to Rajan and Zingales (2001), the banking system is well-suited for manufacturing and market-based systems are more suited for technology-inclined businesses (particularly software) due to lack of collateral and considerable unpredictability. Banking systems are regarded as a superior choice for funding smaller businesses, whereas market systems are deemed as a better option for financing large and creative businesses. Furthermore, governments can have greater influence over capital allocation in banking systems. In terms of financial stability, bank-based systems are prone to runoffs due to poor loans, and market-based systems are also prone to risks arising from speculative bubbles.

Most macroeconomic models exclude banks and other intermediaries; indeed, most macroeconomists appear to model a barter economy. Except for cash payments and crypto asset transfers, which do not require a third party, all money exchanges involve three parties: a seller or receiver, a sender, and the bank/financial intermediary who transfers the number of units of account from the sender's account to the receiver/seller's. However, banks are more than just intermediaries and crisis propagators. Banks create money as well as more purchasing power. Banks desire profit, and their speculative activity can have a significant impact on the economy. The leverage of households and businesses is also critical because over-indebtedness can lead to economic crises without the presence of large shocks in advance. The most significant point is that money supply is endogenous and central banks have no influence over it. Monetary authorities can only influence the liquidity of banks. This was demonstrated by Paul Volcker's unsuccessful monetarist experiments, as well as the Bank of Japan's (BOJ) attempts to end deflation (the failed decades), when the growth rate of

M2 witnessed a decline despite increases in monetary base. Money facilitates exchanges, serves as a unit of account for pricing services and goods, and serves as a store of value.

To answer the question of whether crypto-assets are money, Minsky's straightforward judgment avers that "everyone can produce money; the problem is getting it accepted" (Minsky, 2011, p. 457) and that Bitcoin cannot be categorized as money due to its limited adoption. According to Directive (EU) 2018/843, "virtual currencies" are digital representations of value that are not warranted by a public entity but are recognized as a means of trade.

Monetary aggregates for the United States are the following:

1. M1 includes currency held outside the Federal Reserve, the United States Treasury, and the vaults of depository institutions; traveler's checks issued by nonbank issuers; demand deposits at commercial banks (excluding amounts held by the U.S. government, depository institutions, foreign banks, and official institutions); and other checkable deposits.
2. M2 consists of M1 plus savings deposits, time deposits without the individual retirement account (IRA), and Keogh balances at depository institutions, balances in retail money market mutual funds without the IRA, and Keogh balances at money market mutual funds. M2 will be used in our econometric analyses.

Monetary basis is another type of monetary aggregate. The monetary base is neither a component of M1 nor of M2. Total balances held at the Federal Reserve by depository institutions, currency in circulation, and total borrowings from the Fed comprise the monetary aggregate. This is one of the Fed's tools, the primary one being the Federal Funds rate.

The overnight interbank rate is represented by the Federal Funds rate. The market determines the effective Federal Funds rate, although the Fed guides it through open market operations (Fed acquisitions of governmental bonds will lead to growing liquidity and lower Federal Funds rate while the sales have the opposite effect). The Federal Open Market Committee (FOMC) sets the Federal Funds target rate eight times a year.

The Federal Funds rate influences the prime rate, which is the interest rate that banks charge their best customers, with highest credit ratings. The Federal Funds rate influences the interest rates on loans (including long-term loans) and savings.

Shadow banks are less regulated intermediaries that provide maturity, liquidity, and credit conversion services. Credit hedge funds, finance companies, money market mutual funds, asset-backed commercial paper (ABCP) conduits, special-purpose vehicles (SPSs), and securities lenders are examples of shadow banks (GSEs). Government-sponsored businesses (GSEs) are also included in this category by some economists (Pozsar et al., 2010).

The process of converting loans into tradable assets is known as securitization. Banks, GSEs, or shadow banks choose which loans to omit from their balance sheets and aggregate them into a portfolio (IMF, 2008). The next step is to sell this asset pool to an issuer, which is a special-purpose vehicle (SPV) – a financial institution created particularly to buy the assets and cope with the off–balance-sheet legal and accounting treatment. The SPV issues and sells interest-bearing securities to capital market investors to fund the acquisition of the pooled assets. Typically, the loan originator will collect payments from borrowers and forward them to the SPV (minus the fees). As a result, securitization shifts credit risk from originators to investors. This is a dangerous practice since originators are no longer motivated to maintain high lending standards and may be persuaded to abandon their toxic assets. The information asymmetry between the originator and the investor was exacerbated by rating organizations such as Moody's, which analyzed the securities and rated them with a triple A (the highest rating for the safest assets) only to downgrade 73% of them to junk later on.

While contagion is crucial, it simply accelerates the outbreak of economic crises; it is not the cause of recession, as an economy free of imbalances and bubbles can avoid a crisis regardless of contagion. This is demonstrated with correlations of private debt (including financial corporations)/GDP across nations for 2001 and 2008 as well as for 2008 and 2017 and with private debt (excluding financial corporations)/GDP across countries for the same years. Essentially, for the first correlation, variable Y comprises cross-sectional data for 2008, while variable X includes cross-sectional data for 2001. All available data from the IMF's Global Debt Database are used: 31 countries for debt levels that include financial institutions and 132 countries for debt levels that do not include financial entities. It is proposed to investigate whether the majority of countries followed the same pattern of increasing debt levels from 2001 to 2008 and from 2008 to 2017. The high coefficients for the level of debt, including that of financial institutions – 0.776 for 2001–2008 and 0.92 for 2008–2017 – as well as the level of debt excluding that of financial institutions – 0.88 for both periods – indicate a strong convergence. In 2001, the unweighted mean of private debt for the real economy/GDP was 71.71%, 93.75% in 2008, and 99.12% in 2017. The unweighted averages of private debt, including that of the financial sector/GDP in 2001, 2008, and 2017 are 165.46%, 217.61%, and 220.31%, respectively. The findings show that increased leverage was prevalent not only in the United States but practically in every country around the world, implying that imbalances had been accumulating prior to the Great Recession and are currently accumulating.

This chapter will focus on financial-monetary processes and their impact on economic activity. Policymakers blamed the inability of central banks to achieve constant money growth as a reason for the instability of money demand. A linear regression between money supply and macroeconomic factors is used to estimate money demand. The estimated fitted values represent money demand, and the residuals – the imbalance between money supply and money demand – are used to explain inflation trends. In fact, money demand cannot be less than money supply, and both money demand and banks' intended level of money supply are important.

## 1.2. Financial – monetary economy fundamentals

The economy in which we live is financial-monetary economy and not barter economy. Except for cash and crypto assets, each transaction has three participants: sender (or buyer), recipient of funds, and the bank or financial intermediary.

We live in a monetary system because the creation of money improves the spending capacity of economic agents without transferring purchasing power. Banks generate fresh purchasing power by granting loans. The financial system is extremely crucial in a highly indebted country. Debt affects both production and consumption. The freshly issued debt is absorbed into national income (unless it is used for speculation).

In order for GDP to rise, financial markets must generate continuous gains in real aggregate demand. For aggregate demand to rise, spending plans must be higher than current income, and the excess expenditure must be financed either by debt or by asset sales (Minsky, 1982, p. 6).

Economy is not only monetary; it is also financial, with the banking system being merely one component of the financial system. Because the nonbanking financial system does not generate money, it generates no additional purchasing power. Despite the fact that it just intermediates purchasing power, nonbanking financial institutions are very significant because spending would decrease without their intermediation. Furthermore, banking and nonbanking financial systems are inextricably linked since they finance one another and banks sell assets to SPVs to bypass the central bank's limits.

It is not enough to have brilliant entrepreneurs and technological advancement for economies to expand; it is also necessary to have healthy financial systems that can supply credit to keep the aggregate demand growing.

### 1.2.1 Money supply: Money creation by the central bank and commercial banks

According to works such as Mishkin (2019), the determinants of M2 include the following: changes in monetary base, the minimum required reserve ratio, changes in excess reserves, and changes in currency holdings. The textbook account of money creation begins with an increase in reserves (part of the monetary base) as the central bank purchases governmental bonds from banks. The bank will preserve the necessary reserves and lend the remainder. Its lending act generates checkable deposits (money supply), which end up in another bank, and this process continues to repeat itself. Finally, the deposit creation formula can be stated as follows:

$$Deposits = \frac{1}{Mrrr} * Reserves \tag{1}$$

where *Mrrr* is the minimum required reserve ratio.

Equation (1) illustrates how the money multiplier operates without the premise of excess reserves and without accounting for changes in currency holdings. The money multiplier (M2/M0) specifies how much money supply is created when the monetary base is increased. However, this image is distorted since banks can lend even when the central bank's reserves are not expanded. In fact, banks establish deposits when they make loans and then look for reserves later (Holmes, 1969). The incapacity of central banks to manage money supply was underlined during Paul Volcker's unsuccessful monetarist experiments, when he failed to achieve the targeted percentage of changes in monetary aggregates. In the following subchapters, we will explain how money is created and demonstrate that changes in the money supply determine the monetary base, not vice versa.

### 1.2.2 Money creation and "monetary destruction"

When banks extend loans, money is created. When a bank provides a loan to an agent, the assets increase in the bank's balance sheet – this is the loan – and the liabilities increase by the same amount because the bank creates a new deposit for the borrower or increases the borrower's already existing account with the contracted units of account. There is no intermediation in this procedure. There are two hypotheses about the "destruction" of money:

- When a debt is repaid, money is destroyed (Minsky, 1982). According to Keynes (1937, p. 247), debt payback does not destroy money; rather, the reserves or funds that result from debt repayment might be transferred to another agent.
- Money does not appear to be able to be destroyed, although it can be destroyed in the event of a bank's bankruptcy; however, this is becoming less frequent due to the introduction of deposit guarantee funds and resolution funds.

### 1.2.3 Questioning the money multiplier process

One of the two monetary policy myths is the money multiplier process. According to the textbook story, banks multiply the monetary base, and this is how money is created in a fractional reserve system. Commercial banks have been in existence long before the emergence of central banks; therefore, they do not require the monetary base to provide loans; instead, they use the monetary base for liquidity. Central banks were established to assist governments in financing wars and not to manage the money supply.

The other monetary myth is that the monetary base drives economic expansion. This is  false assumption because central banks respond to changes in GDP by adjusting the Federal Funds rate and the monetary base.

## Research methodology and data

To demonstrate that the monetary processes described above are myths, we begin with an update of Kydland and Prescott's (1990) research to see whether the conclusions of their study are still valid after 29 years. Their research is notable for demonstrating that the monetary base follows the cycle, whereas the monetary aggregates M2 and M2-M1 determine the cycle. They arrived at these conclusions after filtering GNP and monetary aggregates with the HP filter, extracting cycles (deviations from trend), and utilizing the Pearson Correlation Coefficient with lags and leads to establish which variable determines the other.

A minimizing function of Equation (2) is used to calculate the HP trend:

$$Min(\sum_{i=1}^{n}(Yt - \tau_i)^2 + \lambda \sum_{i=2}^{n-1}[(\tau_{i+1} - \tau_i) - (\tau_i - \tau_{i-1})]^2) \quad (2)$$

- Yt is actual data;
- $\tau i$ is the trend component.

The smoothing parameter λ in the HP filter is used to penalize trend acceleration compared to the business cycle component (Ravn & Uhlig, 2002). We follow Hodrick and Prescott's (1997) proposal that λ be equal to 1600.

To evaluate causality between variables, cross-correlations or correlations with lags and leads are used (formula from https://ncss-wpengine.netdna-ssl.com/wp-content/themes/ncss/pdf/Procedures/NCSS/Cross-Correlations.pdf):

$$R = \frac{\sum_{i=1}^{n-k}(X_i - X_m)(Y_i - Y_m)}{\sqrt{\sum_{i=1}^{n}(X_i - X_m)^2 \sum \sum_{i=1}^{n}(Y_i - Y_m)^2}} \quad (3)$$

Kydland and Prescott (1990) used it in their study for monetary aggregate and GNP deviations (data in logs). Although this method has been heavily criticized in the literature (Cogley & Nason, 1995), we believe it is appropriate for this study because we are not attempting to predict the business cycle or anticipate macroeconomic variables (is not suitable for latter since the trend is estimated by using both past and future values).

The findings of their research are as follows (see Figure 1). M2 and GNP have the largest connection ratio, whereas M2-M1 leads the cycle the most (3 quarters). If M(-2) and M2-M1(−3) have the strongest correlations with the GNP of any monetary aggregate and M0 lags, it suggests that variations in M2-M1 and M2 cause fluctuations in GNP, whereas changes in GNP induce deviations from the trend in M0. As a result, controlling M2 with/by targeting M0 is impossible.

Cyclical Behavior of U.S. Monetary Aggregates and the Price Level
Deviations From Trend of Money Stock, Velocity, and Price Level
Quarterly, 1954–1989

| Variable $x$ | Volatility (% Std. Dev.) | Cross Correlation of Real GNP With | | | | | | | | | | |
|---|---|---|---|---|---|---|---|---|---|---|---|---|
| | | $x(t-5)$ | $x(t-4)$ | $x(t-3)$ | $x(t-2)$ | $x(t-1)$ | $x(t)$ | $x(t+1)$ | $x(t+2)$ | $x(t+3)$ | $x(t+4)$ | $x(t+5)$ |
| Nominal Money Stock* | | | | | | | | | | | | |
| Monetary Base | 0.88 | −0.12 | 0.02 | 0.14 | 0.25 | 0.36 | 0.41 | 0.40 | 0.37 | 0.32 | 0.28 | 0.26 |
| M1 | 1.68 | 0.01 | 0.12 | 0.23 | 0.33 | 0.35 | 0.31 | 0.22 | 0.15 | 0.09 | 0.07 | 0.07 |
| M2 | 1.51 | 0.46 | 0.60 | 0.67 | 0.68 | 0.61 | 0.46 | 0.26 | 0.05 | −0.15 | −0.33 | −0.46 |
| M2 - M1 | 1.91 | 0.53 | 0.63 | 0.67 | 0.65 | 0.56 | 0.40 | 0.20 | −0.01 | −0.21 | −0.39 | −0.53 |
| Velocity* | | | | | | | | | | | | |
| Monetary Base | 1.33 | −0.26 | −0.15 | 0.00 | 0.22 | 0.40 | 0.59 | 0.50 | 0.37 | 0.22 | 0.08 | −0.08 |
| M1 | 2.02 | −0.24 | −0.19 | −0.12 | −0.01 | 0.14 | 0.31 | 0.32 | 0.27 | 0.20 | 0.10 | 0.00 |
| M2 | 1.84 | −0.63 | −0.59 | −0.48 | −0.29 | −0.05 | 0.24 | 0.34 | 0.40 | 0.43 | 0.44 | 0.43 |
| Price Level | | | | | | | | | | | | |
| Implicit GNP Deflator | 0.89 | −0.50 | −0.61 | −0.68 | −0.69 | −0.64 | −0.55 | −0.43 | −0.31 | −0.17 | −0.04 | 0.09 |
| Consumer Price Index | 1.41 | −0.52 | −0.63 | −0.70 | −0.72 | −0.68 | −0.57 | −0.41 | −0.24 | −0.05 | 0.14 | 0.30 |

*Based on quarterly data, 1959:1–1989:4.
Source of basic data: Citicorp's Citibase data bank

**Figure 1.** GDP and monetary aggregates cross-correlations
Source: Kydland and Prescott (1990).

We utilize the same smoothing parameter value and substitute GNP with GDP. All monetary aggregate data are obtained from the Federal Reserve (H3 and H6 Tables), whereas nominal GDP and the price deflator are obtained from the BEA (real GDP is calculated by adjusting NGDP with price deflator). All data are seasonally adjusted (we adjusted the monetary base with Tramo/Seats after converting it into quarterly data via average) and are updated quarterly. We selected a sample period of January 1959 to May 2019 and transformed the data into a quarterly frequency.

To demonstrate our point of view, we went one step further and used Granger causality to broaden the analysis of causality between monetary aggregates and bank loans. Granger causality (Granger, 1969) is an appropriate econometric tool for determining whether a variable can be used to forecast another variable.

The variables included in this study are as follows: M0, M2 – currency, M2-M1, lendable reserves (monetary base; total balances maintained), bank credit (FRB H8 Table), and monthly frequency – not seasonally adjusted, as GDP is not considered in this research. Data are logged, and the initial difference is used to assess the effect of changes and to use stationary data (ADF tests confirm the stationarity of the variables).

Simple Granger causality tests (Granger, 1969) can be specified:

$$Y_t = \alpha + \sum_{j=1}^{m} aj\,(Y_{t-j}) + \sum_{j=1}^{m} bj\,(X_{t-j}) + \varepsilon_t \tag{4}$$

$$X_t = \theta + \sum_{j=1}^{m} cj\,(X_{t-j}) + \sum_{j=1}^{m} dj\,(Y_{t-j}) + \eta_t \tag{5}$$

The reported *F* statistics are the Wald statistics for the null hypothesis:

$b_1 = b_2 = b_3 = \cdots = b_j = 0$ for (4) Equation and

$d_1 = d_2 = d_3 = \cdots = d_j = 0$ for (5) Equation

The null hypothesis for the first regression is that X does not Granger cause Y, while the null hypothesis for the second regression is that Y does not Granger cause X. Initially, Y is regressed on its past values – restricted regression – from which we compute SSRr (restricted sum of squared residuals), and then a second regression is estimated that incorporates the past values of Y and X, from which we obtain SSRu (unrestricted sum of squared residuals).

F test is (Foresti, 2007):

$$F = \frac{[SSRr - SSRu]}{m} / \frac{[SSRu]}{[T - (2 * m + 1)]} \tag{6}$$

Where

T = number of observations;
m = number of lags.

The Granger test is highly sensitive to the amount of lags used in regression; thus, we will pick 1 lag because the changes should occur immediately in theory and the second choice will be selected using the lag-length criteria for vector autoregression (EViews 7.2). We will determine the optimal number of lags using the lag-length criteria.

We used the Akaike (AIC), Schwartz (SIC), and Hannan–Quinn criterion (HQC) to choose the best model.

$$\mathrm{AIC} = 2 * \mathrm{k} - 2 * \mathrm{In}(\mathrm{L}) \tag{7}$$

k = number of parameters in the model
L = likelihood value

$$BIC = \ln(n) * k - 2 * \ln(L) \quad (8)$$

n stands for number of observations

$$\mathrm{HQC} = 2 * k * \mathrm{In}(\mathrm{In}(n)) - 2 * L \quad (9)$$

Vector autoregression (VAR) is another model that we use to examine the impact of each variable on the other two. VAR is used for forecasting interconnected time series. Sims argued in favor of the use of this tool (1972, 1980a, 1980b). He saw VAR as a viable alternative to traditional econometric models with questionable exclusion constraints, where a variable was only essential for one side of the market (Christiano, 2012). We chose VAR instead of VECM (Vector Error Correction Model) because we are utilizing log differences and want to describe only the short responses of the selected variables to innovations in each variable.

The following steps are part of the research methodology:

- VAR model estimation
- Performing the VAR model stability test
- Execute impulse–response functions.

We ran the VAR model through a stability test. We checked to see whether we have a stationary stochastic process. When the roots of the matrix equation of the estimated coefficients of the VAR model lie inside the unit circle, the VAR model is stable. When all of the roots are inside the unit circle, the model will converge, which means the values of lagged variables will no longer have a combined influence on one another and will stabilize over time. As a result, within a stable pattern, the impacts of shocks will diminish with time.

Results such as impulse-response standard errors are inconclusive if VAR is not stable.

We use the impulse-response method for 24 months. The fundamental rationale for this choice is that the Federal Reserve Board's MCM model predicts that monetary policy modifications will take at most 2 years to fully affect inflation and real production.

Our ultimate goal is to see how the time series reacts to random shocks.

## Results and discussion

The cross-correlation results are strong in favor of a statistical link between money and GDP and the subsequent causality M2, M2-M1, and M1 ≥ GDP ≥ M0.

Real GDP continues to outperform the monetary base (see Appendix 1), while M1, M2, and M2-M1 lead the cycle (see Appendixes 2, 3, and 4). The cycle is determined by M2-M1 by three quarters is the widest, although the highest reported correlation has been that which occurred between M2 and real GDP (0.3684).

The Granger model with 1 lag (see Figure 2), that is, the likelihood of M0 to Granger causing M -currency is 0.0917>0.05, indicates that the null hypothesis is accepted, and so M0 does not predict future values of M2 – currency, neither does M2-M1; however, both M2 – currency and M2-M1 may be used to predict monetary base.

Pairwise Granger Causality Tests
Date: 06/29/19 Time: 18:19
Sample: 1959M01 2019M05
Lags: 1

| Null Hypothesis: | Obs | F-Statistic | Prob. |
|---|---|---|---|
| DL_M2_CURRENCY does not Granger Cause DL_M0 | 723 | 16.8145 | 5.E-05 |
| DL_M0 does not Granger Cause DL_M2_CURRENCY | | 2.85261 | 0.0917 |
| DL_M2_M1 does not Granger Cause DL_M0 | 723 | 4.30507 | 0.0384 |
| DL_M0 does not Granger Cause DL_M2_M1 | | 0.12842 | 0.7202 |

**Figure 2.** Pairwise Granger causality tests with 1 lag
Source: Authors' computations.

The model with 13 lags indicates that M2 – currency and M2-M1 can be used to forecast M0; however, monetary base can't Granger cause M2-M1 and can improve the forecast of M2 – currency. M0 does not predict the future values of M2-M1 not even in medium term.

Based on the criteria given, the two groups [(M0, M2 – currency and M2-M1) and (bank credit, M2 – currency and Lendable Reserves)] in which the chosen variables are divided have an optimal number of 13 lags (see Appendix 5 and Appendix 6).

The model with 13 delays shows that M2 – currency and M2-M1 may be used to forecast M0, but monetary base cannot Granger cause M2-M1 but can improve M2 – currency forecasting. M0 does not anticipate future M2-M1 values, not even in the medium run (see Figure 3).

Pairwise Granger Causality Tests
Date: 06/29/19 Time: 18:21
Sample: 1959M01 2019M05
Lags: 13

| Null Hypothesis: | Obs | F-Statistic | Prob. |
|---|---|---|---|
| DL_M2_CURRENCY does not Granger Cause DL_M0 | 711 | 4.95256 | 2.E-08 |
| DL_M0 does not Granger Cause DL_M2_CURRENCY | | 2.02369 | 0.0169 |
| DL_M2_M1 does not Granger Cause DL_M0 | 711 | 2.74825 | 0.0008 |
| DL_M0 does not Granger Cause DL_M2_M1 | | 1.53757 | 0.0988 |

**Figure 3.** Pairwise Granger causality tests with 13 lags
Source: Authors' computations.

For the other group, the model with 1 lag demonstrates that bank credit effects the future values of M2, which in turn influences the future values of lendable reserves, although the latter has no effect on either (see Figure 4).

Pairwise Granger Causality Tests
Date: 06/29/19 Time: 17:29
Sample: 1959M01 2019M05
Lags: 1

| Null Hypothesis: | Obs | F-Statistic | Prob. |
|---|---|---|---|
| DL_BANK_CREDIT does not Granger Cause DL_M2_CURRENCY | 723 | 6.78475 | 0.0094 |
| DL_M2_CURRENCY does not Granger Cause DL_BANK_CREDIT | | 3.56774 | 0.0593 |
| DL_LENDABLE_RESERVES does not Granger Cause DL_M2_CURRENCY | 723 | 0.05039 | 0.8225 |
| DL_M2_CURRENCY does not Granger Cause DL_LENDABLE_RESERVES | | 4.17165 | 0.0415 |
| DL_LENDABLE_RESERVES does not Granger Cause DL_BANK_CREDIT | 723 | 1.24758 | 0.2644 |
| DL_BANK_CREDIT does not Granger Cause DL_LENDABLE_RESERVES | | 0.32445 | 0.5691 |

**Figure 4.** Pairwise Granger causality tests with 1 lag, including bank credit
Source: Authors' computations.

We find different results when we apply 13 lags; all variables are linked, except bank credit, which does not Granger cause M2 – currency (see Figure 5). In the near term, this judgment is biased because when a bank grants a loan, it produces a money – liability and a loan – asset (explanation in the second subchapter).

Pairwise Granger Causality Tests
Date: 06/29/19 Time: 17:31
Sample: 1959M01 2019M05
Lags: 13

| Null Hypothesis: | Obs | F-Statistic | Prob. |
|---|---|---|---|
| DL_BANK_CREDIT does not Granger Cause DL_M2_CURRENCY | 711 | 1.19467 | 0.2783 |
| DL_M2_CURRENCY does not Granger Cause DL_BANK_CREDIT | | 4.52601 | 2.E-07 |
| DL_LENDABLE_RESERVES does not Granger Cause DL_M2_CURRENCY | 711 | 4.34140 | 5.E-07 |
| DL_M2_CURRENCY does not Granger Cause DL_LENDABLE_RESERVES | | 3.44755 | 3.E-05 |
| DL_LENDABLE_RESERVES does not Granger Cause DL_BANK_CREDIT | 711 | 3.92093 | 4.E-06 |
| DL_BANK_CREDIT does not Granger Cause DL_LENDABLE_RESERVES | | 1.98861 | 0.0194 |

**Figure 5.** Granger causality tests with 13 lags, including bank credit
Source: Authors' computations.

We use a VAR (13) model. We can see in Figure 6 that for the studied VAR model, no roots lie outside the circle; therefore, the VAR model is stable.

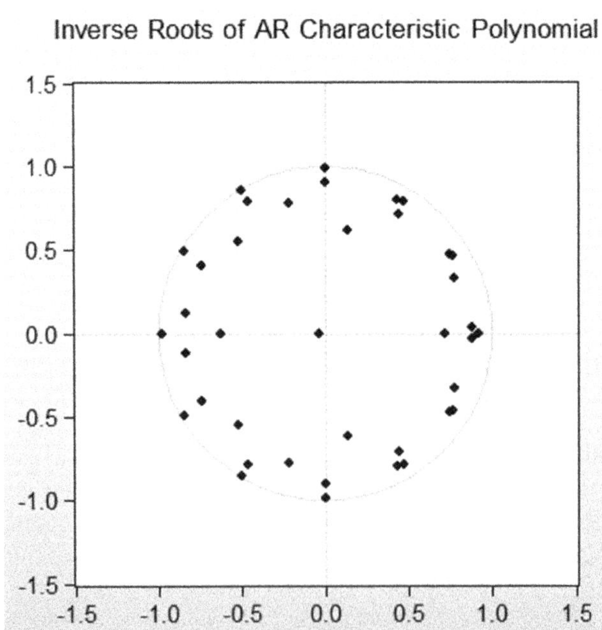


**Figure 6.** Stability test for VAR (13)
Source: Authors' computations.

We compute the impulse responses (see Figure 7) and the accumulated responses (see Figure 8) by using the Cholesky ordering indicated by the Granger causality results: Bank credit contemporaneously affects M2 – currency and Lendable Reserves, while M2 – currency contemporaneously affects Lendable Reserves.

As expected, in response to a positive 1 standard deviation shock to bank credit, M2 – currency increases, while the influence of lendable reserve on M2 – currency is mostly negative proving that this relationship does not hold. The unexpected result is the negative impact of M2 – currency on Lendable Reserves. There are various theories for this phenomena. As Alan Holmes said, bank reserves are required following the creation of deposits through loans. In this instance, the central bank can either satisfy the demand for reserves or influence bank liquidity, resulting in a negative relationship between these variables. Another scenario with a negative association is a lengthy failed attempt by the central bank to incentivize demand by raising the monetary base–liquidity trap or depression.

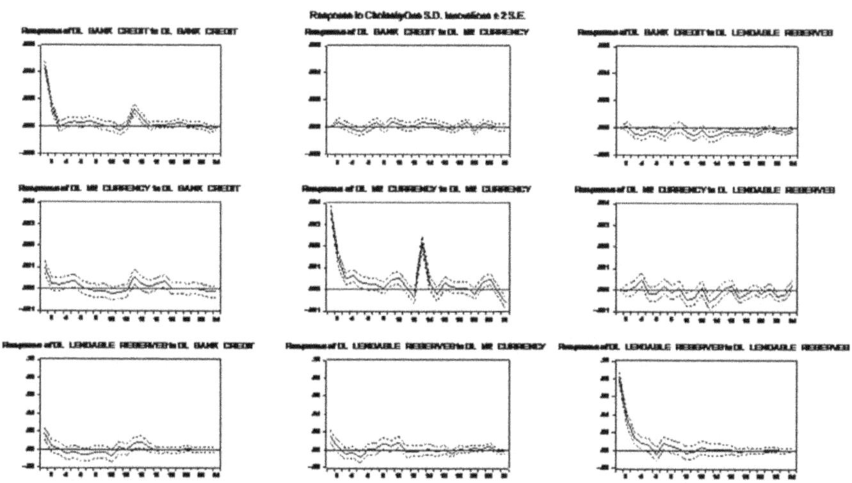

**Figure 7.** Impulse response for VAR (13)
Source: Authors' computations.

We also see a slight negative impact of lendable reserves on bank credit, as well as short-term increases in lendable reserves as a result of M2 – currency and bank credit shocks.

Given all of the empirical evidence, we may conclude that bank liabilities (including M2 and the monetary base) are the result of loans and bank credit, not their cause. The conclusion is that the money multiplier theory is just a myth.

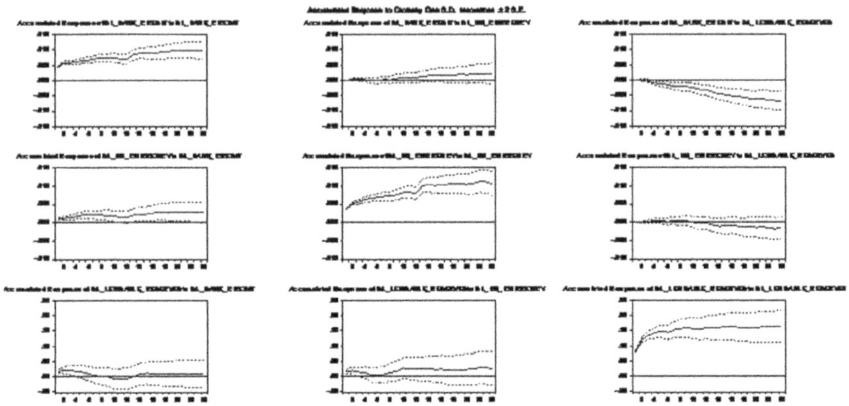

**Figure 8.** Accumulated impulse response for VAR (13)
Source: Authors' computations.

### 1.2.4 Non-neutrality and super non-neutrality of money

According to the neutrality of money theory, changes in the money supply affect only nominal variables in the long term and have no effect on real variables such as real GDP; thus, changes in M2 have an effect exclusively on inflation. According to money super neutrality, changes in money supply growth rates have no influence on output. This subchapter's major purpose is to challenge these beliefs and find logical and factual proof against each theory.

To begin with, money is utilized for more than just commerce; it is also employed for speculating. As a result, money is utilized to build wealth rather than only for production or consumption. Businessmen want to collect riches beyond the boundaries of consumption; thus, the accumulated wealth is not intended to be translated into consumable items through purchases (Veblen, 1909, p. 634)

According to Sims (2009), non-neutrality and bubbles are caused by heterogeneous views. Inflation-averse investors would regard bond sales as a cheap source of finance and will participate in asset markets when they anticipate rising inflation. Those who are pro-inflation will go backwards. Because of the cheap source of money, inflation-averse agents who are not risk averse will invest more in assets than if there was homogeneous confidence in the market and overall stock investment is also larger than in the event of homogeneous beliefs. His conclusion is that central banks can generate bubbles by producing divergences in beliefs, rather than by maintaining low interest rates for extended periods of time.

Another method for combating neutrality and super neutrality is Keynes' two-price system. Keynes' rejection of money neutrality stems from the way money impacts the price level of investment goods and the price level of consumer products. When the price level of investment products is high in comparison to the price level of consumption goods, conditions favor investment; when the process is reversed, a depression or recession may occur. The business cycle is the result of the above-mentioned price levels performing a dance (Minsky, 2011, p. 304). According to Keynes' theory, the flow of money to firms is determined by expectations of future profits; thus, money is linked to the real economy and is more than just a means of exchange.

Minsky expanded on Keynes' theory by introducing three types of financing: hedge, speculative, and Ponzi. A substantial proportion of speculative units can generate a rise in Ponzi units and even a debt deflation process (Minsky, 1993).

Austrian theorists refer to a shift in production structure as the proof against money neutrality. The induced boom caused by bank loan expansion results in resource misallocation. When projects that would be unprofitable in the absence of credit expansion, or interest rate decreases by the central bank, are blooming, it implies that credit booms might lead to resource malinvestment. This misallocation of resources will also alter the production structure at all stages by affecting the relative pricing structure (Huerta De Soto, 2006, p. 550).

Another reason that money may not be neutral is the unexpected inflation. Unexpected inflation makes previously negotiated loans simpler to pay because their real worth has reduced, resulting in a reduction in leverage.

Changes in the money supply, particularly contractions or decreased money growth, can have a significant impact on the economy. Money, as Gurley (1961) put it, is a veil, and, when the veil flutters, the economy shutters. However, because output declines are frequently chronic, money has a long-run impact on output. Due to the Eurozone's delayed response to the crisis, the harmonized unemployment rate is still higher than it was before the crisis (LRHUTTTTEZQ156S series –7.3% in 2008Q1 compared to 7.76% in 2019Q1), whereas in the United States, unemployment is 3.91% in 2019Q1 compared to its lowest level before the crisis outbreak: 4.53% in 2006Q4.

The distribution channel is another method in which changes in the expansion of the money supply affect real output. In general, macroeconomists reject the importance of distribution, but Piketty (2014) has reintroduced it into the discussion. According to Piketty (2014), the rate of return on capital will typically be higher than the rate of economic growth, resulting in wealth concentration. Because wealthy people have a larger proclivity to speculate, wealth concentration can lead to bubbles (Dragoe, 2016). Obviously, there is more to the relationship between increased inequality and financial fragility than meets the eye. Economic inequality and economic growth have a nonlinear relationship. Too much inequality can be bad to human capital (as education becomes too expensive for the poor) and productivity (workers will have less incentive to work harder in this instance). On the other hand, low levels of income disparity may drive away investors and render extremely expensive markets such as diamonds, jewelry, and supercars unworkable. According to Berg and Ostry (2011), more equal economies are associated with growth spells – the interval of trend growth within a country's economy. According to Austrian business cycle theorists (Del Soto, 2006, p. 409), new monetary injections into the economic system caused by new loans would result in a redistribution of buying power in favor of the households/economic agents that contract the loans. Although the rest of society has the same nominal income, prices will rise. Lower-income households are more likely to take out loans in order to maintain their standard of living (Dragoe, 2016). Lower-income households would gain from a shift in monetary policy from low to moderate inflationary conditions. This adjustment would result in changes in consumer preferences and, as a result, in the proportion of industries and sectors at the macroeconomic level; consequently, the neutrality and superneutrality assumptions become invalid.

The connections between changes in the money supply, monetary base, and GDP deflator (all variables are seasonally adjusted) during two monetary policy regimes are shown below. The first regime runs from 1959Q2 to 1984Q3 and has moderate inflation on average. The second regime, which runs from 1984Q4 to 2019Q1, has a low inflation target.

$$R = \frac{\sum_{i=1}^{n}(xi - x\,average)(yi - y\,average)}{\sqrt{\sum_{i=1}^{n}(xi - x\,average)^{2}\sum_{i=1}^{n}(yi - y\,average)}} \qquad (10)$$

Except for the association between monetary base and GDP deflator during the 1959Q2–1984Q3 regime, the correlations do not demonstrate a statistically significant relationship because of the lack of a securitization process, which would have weakened the link between monetary policy and inflation (see Tables 1 and 2).

**Table 1.** Correlation Coefficients of M2 money base and GDP deflator between 1959Q2 and 1984Q3

| | *M2* | *Monetary Base Sa* | *GDP deflator* |
|---|---|---|---|
| M2 | 1 | | |
| Monetary Base Sa | 0.152997086 | 1 | |
| GDP deflator | 0.070488398 | 0.452169554 | 1 |

Source: Authors' computations.

**Table 2.** Correlation Coefficients of M2 money base and GDP deflator between 1984Q4 and 2019Q1

| | *M2* | *Monetary Base Sa* | *GDP deflator* |
|---|---|---|---|
| M2 | 1 | | |
| Monetary Base Sa | 0.248348403 | 1 | |
| GDP deflator | –0.132973534 | –0.109554258 | 1 |

Source: Authors' computations.

Tables 3 and 4 show the average real GDP growth rates under both monetary systems. The average nominal GDP growth is the product of the GDP deflator average and the real GDP average. The figure for the first regime is over 2.5%, whereas the figure for the second regime is 1.2%. When compared to the averages for money supply, it is obvious that the velocity of money grew in the first regime but decreased in the second.

Another two-price system can be used to describe this evolution. We consider the GDP deflator – the price of output – as well as the price of speculative assets in our study. A low-inflation regime is typically associated with higher asset prices because less money is moving into the real economy (nominal GDP), resulting in a decrease in money velocity. A higher GDP deflator indicates that more money is being invested in the real economy rather than in speculation. In the second regime, nominal GDP growth is greater than the change in average money supply, implying that money utilized for speculative purposes was transferred back into the real economy, resulting in a velocity rise.

A comparison between the two periods shows that the money elasticity of real output is 80.81%. A rise of 1 monetary unit results in an increase of 0.8 units in real output. This demonstrates that money is not completely neutral, because changes in money growth cause changes in actual production.

**Table 3.** Averages of M2, GDP deflator, and real GDP, 1959Q2-1984Q3

| **1959Q2–1984Q3** | | |
|---|---|---|
| M2 average | GDP deflator average | RGDP average |
| 2.03% | 1.16% | 0.89% |

Source: Authors' computations.

**Table 4.** Averages of M2, GDP deflator, and real GDP, 1984Q4-2019Q1

| **1984Q4–2019Q1** | | |
|---|---|---|
| M2 average | GDP deflator average | RGDP average |
| 1.37% | 0.54% | 0.66% |

Source: Authors' computations.

Money-neutrality supporters argue that in the long run it will only affect inflation. Inflation, on the other hand, has a significant impact on real variables, and the rate of inflation follows a consistent pattern. We can put this claim to test by doing an autocorrelation test on the GDP deflator (data sample 1959Q2–2019Q1). The autocorrelation coefficients are extremely high, the trend is slow, and the *p* value associated with the *Q* statistics test is less than the chosen level of significance of 5%, rejecting the null hypothesis of no autocorrelation (see Appendix 11).

$$\mathrm{p}_k = \frac{\sum_{i=k+1}^{n}(xt - xmedium) * (xt - k - xmedium) / (n-k)}{\sum_{i=1}^{n}(xt - xmedium) / n} \tag{11}$$

$\mathrm{p}_k$ is the kth order of autocorrelation, *n* represents the number of observations, and *xmedium* is the average inflation rate (Codirlaşu & Moinescu, 2010, p. 34).

According to Minsky, if the inflation rate is high when a crisis occurs, increased cash flows allow for the repayment of debt acquired during expansion despite the economic collapse. This will lead to modest growth and high inflation and only few failures. This is the process of preventing depression (see Keen,

2011). Based on the data presented, we can reject the hypothesis of money and super neutrality in the United States.

Non-neutrality and non-superneutrality, on the other hand, are not bound by borders. The Triffin Dilemma best illustrates its significance. A global currency is required in a global world. The U.S. dollar is both a national currency and a global reserve currency, yet local and international policy do not always coincide. Other countries must hold the reserve currency, resulting in a dollar blackhole. The removal of U.S. money within U.S. borders results in trade deficits, which damage the U.S. economy and the U.S. dollar. The international economy would contract if the United States eliminated its commercial trade imbalances. However, if deficits are continued, the dollar is likely to weaken and confidence in the currency would erode (Triffin, 1959). The current Triffin Dilemma is fiscal in nature because the securities held as reserves by central banks are safe assets – government liabilities. Global reserve expansion necessitates an increase in gross government debt. This procedure has the potential to lead to an unstable fiscal path (Brătian, Bucur, Oprean, & Tănăsescu, 2016).

We still don't have answers to the flaws in the global monetary system. Dragoe and Oprean-Stan's (2018) proposal of G20 expanded SDR and neither Libra (a stable coin) would not function because negative yields account for 27% of global bonds (Obstfeld, 2019). Because bitcoin is a bubble, neither crypto-assets nor cryptocurrencies can be a solution (Dragoe & Oprean-Stan, 2020). Many libertarians support Hayek's proposal to denationalize money (1990). The most significant distinctions between Hayek's (1990, pp. 130–131) private currencies and crypto-assets are that the later compete in terms of technology rather than compete on stability in reference to a basket of products and many crypto-assets are decentralized.

## 1.3. Developments in the current U.S. financial system

### 1.3.1. Loan and bank credit decoupling from money and nonbanking superfinancialisation

Even before the replication of the Hodrick and Prescott's study (1990) began, one point was clear: The relationship between money and production (GDP) is deteriorating. There are numerous elements to examine when attempting to explain this effect. Monetary policy interventions, inventory management improvements, and decoupling of money and bank credit from money and no-banking superfinancialization are some of the reasons for this effect. The term "nonbank superfinancialization" refers to the extraordinary growth of shadow banking and other nonbank financial intermediaries when compared to regular banks. As an abbreviation for credit in the financial industry, we shall use the syntagma "financial credit."

## Research methodology and data

To examine the impact of money, loans, and credit on GDP, we use an ARIMA model (Figure 9). The selected variables are economic growth (dependent variable), the change in money stock/nominal GDP, the ratios of loans (and leases) to M2, the cycle in bank credit, and the change in leverage (total nonfinancial credit/nominal GDP). All variables are seasonally adjusted before being expressed in logs on a quarterly basis from 1959Q1 to 2019Q1.

## Results and discussion

Because partial autocorrelation is strongest at the first lag and continues to remain significant until the third lag (see Appendix 8), we adopt an ARIMA (1,1,3) model. $R^2$, or the coefficient of determination, is very high, at 0.694805. Thus, the selected independent variables predict 69.48% of the variance in GDP.

Dependent Variable: DL_RGDP
Method: Least Squares
Date: 08/14/21 Time: 12:50
Sample (adjusted): 1959Q3 2018Q1
Included observations: 235 after adjustments
Convergence achieved after 8 iterations
MA Backcast: 1958Q4 1959Q2

| Variable | Coefficient | Std. Error | t-Statistic | Prob. |
|---|---|---|---|---|
| C | 0.005492 | 0.001088 | 5.049050 | 0.0000 |
| DL_M2 | 0.202899 | 0.051143 | 3.967312 | 0.0001 |
| D(L_LOANS-L_M2) | 0.108562 | 0.030934 | 3.509450 | 0.0005 |
| CYCLE_HP_BANK_CREDIT | -0.060087 | 0.028682 | -2.094922 | 0.0373 |
| D(L_TOTAL_CREDIT-L_NGDP) | -0.658214 | 0.029247 | -22.50530 | 0.0000 |
| AR(1) | 0.387155 | 0.062788 | 6.166083 | 0.0000 |
| MA(3) | 0.331162 | 0.063907 | 5.181974 | 0.0000 |

| | | | |
|---|---|---|---|
| R-squared | 0.694805 | Mean dependent var | 0.007405 |
| Adjusted R-squared | 0.686774 | S.D. dependent var | 0.008222 |
| S.E. of regression | 0.004602 | Akaike info criterion | -7.895481 |
| Sum squared resid | 0.004828 | Schwarz criterion | -7.792429 |
| Log likelihood | 934.7190 | Hannan-Quinn criter. | -7.853935 |
| F-statistic | 86.51063 | Durbin-Watson stat | 2.095775 |
| Prob(F-statistic) | 0.000000 | | |

| | | | |
|---|---|---|---|
| Inverted AR Roots | .39 | | |
| Inverted MA Roots | .35-.60i | .35+.60i | -.69 |

**Figure 9.** Multivariate linear regression through least-squares method
Source: Authors' computations.

The variables are stationary at the 5% level (ADF and PP tests). The ARIMA model is stable as the AR and MA roots lie inside the circle (see Figure 10). The probabilities associated with the coefficients and with the *F* test (explained variance/unexplained variance) are under the level of significance of 0.05, so the null hypothesis according to which $\beta_i = 0$, is rejected. The probability of committing a type 1 error (to reject the null hypothesis, that is, to assume that the independent variables influence the dependent variable when in fact the relationship does not exist) is zero. GDP does depend on M2, loans, bank credit, and nonfinancial credit (debt securities). With a skewness of 0.052348 and a kurtosis of 3.273214 we can conclude that the residuals are normally distributed (see Appendix 7).

C(2) is the coefficient of the change in money stock. It is positive. A change with 1% in the money stock will lead to a 0.2% change in economic growth. C(3), the loan-to-money ratio is positive (in general) but has a smaller impact on real GDP change than money growth. A 1% change in this ratio results in a 0.108% change in economic growth. This is a liquidity ratio for banks, and while the coefficient is positive, excessive levels of this indicator are not sustainable for banks. A high value indicates that banks rely on debt-to-finance lending ratio. This ratio can rise along with GDP during times of boom and fall during times of recession, but high numbers during booms and bubbles will lead to misallocation of resources and economic crises (huge flows of loans to inefficient sections of the economy and bubbles). It is also worth noting that the loans and leases-to-M2 ratio was always a subunit in the sample of data examined.

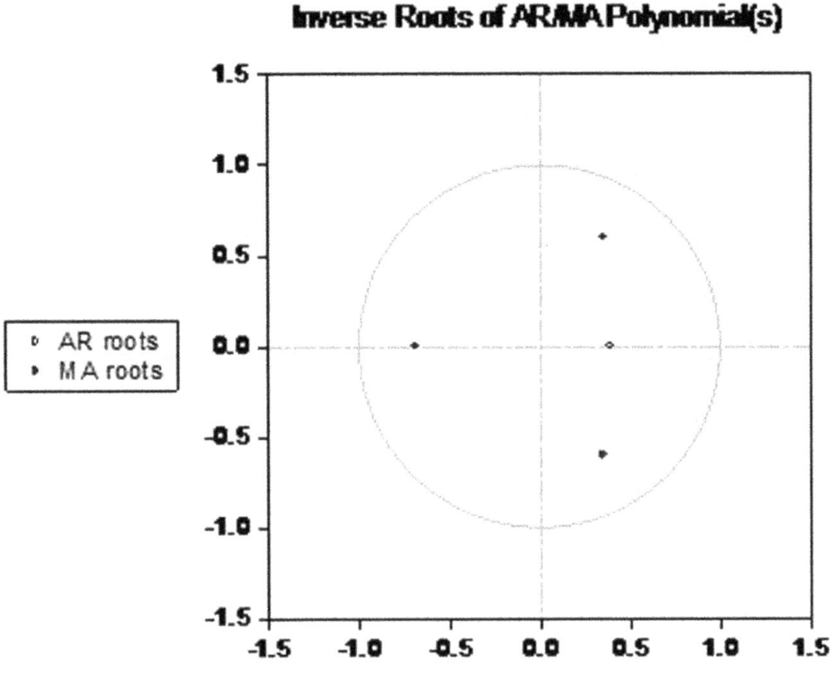


**Figure 10.** AR and MA roots
Source: Authors' computations.

In bank credit, we find a negative coefficient for the two-sided Hodrick–Prescott cycle. The outcome is unsurprising. Extremely high levels of bank lending can be connected with malinvestment, and extremely low levels can also have a negative impact on economic growth.

The coefficient of change in total credit to the nonfinancial sector/nominal GDP is negative. The key reasons for this outcome are that nonbank borrowing does not increase purchasing power and may generate more bubbles than production. The wealth effect, a byproduct of bubbles, has little effect on aggregate demand when compared to an industrial loan or a consumer loan. The negative coefficient also implies that during a period of concurrent banking crisis and a fall in economic activity, economic agents resort to nonbank loans.

The Harvey test for heteroscedasticity is used to assess the validity of our model. The variance of residuals does not remain constant across observations due to heteroscedasticity. The null hypothesis is no heteroscedasticity. This test uses the following regression (see Equation 12) to assess heteroscedasticity:

$$Ln\left(u_i^2\right) = \alpha + \alpha_1 z_{i,1}' + \alpha_m z_{i,m}' + v_i \tag{12}$$

$u_i$ = residual at time I, and z = independent variables used in the primary regression.

As the *p* value is over 0.05, the null hypothesis of homoscedasticity is accepted (see Figure 11).

Heteroskedasticity Test: Harvey

| | | | |
|---|---|---|---|
| F-statistic | 2.291308 | Prob. F(4,230) | 0.0604 |
| Obs*R-squared | 9.005615 | Prob. Chi-Square(4) | 0.0610 |
| Scaled explained SS | 8.497080 | Prob. Chi-Square(4) | 0.0750 |

**Figure 11.** Harvey test for heteroscedasticity
Source: Authors' computations.

Despite the increased volume of nonbank credit to the nonfinancial sector, this study reveals that money still has a significant impact on the actual economy. However, because we have entered an era of unparalleled leverage (Schularick & Taylor, 2009), credit may play a more prominent role in economic cycles, a topic that is different but linked to our study. Since 1945, bank credit has grown faster than money due to funding from nonmonetary liabilities.

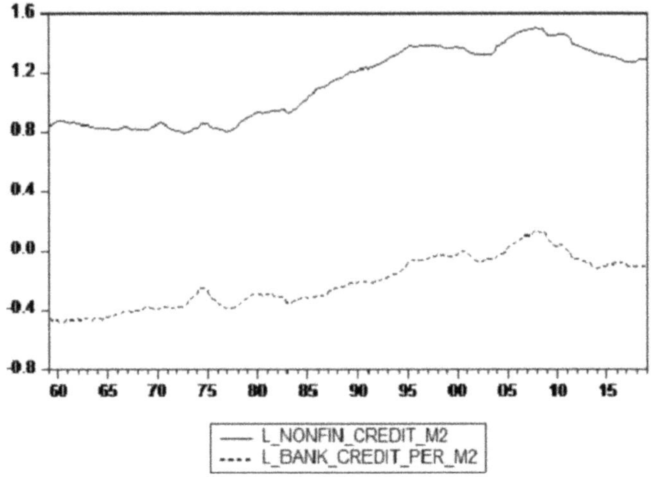


**Figure 12.** Decoupling of credit from money

Source: Authors' computations – M2 from H3, bank credit from H8, and nonfinancial credit from Federal Reserve database; all data are seasonally adjusted, quarterly frequency.

Schularick and Taylor (2009) suggest that since credit aggregates have decoupled from M2, credit holds increasingly relevant information for forecasting financial crises.

Also, as seen in Figure 12, the logged ratios of bank credit/M2 and total nonfinancial credit/M2 have been increasing, although the M2 (difference of logged M2) no longer contracts before or after recessions (see Figure 13 in Appendix 37) due to aggressive monetary policy.

Following our study, we discovered that bank credit/loans and leases make the greatest contribution to GDP and appear to be a better recession predictor than M2.

### *1.3.1.1. Credit aggregates: Suitable for nominal GDP targeting?*

The previous studies' findings confirm a substantial link between bank credit and GDP. The logical next step in our research is to see if policymakers use bank credit or other credit aggregates to target nominal GDP growth. When comparing money and credit as essential variables for targeting GDP, credit has an advantage over M2 in that it may be subdivided into credit for GDP circulation and credit for asset bubbles. The monetarist Equation (13) ignores the speculative sector of the economy:

$$M * V = P * T \tag{13}$$

where M = M2, v = velocity, P = price, and T = quantity.

Because there is no accounting for the money spent in bubbles in Equation (14), the assumption is that all money is employed in production, which is far from true.

Werner (with Voutsinas, 2011) is a credit disaggregation pioneer. Most of the time, he excludes real estate and financial credit. In his 1997 work, he claims that the velocity of the proxy he established for credit used in the real economy is pretty steady between 1979Q1 and 2000Q4. In more recent publications (Ryan-Collins, Werner, & Castle, 2016), the authors discovered a long-term relationship between changes in nominal credit utilized in the real economy and changes in nominal GDP. They have empirically shown, using cointegration methods, that nominal credit growth employed in the real economy has higher explanatory power of nominal GDP growth when compared to M4 (money supply), bank reserves, short-term bank rate, and long-term interest rates.

## Research methodology and data

Our main goal is to estimate better velocities by using GNE instead of GDP because credit is also used to acquire import goods and to see if including loans and debt securities issued by private depository institutions to financial institutions will produce better results because this type of lending also creates money.

$$GNE = C + G + I \tag{14}$$

where GNE = gross national expenditure, C = private expenditure, G = government spending, and I = investment.

The data sample for which the proxies were developed ranges from 1959Q1 to 2019Q1, with all data being seasonally adjusted and on a quarterly basis. The Unique Identifier for Domestic Nonfinancial Credit is Z1/Z1/LA384104005.Q (data from FRB), data for bank credit is taken from H8, FRB, and the components of private depository credit for GDP circulation and Domestic Nonfinancial

Credit for GDP circulation are defined in Appendix 9 and Appendix 10, respectively.

We also computed:

- Private depository – Loans to commercial banks for GNE circulation velocity (Loans to commercial banks from H8 Table, FRB)
- Private depository – Loans to private depository for GNE circulation velocity
- Private depository – Loans to nonbanks for GNE circulation velocity
- Private depository – Loans to financial institutions for GNE circulation velocity

We approximated the financial credit flows ourselves due to a lack of data on the interconnection of financial institutions (and since statistics for loans from commercial banks to non-depository institutions only cover the period 2015Q1–2019Q1). To estimate the velocities, we used the methods developed by Bhatia and Bayoumi (2012) and Herman, Igan, and Sole (2015). The procedure entails computing the percentages of liabilities and assets for each organization. As a result, a matrix is created. The product of the two percentages provides us the proportion of a type of financial institution's assets issued by another type of financial institution for each quarter. The resulting proportion will be multiplied by the value of the specific asset category (loan or debt securities). Tables L.207 to L.222 provide the assets and liabilities for each instrument owned by each sector. We have only estimated the figures for the following categories (albeit for the current analysis, we only utilize loans and securities originated by banks and owned by banks and nonbanks):

- Assets originating from banks and owned by banks
- Assets originating from banks and held by nonbanks
- Assets originating from nonbanks and held by nonbanks
- Assets originating from nonbanks and held by banks
- Assets originating from banks and held by the rest of the world
- Assets originating from nonbanks and held by the rest of the world

The performance of the calculated velocities is measured by the proximity of the STD/MAD ratio to 1.253 (according to Goldstein & Taleb, 2007). The velocity with the closest STD/MAD ratio to 1.253 will be tested for stationarity because it would mean that its variance doesn't change over time – this is a desirable property given that the velocity should be generally stable.

$$\text{Therefore}\,\text{STD}/\text{MAD} = \frac{\sigma}{\sqrt{\frac{2}{\pi}}*\sigma} = \sqrt{\frac{\pi}{2}} \approx 1.253314137 \tag{15}$$

## Results and discussion

The findings confirm that using GNE instead of GDP and including financial credit issued by banks to both banks and nonbanks improve the velocities' stability (see Table 5). The greatest consistent credit velocity is provided by domestic private depository credit to the actual economy.

Despite the early success in producing a normally distributed time series, the logarithmized time series is not stationary (see Figure 14). The null hypothesis "credit velocity has a unit root" is accepted at the 1%, 5%, and 10% levels. The variance of the chosen time series varies over time, meaning that nominal GDP cannot be targeted with private depository credit used in the actual economy.

**Table 5.** Credit Velocities

| **Credit Velocity** | **STD/MAD – square root (π/2)** |
|---|---|
| Total domestic credit GDP velocity | −0.179559287 |
| Domestic nonfinancial sectors GDP circulation velocity | −0.121778343 |
| Bank credit GDP velocity | −0.027906248 |
| Bank credit GNE velocity | −0.006488075 |
| Money velocity | 0.030057841 |
| Private depository for GDP circulation velocity | −0.034857212 |
| Private depository for GNE circulation velocity | −0.002450358 |
| Private depository – Loans to commercial banks for GNE circulation velocity | 0.003163347 |
| Private depository – Loans to private depository for GNE circulation velocity | 0.017458766 |
| Private depository – Loans to nonbanks for GNE circulation velocity | 0.017455731 |
| Private depository – Loans to financial institutions for GNE circulation velocity | 0.02873597 |
| Perfect Normal distribution | 0 |

Source: Authors' computations.

Null Hypothesis: L_VELOCITY_PRIVATEDEP has a unit root
Exogenous: Constant
Lag Length: 0 (Automatic - based on SIC, maxlag=14)

| | | t-Statistic | Prob.* |
|---|---|---|---|
| Augmented Dickey-Fuller test statistic | | -0.376668 | 0.9096 |
| Test critical values: | 1% level | -3.457515 | |
| | 5% level | -2.873390 | |
| | 10% level | -2.573160 | |

*MacKinnon (1996) one-sided p-values.

**Figure 14.** Stationarity of credit velocity
Source: Authors' computations.

In addition to problems in disaggregating credit, there are two main issues such as lack of accounting for injections and leakages from the cyclical flow of income and a change in the propensity to spend, and the latter can vary even if the change in debt is zero. The leakages and injections are both equal. Exports, government spending and investment are examples of injections, while imports, tax payments and savings are examples of leakages (see Equation 16).

$$C+S+T=C+G+Inv+(E-I) \tag{16}$$

$$(E-I)+(G-T)+(\text{Inv}-S)=0 \tag{17}$$

Commercial balance Government deficit Private sector Investment – Savings

where E = exports, I = imports, G = government spending, T = taxes, Inv = private investment, C = private consumption, C + S = disposable income

Although it appears that it is not a suitable tool for targeting nominal GDP, the correlation between domestic private depository credit and GNE/GDP is 0.837248 (see Figure 15), which is slightly lower than the correlation between GNE/GDP and consumer credit (all three variables are expressed in logarithms), indicating that credit aggregates, particularly consumer credit, can be used to target trade deficits. Other variables include the dollar's status as the world's reserve currency and reduced import prices as a result of decreased labor costs.

| | L_CONSUMER_CREDIT_SA | L_GNE_GDP | L_PRIVATE_DEPOSITORY |
|---|---|---|---|
| L_CONSUMER_CREDIT_SA | 1.000000 | 0.837848 | 0.998495 |
| L_GNE_GDP | 0.837848 | 1.000000 | 0.837248 |
| L_PRIVATE_DEPOSITORY | 0.998495 | 0.837248 | 1.000000 |

**Figure 15.** Correlations of GNE/GDP with consumer credit and domestic private depository credit used for real economy

Source: Authors' computations.

### *1.3.1.2. Financial interconnections*

The calculated variables from the previous subchapter's financial flows will be used in our next investigation on financial interconnections.

To gain a better understanding of the connections between various entities in the financial world, we will examine the effect of monetary policy on the dynamics of financial lending.

## Research methodology and data

To investigate the influence of monetary policy on real financial credit flows (credit adjusted with the GDP deflator), we evaluate the impact of a 100-bps unexpected shock to the Federal Funds rate. We chose the Federal Funds rate to reflect monetary policy because Bernanke and Blinder (1992) believed it was the best predictor of monetary policy. Unlike Herman, Igan and Sole (2015), we do not include checkable and time and savings deposits in bank and nonbank holdings because we want to analyze the effect of Federal Funds increases on them separately. We run a VAR (2) with the following variables: Federal Funds rate, change in bank's holdings of assets issued by banks (DL_BANK_FROM_BANK), change in banks' holdings of assets issued by nonbanks (DL_BANK_FROM_NONBANK), change in nonbanks' holdings of assets issued by banks (DL_NONBANK_FROM_BANK), change in nonbanks' holdings of assets issued by nonbanks (DL_NONBANK_FROM_NONBANK), change in bank's holdings assets originating from the rest of the world (DL_BANK_FROM ROW), change in nonbank's holdings assets originating from the rest of the world – DL_BANK_FROM ROW (DL_NONBANK_FROM ROW), and change of the sum of checkable and time and savings deposits. All of the variables, excluding the Federal Funds rate, are expressed in the first difference of the logarithm.

A vector of 1 column and 8 rows with 100 bps in each cell was used for the impulse-response functions.

## Results and discussion

The results (see Figure 16) suggest that a 100-basis point increases in the Federal Funds rate will result in bigger increases in bank funding from nonbanks than in bank funding from banks. Following an increase in the Federal Funds rate, the funding of banks and nonbanks via ROW and deposits likewise accelerates. Although we expected Federal Funds rate shocks to result in less money being generated, we discovered empirically that this theoretical notion did not hold. Rate increases will result in more money being deposited at banks if they do not generate liquidity concerns for the banking system, whereas rate cuts do not always produce the intended results, particularly during liquidity traps. The reactions of asset holdings of nonbanks issued by banks and asset holdings of nonbanks issued by nonbanks appear to be a surprise result. The good effect on credit issued by nonbanks and held by nonbanks is not unexpected; however, the positive effect on credit issued by banks and held by nonbanks is unexpected, as is the fact that the effect on the latter is much larger than the effect on the former.

This reaction of banks and nonbanks to monetary policy shocks can be explained. Monetary tightening may result in increased interconnectivity. Banks relied on securitization to avoid a contraction or slowdown in loan supply growth. Banks turned their illiquid assets into tradable assets that they sold to nonbanks through special purpose vehicles, hence boosting the asset holdings of nonbanks issued by banks. Banks have been funded through this channel and have been able to avoid lowering loan growth despite central bank liquidity constraints.

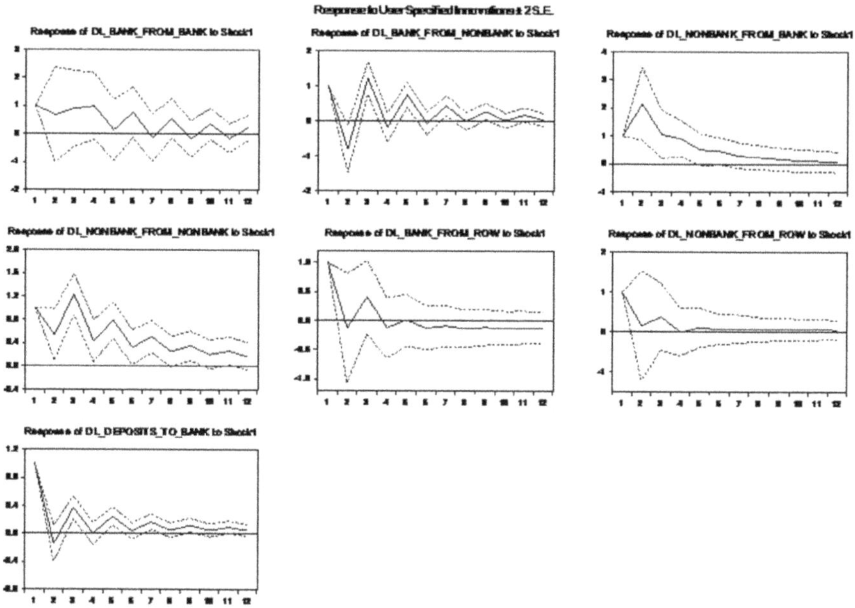


**Figure 16.** Impulse-response functions
Source: Authors' computations.

The evolution of financial credit (1954Q4–2019Q1) demonstrates the banking system's amazing agility to avoid the impacts of monetary tightening. Figure 17 (in Appendix 37) depicts the behavior of financial credit in comparison to the Federal Funds rate. Banking funding by banks was quite volatile from 1954Q4 to 1962Q3. The banks discovered a way to fund Federal Funds rate rises throughout the 1970s (when securitization began) by selling assets to nonbanks. Beginning in the 2000s, whenever banks and nonbanks faced financing challenges as a result of FED rate hikes or crisis outbreaks, there were increases in funding for banks and nonbanks via the rest of the world.

### *1.3.1.3. Securitization, credit origins, and holdings*

The past four decades have seen a period of financial innovation and nonbanking development (nonbanking superfinancialization), but when the extent of securitization is taken into account, the weight of loan origination by private depository institutions has not decreased as much as the share of holdings by private depository loans.

## Research methodology and data

We use a method similar to Unger's (2016) to assess the extent of securitization and the fraction of loans originated by private depository institutions. We use data for private depository institutions, shadow banks (Finance Companies – FC, Security Brokers and Dealers – SBD, and Issuers of Asset Backed Securities – IABS), and Government-sponsored Enterprises (GSE). We compute credit origination for the period sample 1968Q1–2019Q1. Start date is 1968, as this is the first year of mortgage-backed securities issuance (McConnell & Buser, 2011), although IABS, on which we focus, have started their activity in 1984Q4. The methodologies are distinct in the sense that we use aggregate loans for each type of institution (GSELA, IABSLA, SBDOLAA, FCLA, and FL704023005.Q) and have a different allocation into classes. While Unger (2016) has split the origination and the holding of loans into traditional banking (private depository institutions + GSE) and shadow banking, we divide them into private depository and non-private depository institutions (FC, SBD, IABS, and GSE). We compute the loans that originate from private depository by multiplying its share of holdings in total loan holdings to the holdings of IABS. The sum of the resultant amount and the private depository's holdings is divided by total loan holdings in order to obtain the share of loans originating from private depository institutions.

We compute the securitization ratio for private depository institutions as a fraction with the IABS loans originating from private depository institutions as numerator and the sum of balance sheet loans and securitized loans provided by the depository institutions as the denominator.

We estimate the impact of securitization on monetary policy with the help of two regression models for the period 1959Q1–2019Q1. Real economic growth (change after four quarters) is the dependent variable in both models. Real GDP growth is regressed in the first equation on economic growth with 1 lag (expressed in logarithm), on economic growth with 2 lags, and on moving Federal Funds rate (average of the current and last three quarters), also with 1 lag (see Equation 18). In the second regression, we allow the interest elasticity of output to vary with the securitization ratio (see Equation 19). The models used resemble the models developed by Estrella (2002). Estrella's (2002) models investigate the influence of single-family and multi-family securitized mortgages on the real interest elasticity of the output gap, whereas our models investigate the effect of credit originating from private depository institutions on the nominal interest of real GDP growth.

$$\Delta Y = \alpha + \beta_1 \Delta Y_{t-1} + \beta_2 \Delta Y_{t-2+} \beta_3 \Delta \bar{I}_{t-1} \tag{18}$$

Y is real GDP and Ī represents average Federal Funds rate.

$$\Delta Y = \alpha + \beta_1 \Delta Y_{t-1} + \beta_2 \Delta Y_{t-2+} (\beta_3 + \beta_4 S_r)(\Delta \bar{I}_{t-1}) \tag{19}$$

where Sr is securitization ratio.

## Results and discussion

Prior to the Great Recession, the share of private depository loans in loan origination had not declined as substantially (see Figures 18 and 19). Following the Great Recession, the pattern reversed and private depository institutions now dominate in terms of origination and holdings.

A strong peak in loan origination by private depository institutions and loan holdings by nonbanks may be seen in 2010Q1. This is due to the reintroduction of Freddie Mac and Fannie Mae mortgage pools into their balance sheets as a result of new accounting standards.

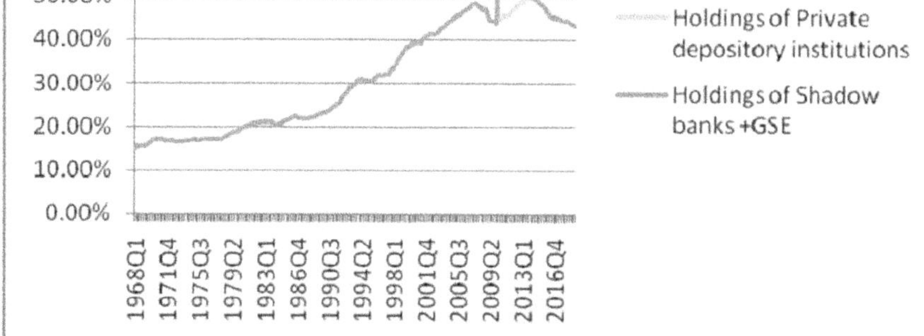


**Figure 18.** The structure of loan holdings

Source: Authors' computations.

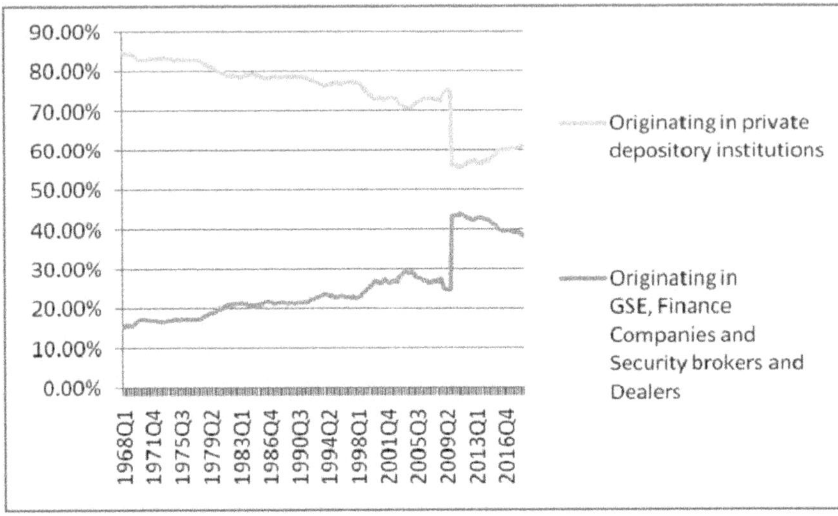


**Figure 19.** The weight of loan origination
Source: Authors' computations.

The greatest value of the securitization ratio was over 29.34% in 2007Q3 (see Figure 20), indicating that securitized loans constituted 41.51% of balance sheet loans.

**Figure 20.** Securitization ratio
Source: Authors' computations.

Following that, we examine how effective monetary policy is now, given that many banks use securitization to avoid monetary policy tightening and capital requirements, as well as to obtain quick funding.

Because the *p* values associated with the model and the coefficients are less than the chosen level of significance of 5%, the model is valid. The high coefficient of determination (above 0.81) indicates that the variables chosen have explanatory power. Although the *p* value linked with the coefficient of interest rate fluctuations is less than 5%, the coefficient value is very close to 0. Changes in interest rates have a slight adverse impact on economic growth, as we can see.

The result is entirely predictable. The securitization has a significant impact on the effectiveness of monetary policy in stimulating economic growth (see Figure 21). When we allow the interest elasticity to fluctuate with the proportion of securitized loans, we find a larger absolute coefficient that is nearly equivalent to −0.3 (see Figure 22). However, because the *p* value is 0.4778, we can conclude that monetary policy no longer has a direct impact on economic activity.

Dependent Variable: L_RGDP-L_RGDP(-4)
Method: Least Squares
Date: 12/26/19 Time: 00:10
Sample (adjusted): 1960Q3 2019Q1
Included observations: 235 after adjustments

| Variable | Coefficient | Std. Error | t-Statistic | Prob. |
|---|---|---|---|---|
| C | 0.004084 | 0.001196 | 3.413685 | 0.0008 |
| L_RGDP(-1)-L_RGDP(-5) | 1.219121 | 0.058910 | 20.69480 | 0.0000 |
| L_RGDP(-2)-L_RGDP(-6) | -0.354594 | 0.061653 | -5.751443 | 0.0000 |
| D(L_FED_FUNDS_AVERAGE(-1)) | -0.011639 | 0.005178 | -2.247839 | 0.0255 |

| | | | |
|---|---|---|---|
| R-squared | 0.810669 | Mean dependent var | 0.029887 |
| Adjusted R-squared | 0.808210 | S.D. dependent var | 0.021887 |
| S.E. of regression | 0.009585 | Akaike info criterion | -6.440343 |
| Sum squared resid | 0.021223 | Schwarz criterion | -6.381456 |
| Log likelihood | 760.7403 | Hannan-Quinn criter. | -6.416602 |
| F-statistic | 329.6941 | Durbin-Watson stat | 2.110635 |
| Prob(F-statistic) | 0.000000 | | |

**Figure 21.** Monetary policy impact on real GDP growth

Source: Authors' computations.

Dependent Variable: L_RGDP-L_RGDP(-4)
Method: Least Squares
Date: 12/26/19 Time: 00:10
Sample (adjusted): 1960Q3 2019Q1
Included observations: 235 after adjustments
L_RGDP-L_RGDP(-4)=C(1)+C(2)*(L_RGDP(-1)-L_RGDP(-5))+C(3)
*(L_RGDP(-2)-L_RGDP(-6))+(C(4)+C(5)*D(SECURITIZATION_RATIO))
* D(L_FED_FUNDS_AVERAGE(-1))

| | Coefficient | Std. Error | t-Statistic | Prob. |
|---|---|---|---|---|
| C(1) | 0.004147 | 0.001201 | 3.453304 | 0.0007 |
| C(2) | 1.224265 | 0.059415 | 20.60535 | 0.0000 |
| C(3) | -0.360483 | 0.062272 | -5.788803 | 0.0000 |
| C(4) | -0.012606 | 0.005359 | -2.352354 | 0.0195 |
| C(5) | -0.305969 | 0.430351 | -0.710977 | 0.4778 |

| | | | |
|---|---|---|---|
| R-squared | 0.811084 | Mean dependent var | 0.029887 |
| Adjusted R-squared | 0.807798 | S.D. dependent var | 0.021887 |
| S.E. of regression | 0.009595 | Akaike info criterion | -6.434027 |
| Sum squared resid | 0.021176 | Schwarz criterion | -6.360419 |
| Log likelihood | 760.9982 | Hannan-Quinn criter. | -6.404352 |
| F-statistic | 246.8676 | Durbin-Watson stat | 2.117533 |
| Prob(F-statistic) | 0.000000 | | |

**Figure 22.** Monetary policy with the degree of securitization's impact on real GDP growth

Source: Authors' computations.

### 1.3.2. The Fed's role in causing the great moderation

Craig S. Hakkio and other economists contend that the Fed played a substantial role in causing the Great Moderation. Our research findings imply differently. Because the Fed has less impact over real GDP growth, it should have less influence over real GDP volatility. Then we ask what the fundamental causes of the Great Moderation were and what role the Fed had in minimizing production volatility.

Kahn (2008) argues for reforms in inventory management, particularly in the durable products sector, as well as shorter lead times for material orders. We build a simple instrument to investigate the volatility associated with changes in real GDP, durable goods output (A354RC1Q027SBEA), and inventories.

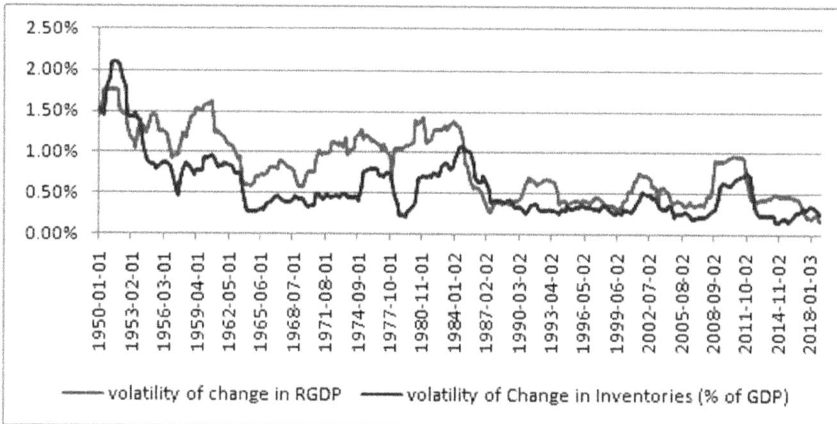


**Figure 23.** The volatilities of output and change in inventories (percentage of GDP)
Source: Authors' computations.

We compute the rolling three-year standard deviations of quarterly growth rates for each of the variables listed above. Following that, we evaluate the correlation coefficients between the volatilities of output and factors throughout two time periods: till 1984Q3 and between 1984Q4 and 2019Q1. Figure 23 shows a strong association between the volatility of changes in real GDP and the volatility of changes in inventories. The computed coefficient values, on the other hand, depict a different image. The value of the coefficient has dropped in the second period (see Table 6).

**Table 6.** Correlation Coefficients

| **Correlation coefficient of volatility of real GDP changes with the following variables:** | | |
|---|---|---|
| | 1950Q1–1984Q3 | 1984Q4–2019Q1 |
| Volatility of the change in inventories | 0.73 | 0.60 |
| Volatility of durable goods GDP | 0.79 | 0.84 |
| | | 1987Q1–2019Q1 |
| Lead time for material orders – average days | | -0.28 |
| | | 1950Q1–1984Q3 |
| Volatility of durable goods GDP | | 0.91 |
| | 1957Q2–1984Q3 | 1984Q4–2019Q1 |
| Volatility of Federal Funds rate | 0.42 | 0.46 |

Source: Authors' computations.

Most likely, the increasing weight of services in GDP, the decreasing share and volatility of change in inventories/GDP, as well as reducing lead time had a significant contribution to decreasing volatility, but in the second period, the strength of correlation has eroded for all of these variables, with the exception of volatility of durable goods GDP, which actually increased (see Figure 24).

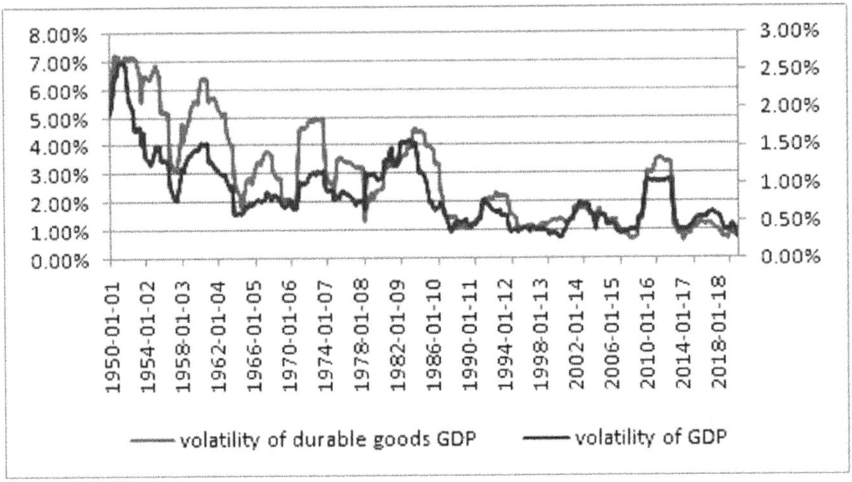


**Figure 24.** The volatilities of output and durable goods GDP (percentage of GDP)
Source: Authors' computations.

Gross domestic product: Durable goods (A354RC1Q027SBEA)

Because durable goods manufacturing is primarily a production-to-order industry rather than a production-to-stock industry, supply chain management advancements have reduced real GDP volatility. Improvements in logistics – such as lean manufacturing, which is characterized by waste reduction; just-in-time (JIT), which is designed to decrease production time and inventories; and the Kanban system, which maintains a minimum level of stockpiles – have ensured smooth production in all firms that use it.

The volatility of the Federal Funds rate is another component with a larger correlation in the second period examined, but the value of correlation is not as high as the logistical factors. Despite the negative impact of securitization on monetary policy transmission, the Federal Reserve System has reduced interest rate variability, which has contributed to a reduction in output volatility. The increased use of interest rates to combat inflation and recessions rather than "go-stop" policy, as well as the release of announcements regarding policy decisions, has helped to stabilize inflation. By always rescuing Wall Street from stock market collapses, a moral hazard was created. Furthermore, the Fed takes an unfair posture by always rising interest rates; when wage share (percentage of GDP) and median wages rise, or unemployment falls, the Fed responds by raising the targeted Federal Funds rate. The Fed has become a slave to the stock market and obsessed with inflation (Cauwels & Sornette, 2012). This behavior resulted in a slowing of what Croitoru (2015) refers to as basic aggregate demand (GDP minus wealth effect) as a result of limited inflation and an increasing wealth effect as a result of Greenspan and Bernanke Put. Despite the rising bubbles, these monetary policy measures ensured that no demand exceeded potential GDP (Summers, 2013), reviving the secular stagnation idea.

If we use the "Potential GDP" concept, the Fed has been cutting both basic aggregate demand and potential GDP by aiming for low and stable inflation, but this has resulted in inflated asset bubbles, bringing the economy to the now-lowered GDP potential. As the Fed, along with other factors such as lower investment and employment required for information and communication technology (Turner, 2014), induced a lower potential GDP or a lower average GDP growth in the medium and long run (if we want to skip the "potential GDP" framework), and always supplied liquidity to the banks so bubbles were able to persist longer and the economic cycle was lengthened (see Figure 25), the real GDP volatility was reduced.

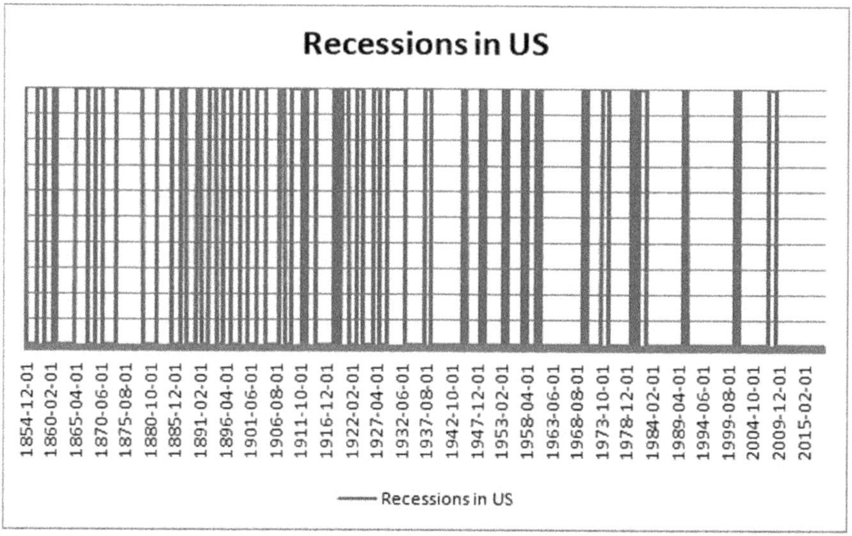


**Figure 25.** U.S. recessions
Source: NBER Data.

This was nicknamed the "Jackson Hole Consensus": It was better to mop up after the disaster than to combat asset bubbles until the Great Recession broke out. However, it is evident that it should adopt a different stance, especially since interest rates are far too low to combat a deep recession. While aiming for a low and consistent inflation rate is necessary to avoid currency depreciation, it is damaging to financial stability because low inflation cannot avoid a liquidity trap. Low inflation at the start of the crisis is detrimental to businesses with a high debt/cash flow ratio. Companies will sell assets and set lower prices in order to pay their debt. These measures will cut inflation while increasing real debt (nominal debt adjusted for inflation), causing the economy to enter a deflationary spiral.

### 1.3.3. The movement of long-term and short-term interest rates

The primary goal of this subchapter is to investigate the relationship between short-term interest rates (3-month Treasury constant maturity rate) and longer-term interest rates (10-year Treasury constant maturity rate). Long-term interest rates typically follow short-term interest rates, at least in theory. Despite this, the Fed was taken aback in 2005 by a paradox, as Alan Greenspan (2005) termed it: Long-term interest rates no longer depended on the Federal Funds rate. Despite the fact that the FOMC raised the target level of the Federal Funds rate by 1.50 percentage points, the 10-year Treasury rate continued to fall. He had no idea that other economists, such as Campbell (1988), Estrella and Hardouvelis (1991), and others, had already solved this conundrum. Short-term interest rates are impacted by monetary policy, whereas long-term interest rates are influenced by both monetary policy and investor sentiment regarding the health of the economy. When investors have a poor outlook on the economy, there is a shift in risk aversion that monetary policy cannot address. Essentially, there is a capital flight to safety. Flows from the equities market and other hazardous markets are flowing into the bond market, particularly long-term bonds. The yield on long-term bonds will reduce as prices climb. There will be an inversion of the yield curve. The yield curve is a major predictor of recession in the United States (Harvey, 1988); but, as we will see in the following chapter, this predictor is effective in all nations, not just the United States. Because banks and nonbanks borrow in the short run and invest in the long run, the inversion of the yield curve will have an impact on their earnings; the flow of credit will become negative, causing consumption and investment to collapse, resulting in a recession.

## Research methodology and data

We will test the dynamic lead-lag patterns between the interest rates by using a modified thermal optimal path (Meng, Zhou, & Sornette, 2014). We standardize the time series and compute the minimum distance with the following formula:

$$\text{Minimum Distance} = \sqrt{(\text{Xtx} - \text{Yty})^2} \tag{20}$$

where

Xtx = standardized value of 3-month interest rate at moment tx
Yty = standardized value of 10-year interest rate at moment ty

For the interest rate distances, we generate a matrix (255 X 255) for the data sample 1954Q4–2018Q1.

## Results and discussion

We find that the maximum difference between interest rates is 20Q, which is feasible given Taylor's (2009) argument that interest rates were excessively low in 2002–2004, which was the primary cause of the Great Recession. The acquired series are too noisy and have large jumps. Although Meng, Su, Zhou, and Sornette (2014) utilize a rotational frame and weighted Boltzmann factors, we simply use an 8-quarter moving average because monetary policy is expected to take impact after no more than 8 quarters (MCM model). This simple process eliminated the majority of the jumps in our created series and prevented deviations from the minimum distance. Positive values in our calculated series indicate that short-term interest rates are ahead of long-term interest rates, whereas the negative values indicate the opposite. Because the mode for our series is 8 quarters and the majority of the negative values occur prior to recessions and yield curve inversions, we may conclude that the constructed time series accurately depicts the general movement and dependency of interest rates. Except in the run-up to a recession, short-term rates usually drive long-term rates. Figure 26 also shows that, beginning in 2017Q2, long rates do not follow short rates. This event occurred prior to the yield curve inversion that began in 2019 Q2.

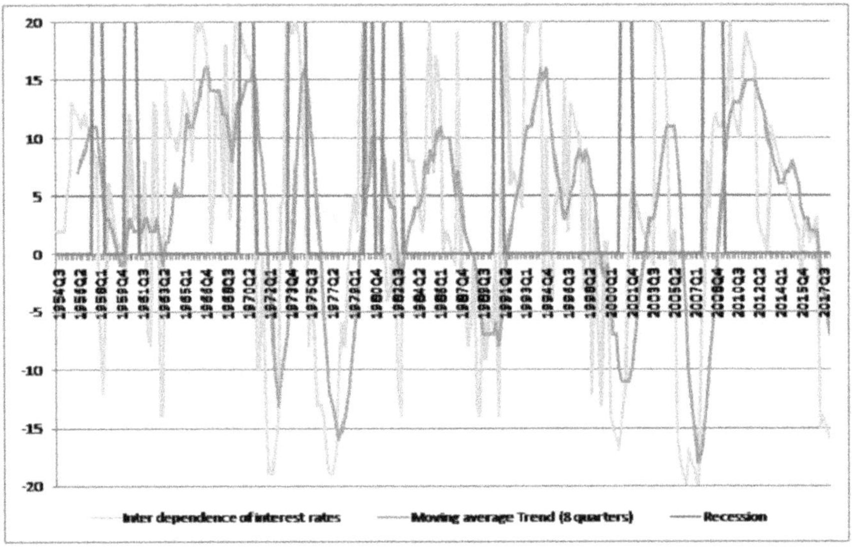


**Figure 26.** Codependence of long-term and short-term interest rates
Source: Authors' computations.

## 1.4. Preliminary conclusions

The financial system in the United States has seen significant changes over the past five decades. Securitization and nonbanking superfinancialization are just two examples of the trends. Regardless of all the improvements, we discovered that money is still important for actual GDP. Because M2 leads the cycle and the monetary base lags, the Federal Reserve (Fed) will respond to changes in real GDP (affected by money supply) by adjusting M0, implying that the money multiplier theory is wrong. The impact of loans and bank credit on economic activity has expanded as the relationship between money and GDP has deteriorated. We examined the stability of the velocity of credit for GDP transactions since the Fed cannot successfully target monetary aggregates. We can conclude that the Fed cannot target credit for GDP transactions due to the volatility of the velocity.

Interconnectivity is another aspect of the financial system. Because of increased interconnectivity, U.S. banks have been able to avoid monetary tightening. Securitization was one of the channels. According to our empirical findings, the Federal Reserve has lost its direct effect on economic activity as a result of securitization. Then it became clear to us that the Federal Reserve did not have a significant role in causing the Great Moderation. The supply-chain improvements played a larger role. The Federal Reserve has reduced output volatility by providing money to banks when needed, inflating bubbles and lowering basic aggregate demand.

We also investigated the Fed's primary tool: short-term interest rates. According to our model, long-term interest rates are typically impacted by short-term interest rates. Inverted yield curves are expected when this rule is breached. Even if the financial world has become more complex, it appears that the Fed can still have an impact on the economy.

# 2 Historical, Conceptual, and Empirical Approaches to Crises

**Abstract:** The purpose of this chapter is to highlight the hazards of the equilibrium paradigm for economic agents and policymakers, as well as to demonstrate the inseparability of the business cycle from the financial cycle. The main goals of this chapter are to investigate the flaws of the equilibrium theory, particularly the underestimation of risks, to demonstrate that the financial system caused almost all of the recessions identified by the NBER in the United States and to investigate the main recession predictors. Business cycles are perceived in the literature, particularly in new classical macroeconomics, as the result of productivity shocks (Stadler, 1994). Borio (2012) classified recessions as business cycles and financial cycles, whereas we believe that almost all recessions are caused by lower levels of credit availability and tighter credit standards. Given that the central element of this research is proving that the financial system is the source of economic crises, the purpose of this chapter is to demonstrate with evidence that nearly all recessions have financial roots and, thus, financial variables used as recession indicators should have longer leads than real variables. The recession process begins with significant shifts in risk aversion (shown by an inverted yield curve), which leads to a fall in the profitability of financial institutions. Financial institutions will respond by tightening lending standards and limiting credit availability, resulting in a fall in investment and consumption. In this setting, determining the best recession predictions and the lag between predictors and crises is critical. Starting with the stated goal and objectives, this chapter is structured as follows:

(a) Stressing the challenges raised by the equilibrium approach
(b) Arguing against the separation of business and financial cycles.

**Keywords:** business cycle, financial cycle, crises, yield curve, equilibrium theory

## 2.1. The influence of the financial system on economic crises: The historical context

We examine six major crises to assess the relevance of the financial system in economic declines. We begin with the most well-known disaster in history, the Tulip Crisis, due to irrational exuberance. We also investigate the Panic of 1907 because of bank crashes and because it resulted in the establishment of the Federal Reserve in 1913, the Great Depression because of its severity, the Great Stagflation because of its various causes (both financial and supply side), the Dotcom crisis because of irrational exuberance, and the Great Recession because it was the second most severe crisis that the U.S. economy faced in the last 100 years.

### 2.1.1. Tulip crisis

The Tulip Mania of the 17th century was described by Charles Mackay in 1841 and is considered one of the earliest speculative bubbles. Tulip bulb prices jumped at the time, only to collapse again. According to Mackay, people were so obsessed with Dutch tulips that the country's usual businesses were neglected (Mackay, 1841, p. 142). However, Mackay did not present evidence that the mania was caused by a market deviation from fundamentals.

According to Garber (2000), rare types of tulips with unusual coloring caused by mosaic virus infection were pricey. These tulips were quite unusual. These peculiar flowers held significant cultural significance in Holland. As a result, high tulip prices are comparable to high prices for rare art pieces. However, economists were unable to blame all tulip price changes on rational behavior. According to Peter Garber (1989), in January 1636, the price of ordinary bulbs jumped twentyfold and then dropped substantially and it is difficult to find rational reasons for this event.

### 2.1.2. The Panic of 1907

The Panic of 1907 was precipitated by a series of rash financial actions and huge withdrawals fueled by public skepticism about the banking system. Each bank's failure eroded trust in the others.

The crisis began in New York institutions known as "trusts," which functioned on deposits but had the goal of managing inheritances for rich customers. In comparison to national banks, they had fewer rules and weaker cash reserves. Because the economy grew greatly in the first decade of the 20th century, trusts began to speculate in the stock market and real estate. Trusts could have given larger yields since they were not as regulated as banks. As a result, trusts quickly expanded: by 1907, the whole value of trust assets in New York was equal to the total value of national bank assets (Krugman, 2009, p. 155).

The Knickerbocker Trust, a prominent New York City trust that fell when it financially supported large-scale stock market speculation, triggered the 1907 Panic. This tragedy eroded the confidence of other investors, who withdrew large sums of money. This resulted in the stock market meltdown because stock traders were unable to acquire credit for their trades.

J. P. Morgan's assistance in putting a stop to the panic improved the situation. He recognized that the panic would impact healthy institutions as well; therefore he, along with other rich bankers, contributed to the building of banks' and trusts' reserves, so that they could withstand the attack of massive withdrawals. The panic subsided after investors realized they could withdraw their funds. The panic lasted only a few days, but it had a significant impact on the economy. Four years of recession followed, with unemployment rising from 3% to 8%.

The 1907 Panic resulted in banking reform. The Federal Reserve System was established in 1913. As a result, all deposit-taking banks were required to maintain bigger reserves and to be examined by regulators (Krugman, 2009, p. 155).

### 2.1.3. Great Depression of the 1930s

The effects of the Great Depression were felt all around the world. It was the impetus for the New Deal in the United States, as well as a factor in the outbreak of World War II.

The Great Depression was the longest and most painful depression in Western history. Even though the crisis began in the United States, it spread and resulted in substantial declines in production, high unemployment, and deflation in practically all states throughout the world. The Great Depression was the second major crisis in the United States following the Civil War. The depths of the Great Depression differed by country. The Great Depression lasted longer and was more severe in the United States and Europe than in Japan, South and Central America, and Asia.

The fall in the stock market was not the sole cause of the Great Depression. There are additional factors that contributed to this depression. During the 1920s, American firms made great profits and reinvested large sums in expansion. By 1929, businesses had grown tremendously. A slowdown was unavoidable, as workers couldn't keep up with such rapid growth. While corporate profits fell, wages gradually rose, resulting in a widening of the wealth distribution.

American banks operated without providing guarantees to their consumers, causing uncertainty. They also lent money to stock traders. Another element that added to the intensity of the issue was that as the depression spread over America, Europeans began to buy fewer American items.

In the United States, the economy would not recover until after 1939, when World War II stimulated American industry.

### 2.1.4. Great stagflation

Blinder (1979, 1982), Blinder and Rudd (2008) concluded that the two OPEC shocks, as well as the cancellation of wage-price controls, had a significant impact on the commencement of the Great Stagflation. Aside from the supply shock, another element that contributed to the Great Stagflation was increased demand, whether through monetary or fiscal policy.

According to Barsky and Kilian (2000), the main causes of the 1970s Great Stagflation were monetary expansions and contractions. Oil price increases, in their opinion, could not have caused stagflation if the Federal Reserve had avoided expansionary monetary policy. Furthermore, Barsky and Kilian argue that a prolonged increase in the price of oil is not achievable in the absence of a favorable macroeconomic environment, particularly robust economic growth and low interest rates. As the monetarists gained influence, the banking system's implicit deregulation led to debt accumulation. Credit crunches, along with increased inflation at the start of crises and low interest rates, ensured quick debt-based recoveries.

### 2.1.5. Dotcom mania

The dotcom bubble was a speculative bubble that affected the shares of early Internet companies. It was most severe in the United States. It primarily occurred between 1994 and 2000, a period marked by a significant increase in Internet usage.

In March 2000, the Nasdaq index, which contained largely firms with Internet-related activity, crashed. Many dotcom companies lost money because they spent a lot of money on advertising to gain a larger market share. Furthermore, many businesses provided services or products at reduced cost or no cost in order to gain the necessary popularity to allow them to raise their pricing in the future.

By the year 2000, investors had lost faith after realizing that the dotcom boom was a speculative bubble. Panic broke out as the stock market's value dropped by trillions of dollars. Furthermore, a slew of reports appeared claiming that tech corporations had artificially raised their profits. In 2001, the United States experienced a post-dotcom-bubble recession. This occurrence prompted the Fed to lower interest rates in order to mitigate the losses. Many IT workers lost their jobs, as well as a significant portion of their funds, as a result of investing in tech stocks. As a result, the new economy theory was revealed to be incorrect.

### 2.1.6. The great recession

The development of the global economic and financial crisis, commonly known as the Great Recession, was precipitated by the collapse of the subprime mortgage bubble in the United States and its spread around the world. The Great Recession began in August 2007 in the United States and touched all sectors of international economic life. Financial markets confronted numerous issues that had a significant impact on company success.

The economists who were unable to predict the recession attempted to understand why they were unable to predict the event and its duration. From late 2007 through the third quarter of 2009, the global economy was severely impacted by the Great Recession. Consumption, investment, and employment all fell precipitously.

Economists believe that the Great Recession was caused by a drop in housing prices as well as a banking system that was vulnerable to bank runs. Because households were unable to increase spending, this recession lasted longer than any previous recessions. Many economists feel that the crisis could not have been predicted since the scale and volatility of the banking sector were not detected in time. The Great Recession had an unexpected effect on macroeconomics in that it forced economists to incorporate the financial sector into their models (Christiano, 2017).

All of the given crises have overindebtedness and irrational exuberance at their foundation. The ability of debtors and borrowers to fulfill their promises determines the functioning of any economy (Minsky, 1980).

## 2.2. Considerations about equilibrium illusions

The junction of supply and demand is represented by economic equilibrium. This word, however, is an illusion; it is a simple and beautiful means of conducting analysis, but it is faulty. It is all an illusion. Policymakers can smooth the inflation rate and GDP growth, but they are actually masking concerns. The low and stable inflation rate combines with relatively continuous fiscal deficits, with central banks providing liquidity to the market when the stock market falls and tightening monetary policy when wages expand. Investors are given a false sense of security by policymakers. It provides the idea that the economy can develop at a stable rate and that the central bank and government can back this up. In reality, this is not always the case, particularly in heavily indebted economies with a fragile financial structure. However, governments and central banks are simply amplifying a sentiment that has already been established by banks and other financial entities. Their euphoria offers the sense of continuous growth, persuading us that "this time is different." As a result, investors are fooled by credit institutions' euphoria. Because euphoria hinders the market from making regular corrections, markets can be overoptimistic or overpessimistic for extended periods of time.

Credit availability and lax credit criteria assist underperforming companies remain in the market by providing them with financing and allowing them to use high leverage. Credit expansions prevent real estate from following the law of supply and demand, whereas credit, financial innovations, and Fed interventions cause stock market bubbles. Markets are never in equilibrium; we are simply fooled by economic growth and credit-fueled booms into believing that the economy is in equilibrium. The markets are seeking balance, but this equilibrium may simply be an unsustainable state of the economy sustained solely by credit. The economy's disequilibrium can be seen in the form of long-term imbalances such as stock market bubbles, home price booms, and current account deficits. Another sign is the credit-to-GDP ratio, which indicates that more funds (e.g., from debt) are flowing into asset price speculations, are poorly invested, or are funding commercial deficits.

Most of us believe the economy is in disequilibrium only during a recession, which is comparable to the corridor hypothesis suggested by Leijonhufvud (1973). According to the corridor hypothesis, the economy may regulate itself toward equilibrium within a corridor, but, outside of the corridor, the economic system loses its self-regulating mechanism. However, Austrian business cycle theorists view recessions as a means of restoring equilibrium and eliminating misinvestments (Huerta de Soto, 2006, p. 416). Instead, if the mechanisms are self-reinforcing, such as debt deflation and stagflation, this process can also lead to disequilibrium.

There are various statistical methods to detect disequilibrium, but most of them represent disequilibrium as small deviations from long-run equilibrium. Some of the methods in this regard include the error correction toward long-term equilibrium models, for example, or deviations from the trend predicted with band-pass filters, the latter of which is also used to detect bubbles.

The fundamental advantage of these statistical techniques is that they are dynamic; yet, they never reflect big and long-lasting deviations from equilibrium induced by the financial system's excitement. Also, some variation is required to ensure that commercial possibilities do not slide through the cracks. The conclusions drawn from the use of band-pass filters and long-run equilibrium models imply that businesses should not take advantage of these fluctuations and that policymakers should eradicate them (New Keynesians).

Macroeconomic equilibrium necessitates market clearing prices and economic growth that is equal to or nearly equal to potential economic growth at a steady state rate. Prices are not always flexible; in these circumstances, markets do not clear, and, in some cases, such as debt deflations, price flexibility worsens the economic situation because debt becomes more difficult to pay as prices and wages fall.

Normality tests can be used to put the steady-state growth-rate theory to the test. If the economic growth time series does not follow a Gaussian bell curve, it suggests that extreme events occur more frequently than a normal distribution would imply/predict and the time series has undergone considerable deviations from a steady-state rate or its average rate.

The Markowitz model (1952) and the Arrow–Debreu equilibrium model (1954) dominated asset pricing in microeconomics and finance, with normality assumptions applied. The Arrow–Debreu model predates and serves as a foundation for real business cycle models, the macroeconomic theory that has dominated over the previous 30 years. The impulses in these models are normally distributed (Haldane, 2012). The DSGE models produce a unique and stationary equilibrium with regular oscillations around it (Haldane, 2016). DSGE models include both RBC and New Keynesian models; the latter are basically the same as RBC but only include frictions like sticky prices.

Output volatility decreased dramatically during the Great Moderation as a result of economic policies, supply chain, and industry innovations (see subchapter 1.2.4). Suppressing volatility, on the other hand, might lead to fragile systems (Taleb & Blyth, 2011). As a result, volatility suppression will not result in a normal distribution since low volatility would conceal risks and produce huge deviations from the target economic growth rate.

## Research methodology and data

In order to test for normality, we apply the Jarque–Bera test on daily and monthly S&P returns, real GDP growth, unemployment rate, and total unemployment rate time series. We used 20,087 observations from March 1, 1928 to December 31, 2007 for daily S&P (we use it instead of S&P 500 in order to have more observations). The period was chosen because we know that there were large changes in S&P returns in 2008, and we want to estimate VAR and the probabilities of extreme events occurring using past data.

## Results and discussion

As we can observe in Figure 27, with a skewness of –0.086 and a kurtosis of 21.63, the distribution of S&P daily returns isn't normal.

The largest losses that occurred in 2008 include the following: 8.81% on September 29, 2008; 9.03% on October 15, 2008; and 8.93% on January 12, 2008.

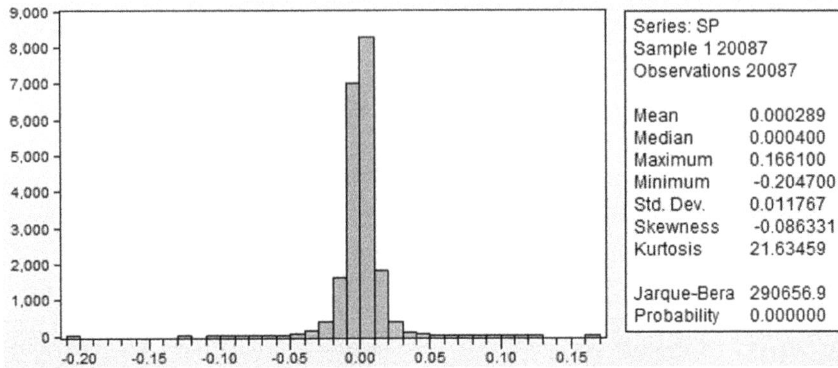


**Figure 27.** Distribution of daily returns for S&P for March 1, 1928–December 31, 2007
Source: Authors' computations using data from Yahoo Finance.

We have estimated historical, normal Value at Risk, as well VaR based on a symmetrical Chebyshev distribution by using the formula (Equation 21):

$$VaR\alpha = \mu - Z\alpha^{*}\sigma \qquad (21),$$

where α is the confidence interval, Z is the distance between confidence interval, mean expressed in standard deviations, and σ is standard deviation.

Chebyshev's inequality states maximum $1/k^2$ of the distribution's values will beat a distance of k standard deviations away from the mean.

The results presented in Table 7 show that normal distribution underestimates risks. Using a Chebyshev $VaR_{1\%}$ would have anticipated the large swings in price in 2008. But this is a highly unlikely event according to Gauss bell, because it is seven standard deviations away from average. In fact, these price movements seem to be random events.

**Table 7.** Value at Risk for daily S&P

| Count | 5% potential losses | 1% potential losses | 0.07% potential losses |
|---|---|---|---|
| 20087 | 1004 | 201 | 14 |
| Historical VaR | −1.64% | −3.36% | −8.02% |
| Normal VaR | −1.91% | −2.71% | −3.73% |
| Chebyshev VaR | −3.69% | −8.29% | −31.42% |

Source: Authors' computations.

We estimate the occurrence of a Z sigma event in a normal distribution by dividing 1/probability corresponding to Z sigma events. We find out that 2 sigma events occur once every 44 trading days, 3 sigma events occur once every 741 trading days, while 7 sigma events should happen once every 3.1 billion trading years (see Table 8).

**Table 8.** Event occurrence according to a normal distribution

| Z | Probability | Occurrence according to bell curve |
|---|---|---|
| 2 | 2.275013194818% | 43.96 |
| 3 | 0.134989803163% | 740.80 |
| 4 | 0.003167124184% | 31574.39 |
| 5 | 0.000028665157% | 3488555.79 |
| 6 | 0.000000098659% | 1013594634.89 |
| 7 | 0.000000000128% | 781332343402.24 |

Source: Authors' computations

However, it occurred three times in 2008 for S&P returns (when only the left half of the distribution was considered). Figure 28 shows the enormous contrast between the histogram of historical returns and a Gaussian distribution with the same mean and standard deviation, where the density (frequency/bin width) is much larger at the tails for the historical returns.

When we examine monthly returns for the S&P (January 1928–December 2007), we see that, when compared to daily returns, the extreme events in this case are less frequent, despite the fact that the distribution is also not normal (see Figure 28 and 29).

The risks are still being understated, as the largest monthly loss recorded in 2008 is 16.94% (October 2008), which is greater than the expected historical and normal VaR. Using a Chebyshev VaR with a 5% confidence interval would have predicted a loss of 16.78%, which is pretty close to the actual result (see Table 9).

Extreme financial events, such as financial scandals and bankruptcies of financial institutions, can lead to extreme events in the real economy (recessions), whereas stock market crashes can cause recessions or exacerbate them through the wealth effect and diminished market confidence.

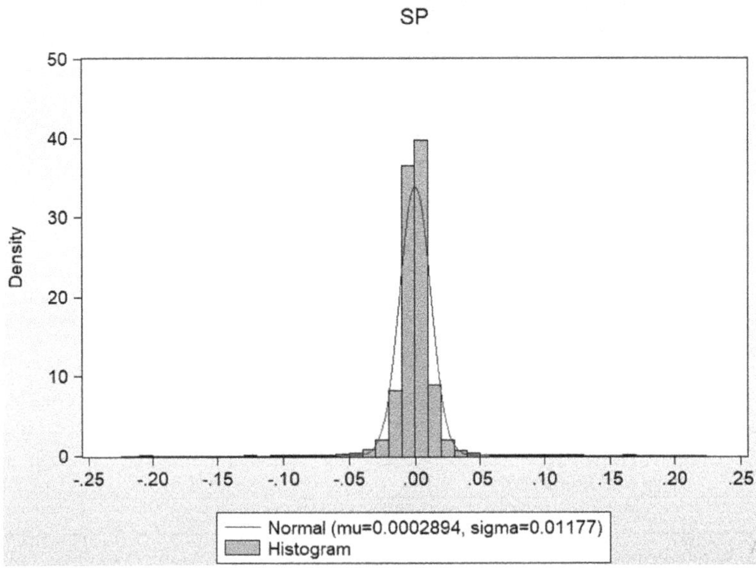


**Figure 28.** S&P histogram of daily returns and normal distribution
Source: Authors' computations.

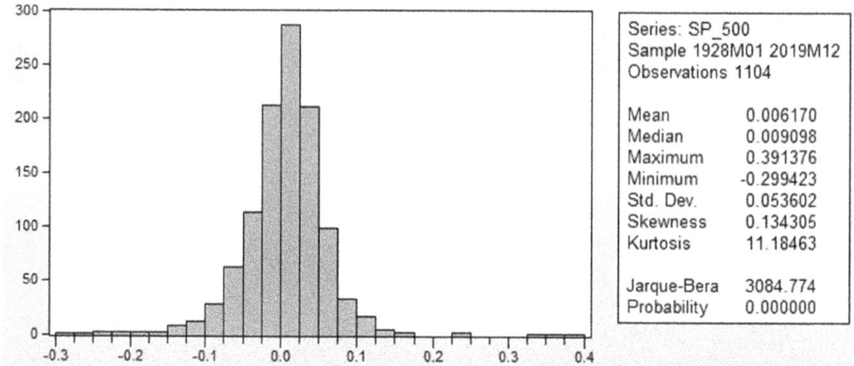


**Figure 29.** S&P returns – histogram

Source: Authors' computations.

**Table 9.** Value at risk for S&P monthly returns

| VaR | 5% | 1% |
|---|---|---|
| Historical | −7.78% | −14.58% |
| Normal distribution | −8.44% | −12.18% |
| Chebyshev | −16.78% | −38.29% |

Source: Authors' computations.

The distribution of quarterly GDP growth (annual change) for the period 1948Q1–2019Q3 is not normal (see Figure 30).

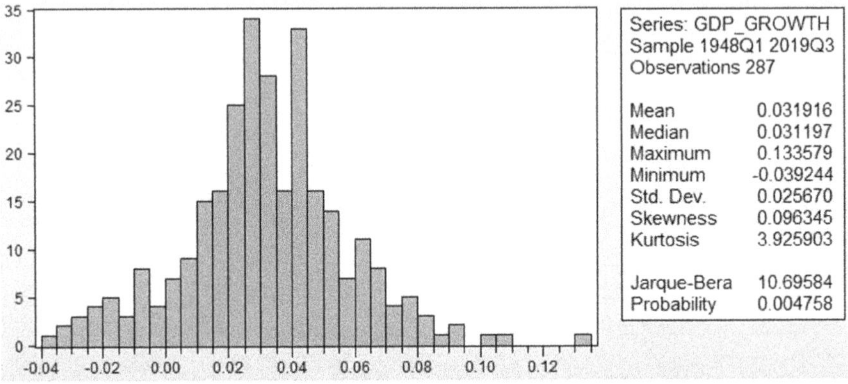


**Figure 30.** Distribution of GDP growth

Source: Authors' computations; raw data from St. Louis Fed.

Normality can also be analyzed in a dynamic way. We use 30 quarters for a rolling STD/MAD and compare it with the normal level of 1.253 (see Figure 31).

There are also other ways of proving the disequilibrium.

In order to show that equilibrium is rarely achieved and that there is no path to equilibrium, we compute a coefficient of synchronization (see Equation 22) for Output Gap/Real Potential GDP 1949Q1–2019Q3.

$$\text{Synchronization} = \frac{T}{N} \tag{22}$$

where T = number of observations within the chosen target of Output Gap and N = total number of observations.

We use targets of ±0.1% and ±0.01% of Real Potential GDP, as we can consider that Output Gap is close to 0 in these two cases.

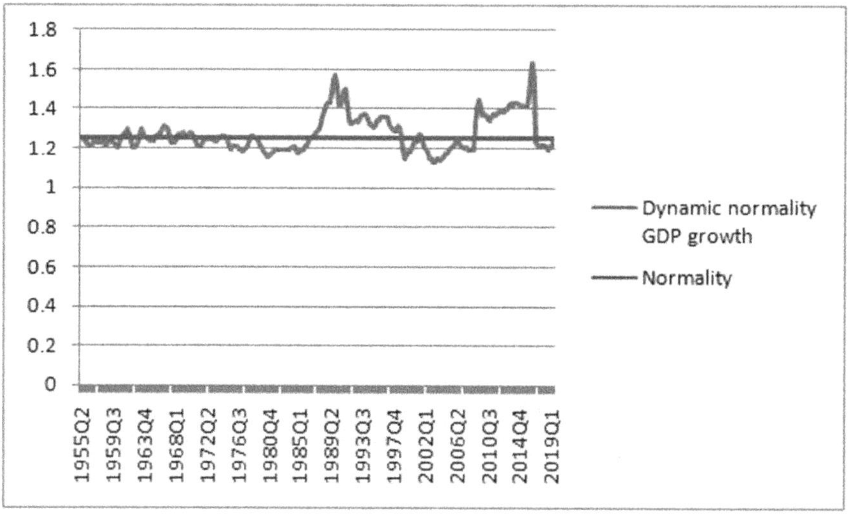


**Figure 31.** STD/MAD for real GDP growth
Source: Author's calculation; raw data from St. Louis Fed.

The synchronization coefficient is 3.89% for a target of 0.1% of Real Potential GDP, which means that only 3.89% of the time the output was within this target and 0.35% for a target of 0.01%.

Another confirmation is the autocorrelation coefficient of Output Gap/Real Potential GDP for the same period (see Appendix 16). Because the output gap exhibits substantial autocorrelation (the autocorrelation at the first lag is 0.931 and subsequently decays to 0), it indicates that the output gap is clustering – good times will follow good times and bad times will follow bad times (Grauwe, 2010). This demonstrates the persistence of the output gap, which indicates that the economy works far from equilibrium (or at a steady-state rate) for extended periods of time. The lack of normality, low synchronization coefficient, and autocorrelation of Output Gap/Real Potential GDP suggest significant and continuous deviations from the equilibrium path (see Appendix 12). Even when economic development is suboptimal, economists always use the term "equilibrium" rather than "disequilibrium."

Another method of demonstrating disequilibrium is to refute Say Law. According to Say Law, supply generates its own demand. Because the supply of some goods and services is limited, the income generated by the production of those goods and services will finance the demand for other goods and services.

Essentially, there cannot be a universal glut. However, this would imply that all funds are spent for product manufacture and purchase. However, money is also used for wealth growth, particularly the use of money for unproductive profits, that is, speculating. This alternative money circuit indicates that lesser funds are accessible for the purchase of goods and services.

Very high levels of income inequality would widen the gap between aggregate supply and aggregate demand in a barter economy or a very restrictive finance system. The complicated financial environment in which we now live has the potential to solve or postpone these issues in the short and medium term. However, rising inequality, along with increased leverage on the part of low-income households in order to maintain their standard of living, will pose financial dangers and is an unsustainable process. It is not by chance that the two most severe crises in the last century – the Great Depression and the Great Recession – were preceded by high levels of income and wealth inequality.

Misallocation of financial resources to unsustainable industries is another way the financial system produces the illusion of equilibrium. Banks and other financial organizations may undervalue risks, grow overconfident, and oversupply one or more industries with loans. Reduced credit availability for these sectors, if these sectors play a significant role in the economy, could lead to a recession.

In fact, we know that:

*Output (Production or GDP) – Demand (Final Sales) = Change in stocks* (23)

Following a dramatic drop in demand, firms are producing less in order to consume their stocks and reduce their high levels of inventory. Figure 32 shows that throughout each recession, the change in stocks was negative as a result of inventories being adjusted due to the prior reduction in demand. This assumption is also confirmed by the co-movements (analyzed period 1954Q3–2019Q3) between changes in inventories and NBER recessions (see Appendix 13) and the comovements between changes in inventories and real GDP contractions from the previous quarter (see Appendix 14). The annexes show that negative changes in inventories follow real GDP contractions and are more closely connected with real GDP contractions than with recessions.

Despite the availability of data on new orders and inventory changes, predicting the equilibrium based on these signs is impossible. Changes in inventories are affected by causes other than demand, such as technical adjustments, lead-time changes, logistics improvements, strategy changes (production-to-stock vs. production-to-order), and services.

$$Coefficient\ of\ variation = Standard\ deviation/Average \tag{24}$$

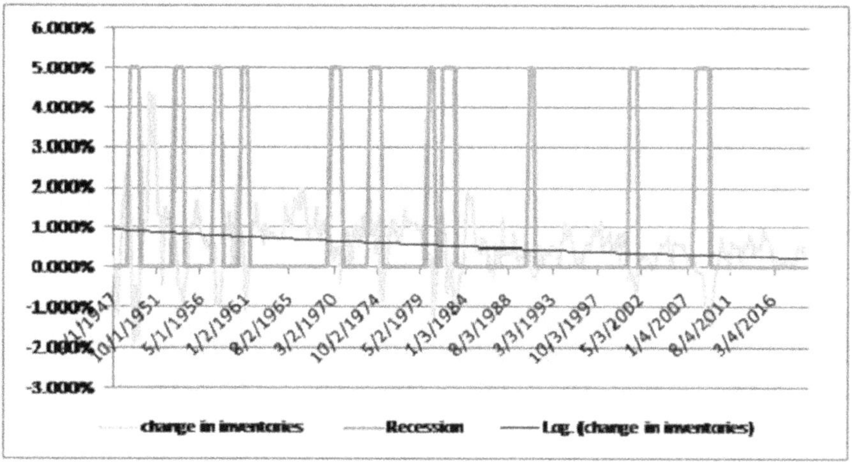


**Figure 32.** Change in inventories/GDP
Source: Authors' computations; primary data from St. Louis Fed.

Changes in stocks near to zero may not indicate equilibrium; they may be part of adjusting or progressively reducing inventories, or they may indicate technological advancements and a general drop in lead times. Inventories allow for production. For the period 1947Q2–2019Q3, the variation coefficient for change in stocks (change in stocks/GDP) is 142.38%, compared to 70.70% for production (nominal GDP, growth, change from a quarter ago) and 61.58% for sales (nominal final sales growth, change from a quarter ago; data from St. Fed Louis).

Increasing changes in inventories are not usually the result of a drop in demand. Positive adjustments in inventory have been sustained as a result of received and predicted increased orders. Both the pattern of inventory change and the tendency of economic growth slowed with time. This implies not only better inventory management but also slower demand growth. The opposite of Say Law is true: A lack of demand leads to a lack of supply. In fact, supply-side shocks do occur but occur less often.

Because the equilibrium of demand and supply should provide full employment, the short-term multiplier of government deficit should be zero (government deficit inelasticity of GDP growth) in order to achieve full employment and/or the difference between job openings and unemployment rate should be zero, implying that involuntary unemployment is equal to zero.

Since the government deficit elasticity of GDP growth is usually greater than zero and the job openings–unemployment rate is always positive, except for the period 2018Q1–2019Q3, and the capacity utilization rate is always less than 100% (see Appendix 15), full employment demand is rarely attained.

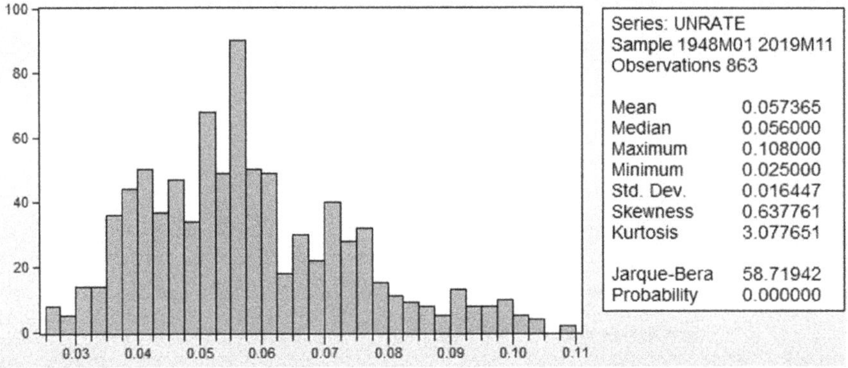


**Figure 33.** Unemployment rate, percentage, monthly, s.a.
Source: Authors' computations; data from St. Louis Fed.

We may see evidence for this claim in the distribution of the unemployment rate and the true unemployment rate, both of which are not normal (Figures 33 and 34). Another piece of evidence is the fact that actual unemployment time series have a unit root (see Figure 35). True unemployment is non-stationary, implying that time series have a constant mean and variation across time, implying that changes are not temporary but permanent. These findings are consistent with a sustained lack of demand and unappealing salaries.

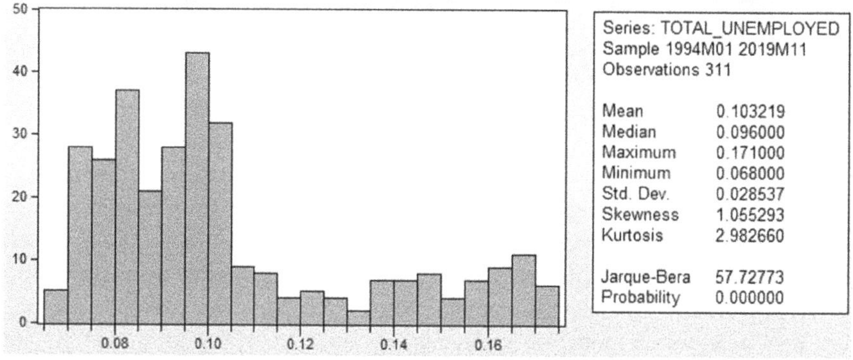


**Figure 34.** Distribution of true unemployment rate
Source: Authors' computations; data from St. Louis Fed.

Null Hypothesis: TOTAL_UNEMPLOYED has a unit root
Exogenous: Constant
Lag Length: 5 (Automatic - based on SIC, maxlag=15)

| | | t-Statistic | Prob.* |
|---|---|---|---|
| Augmented Dickey-Fuller test statistic | | -1.745732 | 0.4072 |
| Test critical values: | 1% level | -3.451632 | |
| | 5% level | -2.870805 | |
| | 10% level | -2.571777 | |

*MacKinnon (1996) one-sided p-values.

**Figure 35.** Unit root test of true unemployment
Source: Author's calculation; data from St. Louis Fed.

The supply and demand imbalance explains why the economy is usually never at full employment and why recessions occur but not how they occur. In the following chapter, we will look at the causes of recessions.

## 2.3. The current status of the literature on economic and financial crises and its critique

Over the previous seven decades, macroeconomics has deteriorated considerably. At the moment, macroeconomists believe that technological change is the source of recessions. Solow's residual (1957) is regarded as the technological change. GDP is deflated by capital and labor inputs. The residual, also known as technical change, is the difference between actual GDP and the predicted time series, and it accounts for 87.5% of the variation in GDP between 1909 and 1949. All of this was attributed to technology without taking into account the demand side or the effectiveness of the institutions. But, more significantly, there can't be any negative technology shocks in our economy since information storage has developed and we have patents. Negative technological shocks happened only when ancient civilizations fell due to the loss of their technologies. Only an extremely intense solar electromagnetic pulse would leave our technology obsolete now, as it can no longer be ignored.

Money supply contractions, according to monetarists, are the root cause of crises. Credit and money were nearly similar until 1970, before the development of nonmonetary liabilities. However, they believed that money is exogenous and that economic crises are the consequence of the central bank's poor management of the money supply. Money is endogenous, as Volcker's tests have shown.

Borio (2012) differentiated recessions into business and financial cycles. This categorization is incorrect. The cycle is derived using trend filters and applied to a composite financial index that incorporates the credit-to-GDP ratio, where real credit and house prices are not always relevant. Due to the superior growth rate of GDP compared to the credit growth rate, the economy might see substantial changes in credit flows even when credit to GDP is on the decline.

Financial crises/cycles occur when financial markets experience significant disruptions in information flows, resulting in increased credit spreads and limited liquidity. The total level of economic activity will then fall (Mishkin, 2018, p. 207). It begins with credit booms or asset price booms and busts caused by financial breakthroughs or bankruptcy of large financial organizations (Mishkin, 2018, p. 207). It appears that, while financial crises can lead to economic crises, they do not always occur at the same time. According to the literature, business cycles have a frequency of up to 8 years, whereas financial cycles have a frequency of around 16 years (Borio, 2012).

There are numerous definitions for recessions, depressions, economic crises, and economic contractions. They differ depending on the geographical region, the economic theory, and the macroeconomic condition. Most commonly, a recession is defined as a decrease in real GDP for at least two consecutive quarters. The NBER defines a recession as "two or more consecutive quarters of negative real GDP growth." A recession, according to the NBER, is a significant decline in economic activity that lasts more than few months and has an influence on real GDP, industrial output, sales, and employment. The NBER's definition of recession will be used. We also define an economic downturn as a fall in real GDP that is not always classified as a recession.

Most recessions are caused by a decrease in demand. But what is causing this drop in demand? The inverted yield spread is the best recession predictor because it signals future decreases in financial institution's profitability and, as a result, an increase in credit standards, an increase in debt service ratio, and a decrease in credit availability, all of which will lead to a sharp decrease in aggregate demand. The fact that yield spread inversions precede recessions shows that nearly all crises have financial origins. Except for pandemics and wars, all crises are financial in nature.

There are several hypotheses as to why the yield curve inverts. The majority of these point to tightening monetary policy, yield curve predictability impacted by monetary regimes (Bordo & Haubrich, 2004), and expectations theory.

According to the monetary regimes theory, in both the gold standard and the fiat standard with credible monetary policy regimes, both real and inflation shocks will increase short-term interest rates and long-term interest rates will remain constant, allowing for inversions and rendering the yield spread an unreliable indicator. However, under a fiat standard with no credibility, inflation shocks will not result in inversions since both short- and long-term interest rates would rise, whereas real shocks will result in inversions. As a result, the inverted yield curve is a powerful statistical indicator in the third regime.

Monetary regimes, we argue, have a substantial effect on the predictability of the yield spread, although not in the same way. We expect that targeting long-term interest rates will reduce, but not eliminate, its predictive power. Before a recession, the yield curve would partially invert.

The idea of tightening monetary policy is equally unconvincing to us, given that long-term interest rates often follow short-term interest rates. Tightening monetary policy can cause recessions, but the phenomenon of inversion should be explained before a crisis occurs. Why does the spread not remain constant or expand prior to recessions if short-term interest rates rise? Most significantly, why did long-term interest rates fall concurrently with short-term interest rates prior to the previous three recessions (see Figure 36)?

**Figure 36.** 10-year Treasury bonds, 3-month Treasury bond-equivalent basis, and recessions

Source: Author's calculation; data from Federal Reserve Database, H15, http://www.federalreserve.gov/releases/h15/data.htm. Recessions from NBER.

It is due to risk aversion, as long-term rates also represent future production and inflation expectations. During expansions, investors shift from bonds to more risky and illiquid assets such as stock options and real estate, among others. During a boom, the yield gap is wide because default risk is extremely improbable in the near future, and, hence, short-term interest rates are low. At the same time, long-term interest rates also rise since the economic outlook may worsen in the future. As a result, investors who are not afraid of taking risks will be rewarded with greater dividends.

Furthermore, as investors' alternatives expand, they will choose a combination of higher-return assets with short-term bonds, stocks, and other riskier assets.

Short-term interest rates are high before recessions because the anticipated risk of default (depending on income and debt) is high for the near future. This time, investors would abandon riskier assets and migrate to the bond market, particularly long-term bonds, which are now safer than short-term debt instruments since governments may cut debt in the future, lowering the chance of failure. Because long-term bonds are in great demand, they will be less expensive (have a lower yield) than short-term bonds. After the inversion, long-term rate bonds will be more beneficial for investors, which might be another cause.

There is also a supply–demand mismatch, since governments typically reduce bond maturities when the yield spread is downward sloping and lengthen them when it is upward sloping, as demonstrated by Arellano and Ramanarayanan (2012). The authors attribute the move to long-term bonds to insurance against short-term interest rate volatility and attribute the choice of shorter maturities to liquidity needs and the need to stimulate consumption during inversions. Broner et al. (2007) believe that short-term borrowing is less expensive even during economic downturns because inverted yield curves do not endure for long.

What occurs following the inversion is what is most important. Banks and other financial institutions fund themselves in the near term and lend/invest in the long term. Financial firms suffer loss of earnings as a result of spread inversion. Financial institutions will tighten credit criteria and reduce credit availability (see Figure 37, Appendix 16 and Figure 40). The yield spread is a leading indicator of tighter credit standards. The tightening of credit standards and the reduction in credit availability will result in a drop in aggregate demand.

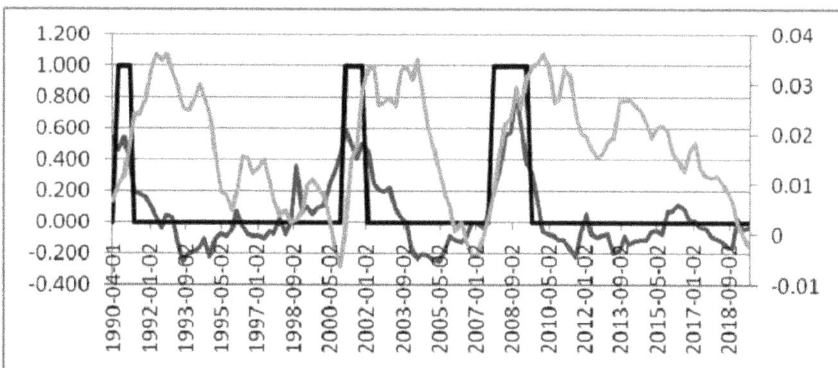


**Figure 37.** Yield spread, credit tightening standards for commercial and industrial loans to large and middle-market firms, and recessions

Source: St. Louis Fed.

Demand for loans is another high-level performance indicator for anticipating recessions. However, the implications of the yield curve, namely, the rise in credit-tightening criteria and the scarcity of credit availability, are more powerful primary predictors of recessions.

Net percentage of domestic banks reporting stronger demand for:

- C&I loans from large- and middle-market firms + small firms (data beginning in 1991Q4);
- demand for auto loans, credit card loans, and consumer loans, excluding credit card and auto loans (data beginning in 2011Q2);
- demand for commercial real estate loans for construction and land development purposes, commercial real estate loans secured by nonfarm nonresidential structures, and commercial real estate loans secured by multifamily residential structures (data beginning in 2013Q4);
- demand for GSE-eligible mortgage loans; government mortgage loans; QM non-jumbo, non–GSE-eligible mortgage loans; QM jumbo mortgage loans; non-QM jumbo mortgage loans; and non-QM non-jumbo mortgage loans (data beginning in 2015Q1).

As shown in Figure 38 (see Appendix 37), the nonweighted average of domestic banks reporting greater demand for loans in the United States turned negative during 2017Q1–2019Q2, yet no recession followed.

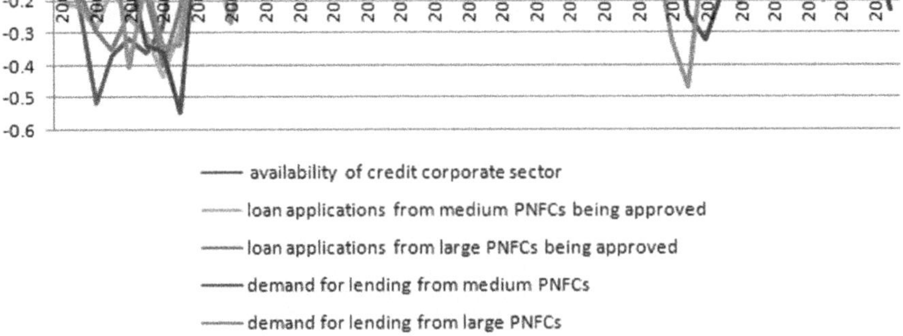


**Figure 39.** Demand for loans

Source: Bank of England; Credit Conditions Survey – 2019Q3.

We see similar tendencies in the United Kingdom, where a drop in demand for private nonfinancial company loans followed a drop in credit supply. The latter began to fall in 2018Q3, but it was a minor dip (see Figure 39).

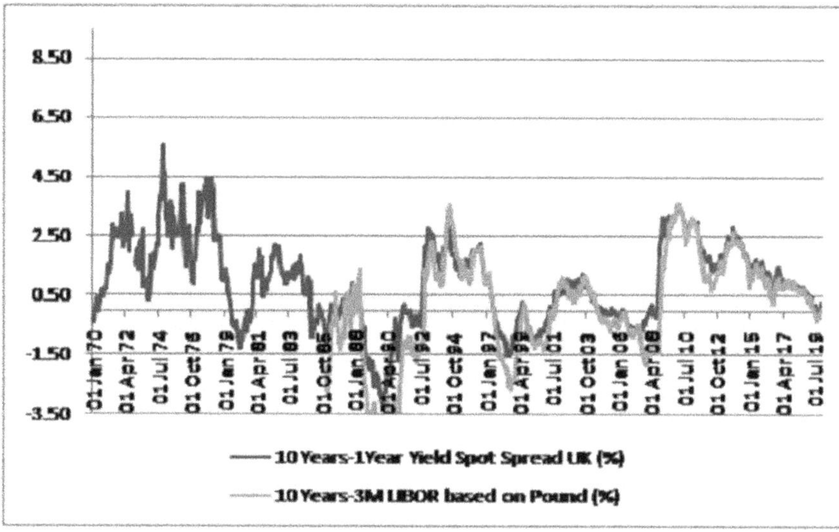


**Figure 40.** Yield curve in the United Kingdom
Authors' computations; data from Bank of England.

Reduced loan availability and stricter criteria have a greater impact than a drop in credit demand. Aside from recession-related factors such as excessive debt payment, a reduction in loan demand may be attributed to financing investments in fixed assets from personal funds if the loan is deemed too expensive. In this instance, a drop in loan demand would result in sluggish growth rather than a recession.

## 2.4. An examination of relevant indicators to forecast the crisis

We will look at the following recession predictors in this chapter: yield spreads, credit cycles, New Housing Units, Housing Starts, Monthly Supply of Houses, initial claims, Aruoba–Diebold–Scotti Index (ADS), Chicago Fed National Activity Index (CFNAI), Margin Debit changes, excess bond premium, and production indexes (New Orders–Inventories Index, Industrial Production Index, and Purchase M). We will focus on yield spreads in particular because they appear to be an almost omnipresent recession indicator (10-year Treasury rates constant maturity – 3-month bill secondary market rate) and discuss the cases where they fail to predict recessions.

### 2.4.1. The omnipresence of a financial indicator, as a proof of the inseparability of business cycle from financial cycle

In order to demonstrate that the business cycle cannot be separated from the financial cycle, we conducted a study showing the prevalence of a financial recession indicator.

## Research methodology and data

To assess the relationship between yield curve inversions and recessions, we employ the methods of Estrella and Trubin (2006). We apply probit equations, which use the Gaussian distribution to convert (in the model) the yield spread value into the probability of recession during the next 12 months. The recession is the dependent variable in this regression, denoted as 1 when there is a recession and 0 when there is no recession.

$$Recession_{t+h} = F(\alpha+\beta^{*}Yield\ Spread) \quad (25)$$

or

$$Recession_{t} = F(\alpha+\beta^{*}Yield\ Spread_{t-h}) \quad (26)$$

$$F(z) - \int_{-\infty}^{z} 1/\sqrt{2\pi}\ \exp(-x^{2}/2)dx \quad (27)$$

For recessions we will use the NBER database. The independent variable in this regression is the value of the yield spread, which can be the 10-year Treasury rates constant maturity (10Y) – 3-month Treasury rates (3 MO) or 10Y – Fed Funds or 10Y – 2Y, and so on. Because of data availability, we will use the 3-month bill secondary market rate. Equation (28) will be used to express it on a bond-equivalent basis:

$$Bond\,equivalent_t = 100 * \left( \frac{365 * Short\,term\,Bill\,Rate_t}{100} \right) / \left( 360 - \frac{91 * Short\,term\,Bill\,Rate_t}{100} \right) \tag{28}$$

With the information provided in month $t$, the model will calculate the likelihood of a recession occurring over a set time period. The time span under consideration is 194M07–2019M10. The McFadden $R^2$ and graphs will be used to compare the prediction capacities of indicators. According to McFadden (1977), values of $\rho^2$ between 0.2 and 0.4 signify an excellent fit.

$$R^2 = 1 - \frac{\ln L(\text{Full Model})}{\ln L(\text{Model Intercept})} \tag{29}$$

where L is the estimated likelihood and $R^2$ has values in the range of 0–1.

## Results and discussion

The null hypothesis "$\beta = 0$" is rejected since the probability associated with the LR test and the $p$ values associated with the coefficients are both 0.0000.

Dependent Variable: RECESSION(12)
Method: ML - Binary Probit (Quadratic hill climbing)
Date: 12/28/19 Time: 11:39
Sample (adjusted): 1954M07 2018M10
Included observations: 772 after adjustments
Convergence achieved after 5 iterations
Covariance matrix computed using second derivatives

| Variable | Coefficient | Std. Error | z-Statistic | Prob. |
|---|---|---|---|---|
| C | -0.472861 | 0.075453 | -6.266927 | 0.0000 |
| S_10Y_3M | -69.77477 | 6.420693 | -10.86717 | 0.0000 |

| | | | |
|---|---|---|---|
| McFadden R-squared | 0.264084 | Mean dependent var | 0.142487 |
| S.D. dependent var | 0.349776 | S.E. of regression | 0.304621 |
| Akaike info criterion | 0.607827 | Sum squared resid | 71.45140 |
| Schwarz criterion | 0.619871 | Log likelihood | -232.6213 |
| Hannan-Quinn criter. | 0.612462 | Deviance | 465.2426 |
| Restr. deviance | 632.1949 | Restr. log likelihood | -316.0974 |
| LR statistic | 166.9523 | Avg. log likelihood | -0.301323 |
| Prob(LR statistic) | 0.000000 | | |

| | | | |
|---|---|---|---|
| Obs with Dep=0 | 662 | Total obs | 772 |
| Obs with Dep=1 | 110 | | |

**Figure 41.** Predictive power of yield curve (10Y-3M)
Authors' computations; data from St. Louis Fed.

When employing the 12-month lead, the maximum McFadden $R^2$ coefficient is attained. This suggests that the yield curve can predict recessions up to a year in advance. The yield spread has a high forecasting capacity, as illustrated in Figures 41 and 42. We anticipate the recession likelihood for 2019M11–2020M10 using the equation shown in Figure 42. We discover that the biggest probability of a recession is 41.14% for 2020M08 (see Figure 43).

Dependent Variable: RECESSION
Method: ML - Binary Probit (Quadratic hill climbing)
Date: 12/29/19 Time: 02:33
Sample (adjusted): 1955M07 2019M10
Included observations: 772 after adjustments
Convergence achieved after 5 iterations
Covariance matrix computed using second derivatives

| Variable | Coefficient | Std. Error | z-Statistic | Prob. |
|---|---|---|---|---|
| C | -0.472861 | 0.075453 | -6.266927 | 0.0000 |
| S_10Y_3M(-12) | -69.77477 | 6.420693 | -10.86717 | 0.0000 |

| | | | |
|---|---|---|---|
| McFadden R-squared | 0.264084 | Mean dependent var | 0.142487 |
| S.D. dependent var | 0.349776 | S.E. of regression | 0.304621 |
| Akaike info criterion | 0.607827 | Sum squared resid | 71.45140 |
| Schwarz criterion | 0.619871 | Log likelihood | -232.6213 |
| Hannan-Quinn criter. | 0.612462 | Deviance | 465.2426 |
| Restr. deviance | 632.1949 | Restr. log likelihood | -316.0974 |
| LR statistic | 166.9523 | Avg. log likelihood | -0.301323 |
| Prob(LR statistic) | 0.000000 | | |

| | | | |
|---|---|---|---|
| Obs with Dep=0 | 662 | Total obs | 772 |
| Obs with Dep=1 | 110 | | |

**Figure 42.** Predictive power of yield curve (10Y-3M) model with a lagged independent variable

Authors' computations; data from St. Louis Fed.

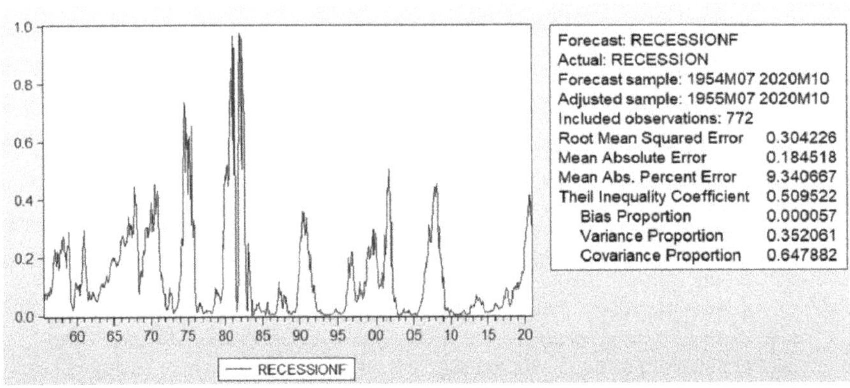


**Figure 43.** Predictive power of yield curve (10Y-3M), model with a lagged independent variable, estimated recession probabilities

Authors' computations, data from St. Louis Fed.

We discovered that recession forecasting based on the yield spread performs reasonably well by applying the Theil inequality coefficient (see Equation 30), since the coefficient is equal to 0.509522. The coefficient's values are always between 0 and 1. A value of 0 indicates a perfect fit, whereas a value of 1 indicates the worst fit.

$$U = \frac{\sqrt{\frac{1}{n} * \Sigma(Y_t - F_{t)}^2}}{\sqrt{\frac{1}{n} * \Sigma(Y_t)^2} + \sqrt{\frac{1}{n} * \Sigma(F_t)^2}} \tag{30}$$

where Ft is predicted at time *t*.

When we compare the estimated recession probabilities from the model to the actual recessions (see Figure 44), we can see that the yield spread is a good recession predictor and that a computed probability of more than 40% is frequently linked with a recession.

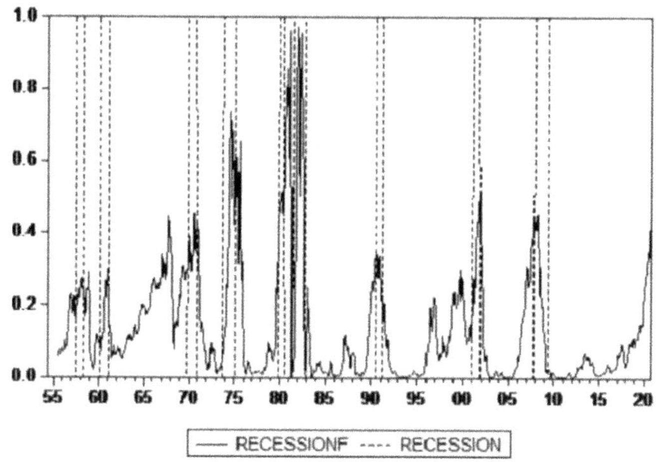


**Figure 44.** Recession probability based on 10Y–3MO probit model
Authors' computations.

Dependent Variable: RECESSION(12)
Method: ML - Binary Probit (Quadratic hill climbing)
Date: 12/28/19 Time: 02:57
Sample (adjusted): 1954M07 2018M10
Included observations: 772 after adjustments
Convergence achieved after 5 iterations
Covariance matrix computed using second derivatives

| Variable | Coefficient | Std. Error | z-Statistic | Prob. |
|---|---|---|---|---|
| C | -0.827941 | 0.065267 | -12.68552 | 0.0000 |
| S_10Y_FEDFUNDS | -47.18487 | 4.189155 | -11.26358 | 0.0000 |

| | | | |
|---|---|---|---|
| McFadden R-squared | 0.251759 | Mean dependent var | 0.142487 |
| S.D. dependent var | 0.349776 | S.E. of regression | 0.308777 |
| Akaike info criterion | 0.617920 | Sum squared resid | 73.41428 |
| Schwarz criterion | 0.629964 | Log likelihood | -236.5171 |
| Hannan-Quinn criter. | 0.622554 | Deviance | 473.0342 |
| Restr. deviance | 632.1949 | Restr. log likelihood | -316.0974 |
| LR statistic | 159.1607 | Avg. log likelihood | -0.306369 |
| Prob(LR statistic) | 0.000000 | | |

| | | | |
|---|---|---|---|
| Obs with Dep=0 | 662 | Total obs | 772 |
| Obs with Dep=1 | 110 | | |

**Figure 45.** Predictive power of yield curve (10Y-Fed Funds), 12 months lead
Authors' computations; data from St. Louis Fed.

The 10-year Treasury constant maturity – Federal Funds rate is another yield spread with predictive ability. McFadden $R^2$ for the 12-month model is 0.251759 (see Figure 45), which is less than the $R^2$ value for 10Y – 3M. However, the model with an 8-month lead (shown in Figure 46) has the greatest $R^2$ for 10Y – Fed Funds, 0.295123, which is more than the coefficient for 10Y – 3M. Despite this conclusion, the 10Y – 3M yield spread is still a superior indication because it predicts better recessions with 12 months and, more crucially, the former yield spread provided a false warning between 1988M06 and 1998M12 (see Figure 47). After that, it reversed again between 2000M04 and 2001M03, followed by a recession from 2001M03 to 2001M11, whereas 10Y – 3M inverted between 2000M07 and 2001M01.

Dependent Variable: RECESSION(8)
Method: ML - Binary Probit (Quadratic hill climbing)
Date: 12/28/19 Time: 03:01
Sample: 1954M07 2018M10
Included observations: 772
Convergence achieved after 5 iterations
Covariance matrix computed using second derivatives

| Variable | Coefficient | Std. Error | z-Statistic | Prob. |
|---|---|---|---|---|
| C | -0.801171 | 0.067364 | -11.89314 | 0.0000 |
| S_10Y_FEDFUNDS | -53.07589 | 4.576951 | -11.59634 | 0.0000 |

| | | | |
|---|---|---|---|
| McFadden R-squared | 0.295123 | Mean dependent var | 0.142487 |
| S.D. dependent var | 0.349776 | S.E. of regression | 0.292257 |
| Akaike info criterion | 0.582409 | Sum squared resid | 65.76877 |
| Schwarz criterion | 0.594453 | Log likelihood | -222.8098 |
| Hannan-Quinn criter. | 0.587043 | Deviance | 445.6197 |
| Restr. deviance | 632.1949 | Restr. log likelihood | -316.0974 |
| LR statistic | 186.5752 | Avg. log likelihood | -0.288614 |
| Prob(LR statistic) | 0.000000 | | |

| | | | |
|---|---|---|---|
| Obs with Dep=0 | 662 | Total obs | 772 |
| Obs with Dep=1 | 110 | | |

**Figure 46.** Predictive power of yield curve (10Y-Fed Funds)
Authors' computations; data from St. Louis Fed.

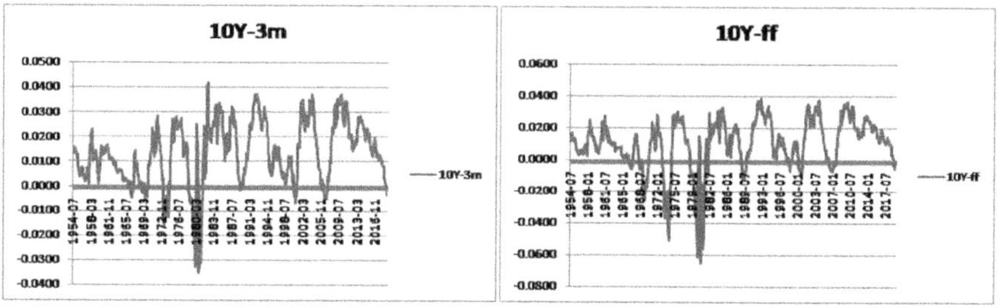


**Figure 47.** 10Y-3M versus 10Y-Fed Funds
Authors' computations; data from St. Louis Fed.

When we compare yield spreads to credit deviations, we discover that while the model with the strongest $R^2$ has a 17-month lead (see Figure 48), the McFadden coefficient is much smaller than $R^2$ yield spreads, especially 10Y – 3M and 10Y – Fed Funds. As seen in Figure 49, variations from trend in bank credit do not always precede recessions; they can also follow them, as in the case of the Great Recession. The bank credit cycle is built by using a Hodrick Prescott one-sided filter to calculate deviations from the trend in bank credit. The deviations are then divided by nominal GDP.

Dependent Variable: RECESSION(17)
Method: ML - Binary Probit (Quadratic hill climbing)
Date: 01/05/20 Time: 01:33
Sample (adjusted): 1954M07 2018M05
Included observations: 767 after adjustments
Convergence achieved after 5 iterations
Covariance matrix computed using second derivatives

| Variable | Coefficient | Std. Error | z-Statistic | Prob. |
|---|---|---|---|---|
| C | -1.800669 | 0.119164 | -15.11079 | 0.0000 |
| CYCLE_2073600_BCREDIT | 16.92439 | 2.105578 | 8.037881 | 0.0000 |

| | | | |
|---|---|---|---|
| McFadden R-squared | 0.129426 | Mean dependent var | 0.143416 |
| S.D. dependent var | 0.350725 | S.E. of regression | 0.328609 |
| Akaike info criterion | 0.721029 | Sum squared resid | 82.60763 |
| Schwarz criterion | 0.733135 | Log likelihood | -274.5148 |
| Hannan-Quinn criter. | 0.725689 | Deviance | 549.0295 |
| Restr. deviance | 630.6523 | Restr. log likelihood | -315.3261 |
| LR statistic | 81.62273 | Avg. log likelihood | -0.357907 |
| Prob(LR statistic) | 0.000000 | | |
| Obs with Dep=0 | 657 | Total obs | 767 |
| Obs with Dep=1 | 110 | | |

**Figure 48.** Deviations from the trend of bank credit and recessions
Authors' computations; data from FRB H8.

Because it is a one-sided filter, we take the recommendations of Ravn and Uhlig (2002) and use power 4. Because the periodicity is monthly and the credit cycle is twice as long as the business cycle, the base is 6 (2*3); thus, we use a lambda of 2 073 600 (see Equation 31).

$$(2*3)^4 * 1600 = 2\ 073\ 600 \tag{31}$$

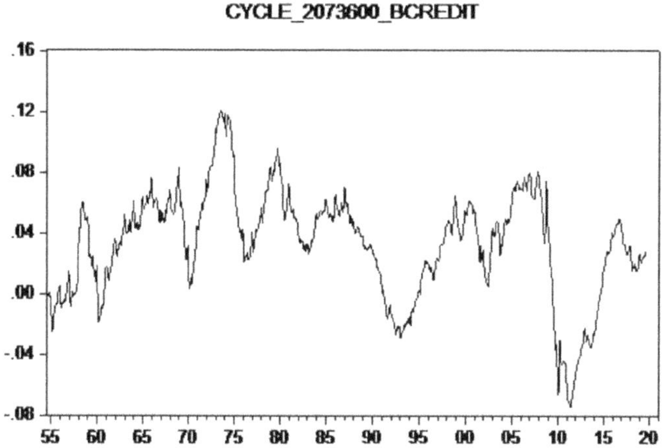


**Figure 49.** Deviations from the trend of bank credit
Authors' computations; data from FRB H8.

When we compare the yield spread prediction power to real-world factors, we find that it outperforms them. As significant key indicators for industrial output, we use the St. Louis Fed's Industrial Production Index and the ISM Institute's New Orders–Inventories Index. For the Industrial Production Index, we calculate the change as the current month's value minus the average of the previous 12 months. Declines in the changes of the Industrial Production Index are related to recessions, but they do not cause them (see Figure 50). We also used a probit regression to test this theory practically. After doing numerous tests on data from 1954M10 to 2019M10, we can infer that drops in industrial production follow recessions, since the model with 3 lags has the highest $R^2$ (see Figure 51).

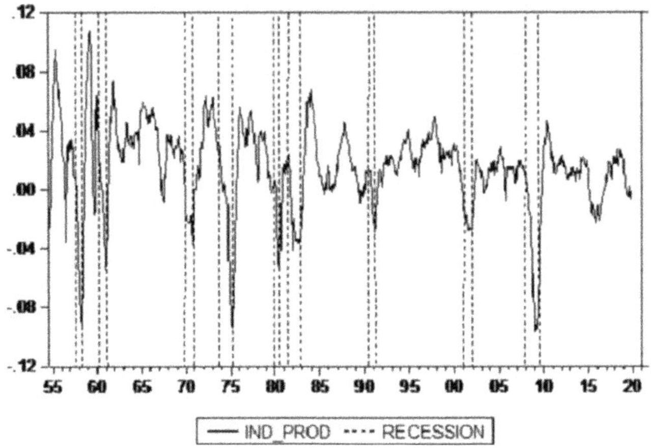


**Figure 50.** Industrial production and recessions
Source: Authors' computations; data from St. Louis Fed.

The Industrial Production Index is unsuitable for predicting recessions since a model with 1 lead has an $R^2$ of 0.28999, a model with 2 leads has an $R^2$ of about 0.202930, and a model with 3 leads has an $R^2$ of 0.13566 (see Figures 51 and 52).

Dependent Variable: RECESSION(-3)
Method: ML - Binary Probit (Quadratic hill climbing)
Date: 02/01/20 Time: 23:26
Sample (adjusted): 1954M10 2019M10
Included observations: 781 after adjustments
Convergence achieved after 6 iterations
Covariance matrix computed using second derivatives

| Variable | Coefficient | Std. Error | z-Statistic | Prob. |
|---|---|---|---|---|
| C | -1.143583 | 0.103453 | -11.05413 | 0.0000 |
| IND_PROD | -77.50716 | 6.756680 | -11.47119 | 0.0000 |

| | | | |
|---|---|---|---|
| McFadden R-squared | 0.661488 | Mean dependent var | 0.140845 |
| S.D. dependent var | 0.348085 | S.E. of regression | 0.205016 |
| Akaike info criterion | 0.280328 | Sum squared resid | 32.74266 |
| Schwarz criterion | 0.292263 | Log likelihood | -107.4682 |
| Hannan-Quinn criter. | 0.284918 | Deviance | 214.9364 |
| Restr. deviance | 634.9445 | Restr. log likelihood | -317.4723 |
| LR statistic | 420.0081 | Avg. log likelihood | -0.137603 |
| Prob(LR statistic) | 0.000000 | | |

| | | | |
|---|---|---|---|
| Obs with Dep=0 | 671 | Total obs | 781 |
| Obs with Dep=1 | 110 | | |

**Figure 51.** Industrial production model with 3 lags

Dependent Variable: RECESSION(1)
Method: ML - Binary Probit (Quadratic hill climbing)
Date: 02/13/20 Time: 08:55
Sample (adjusted): 1954M07 2019M09
Included observations: 783 after adjustments
Convergence achieved after 5 iterations
Covariance matrix computed using second derivatives

| Variable | Coefficient | Std. Error | z-Statistic | Prob. |
|---|---|---|---|---|
| C | -0.963123 | 0.065764 | -14.64507 | 0.0000 |
| IND_PROD | -28.62602 | 2.440864 | -11.72782 | 0.0000 |

| | | | |
|---|---|---|---|
| McFadden R-squared | 0.289999 | Mean dependent var | 0.140485 |
| S.D. dependent var | 0.347712 | S.E. of regression | 0.296487 |
| Akaike info criterion | 0.581407 | Sum squared resid | 68.65328 |
| Schwarz criterion | 0.593318 | Log likelihood | -225.6208 |
| Hannan-Quinn criter. | 0.585987 | Deviance | 451.2417 |
| Restr. deviance | 635.5509 | Restr. log likelihood | -317.7755 |
| LR statistic | 184.3092 | Avg. log likelihood | -0.288149 |
| Prob(LR statistic) | 0.000000 | | |

| | | | |
|---|---|---|---|
| Obs with Dep=0 | 673 | Total obs | 783 |
| Obs with Dep=1 | 110 | | |

**Figure 52.** Industrial production model with 1 lead

It is also worth noting that the Industrial Production Index fell from 2015M03 to 2016M09 (see Figures 50 and 53), but this was not followed by a recession. A downturn in industrial production is not always followed by a downturn in other economic sectors. Recessions in industrial production will not result in a general recession unless the manufacturers are heavily indebted and damage the financial system, which would then affect the rest of the economy.

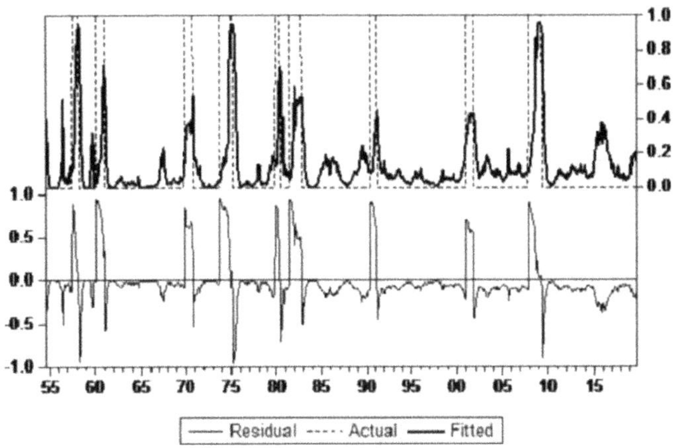


**Figure 53.** Recession probabilities based on probit regression with 1 lead, independent variable: Industrial production

Source: Authors' computations; data from Quandl.

The New Orders–Inventories Index is another real indicator that is important for industrial output. When this index registers negative values, a recession usually follows. This measure is a better predictor of recessions than changes in the Industrial Production Index, but it falls short of the yield spread. The models used for the periods 1948M01–2019M10 (see Figure 54) and 1954M07–2019M10 (see Figure 55) had a lower $R^2$ and higher Akaike and Schwarz criterion than the yield spread models.

The number of leads between negative fluctuations in the index and recessions are another crucial factor in how New Orders–Inventories precede recessions. When opposed to the yield spread, the index has a shorter duration (2–4 months, see Figures 54 and 55).

Dependent Variable: RECESSION(4)
Method: ML - Binary Probit (Quadratic hill climbing)
Date: 12/28/19 Time: 03:34
Sample (adjusted): 1948M01 2019M06
Included observations: 858 after adjustments
Convergence achieved after 5 iterations
Covariance matrix computed using second derivatives

| Variable | Coefficient | Std. Error | z-Statistic | Prob. |
|---|---|---|---|---|
| C | -0.491981 | 0.070747 | -6.954108 | 0.0000 |
| NEW_ORDERS_INVENTORIES | -0.084192 | 0.008478 | -9.930879 | 0.0000 |

| | | | |
|---|---|---|---|
| McFadden R-squared | 0.164131 | Mean dependent var | 0.155012 |
| S.D. dependent var | 0.362127 | S.E. of regression | 0.333712 |
| Akaike info criterion | 0.725691 | Sum squared resid | 95.32752 |
| Schwarz criterion | 0.736774 | Log likelihood | -309.3213 |
| Hannan-Quinn criter. | 0.729934 | Deviance | 618.6426 |
| Restr. deviance | 740.1189 | Restr. log likelihood | -370.0594 |
| LR statistic | 121.4762 | Avg. log likelihood | -0.360514 |
| Prob(LR statistic) | 0.000000 | | |
| Obs with Dep=0 | 725 | Total obs | 858 |
| Obs with Dep=1 | 133 | | |

**Figure 54.** New orders – inventories, probit regression

Source: Authors' computations; data from Quandl.

Dependent Variable: RECESSION(2)
Method: ML - Binary Probit (Quadratic hill climbing)
Date: 02/01/20 Time: 10:10
Sample (adjusted): 1954M07 2019M08
Included observations: 782 after adjustments
Convergence achieved after 5 iterations
Covariance matrix computed using second derivatives

| Variable | Coefficient | Std. Error | z-Statistic | Prob. |
|---|---|---|---|---|
| NEW_ORDERS_INVENTORIES | -0.094830 | 0.009735 | -9.741451 | 0.0000 |
| C | -0.515618 | 0.076876 | -6.707099 | 0.0000 |

| | | | |
|---|---|---|---|
| McFadden R-squared | 0.189323 | Mean dependent var | 0.140665 |
| S.D. dependent var | 0.347898 | S.E. of regression | 0.314707 |
| Akaike info criterion | 0.663658 | Sum squared resid | 77.25142 |
| Schwarz criterion | 0.675581 | Log likelihood | -257.4904 |
| Hannan-Quinn criter. | 0.668244 | Deviance | 514.9808 |
| Restr. deviance | 635.2479 | Restr. log likelihood | -317.6240 |
| LR statistic | 120.2671 | Avg. log likelihood | -0.329272 |
| Prob(LR statistic) | 0.000000 | | |
| Obs with Dep=0 | 672 | Total obs | 782 |
| Obs with Dep=1 | 110 | | |

**Figure 55.** New orders – inventories, recession model

Source: Authors' computations; data from Quandl.

**Figure 56.** New orders – inventories
Source: Authors' computations; data from Quandl.

As illustrated in Figure 56, the New Orders–Inventories Index is highly variable, suggesting that it may be connected with real GDP downturns rather than recessions. To put this idea to the test, we must first decide how these economic contractions will manifest themselves.

Because the quarterly real GDP change (change from Year Ago – Contract 4 Quarters) misses the 1970 and 2001 recessions, as well as periods of economic volatility without recessions, the quarterly real GDP change (change from the preceding quarter – real GDP contraction) is a better fit.

- The probit regressions used for the quarterly (monthly average) New Orders–Inventories Index and the yield spreads reveal the following facts:
- The New Orders–Inventories Index is slightly more closely related to real GDP declines than to recessions (compare Figure 57 with Figure 58).
- Yield spreads are significantly more closely connected with recessions than with negative real GDP changes (compare Figures 59 and 60 with Figures 61 and 62); therefore, negative yield spreads suggest recessions rather than temporary decreases in economic activity.
- According to econometric assessments, financial factors, specifically the yield spread, tend to lead recessions by a greater margin than actual variables such as the New Orders–Inventories Index (three quarters for financial variables compared to one quarter for real variables).

Dependent Variable: RECESSION(1)
Method: ML - Binary Probit (Quadratic hill climbing)
Date: 12/28/19 Time: 09:09
Sample (adjusted): 1954Q3 2019Q2
Included observations: 260 after adjustments
Convergence achieved after 5 iterations
Covariance matrix computed using second derivatives

| Variable | Coefficient | Std. Error | z-Statistic | Prob. |
|---|---|---|---|---|
| C | -0.248100 | 0.145876 | -1.700753 | 0.0890 |
| NEW_ORDERS_INVENTORIES_Q | -0.119301 | 0.019382 | -6.155221 | 0.0000 |

| | | | |
|---|---|---|---|
| McFadden R-squared | 0.224757 | Mean dependent var | 0.161538 |
| S.D. dependent var | 0.368737 | S.E. of regression | 0.324936 |
| Akaike info criterion | 0.701028 | Sum squared resid | 27.24048 |
| Schwarz criterion | 0.728418 | Log likelihood | -89.13370 |
| Hannan-Quinn criter. | 0.712040 | Deviance | 178.2674 |
| Restr. deviance | 229.9504 | Restr. log likelihood | -114.9752 |
| LR statistic | 51.68296 | Avg. log likelihood | -0.342822 |
| Prob(LR statistic) | 0.000000 | | |

| | | | |
|---|---|---|---|
| Obs with Dep=0 | 218 | Total obs | 260 |
| Obs with Dep=1 | 42 | | |

**Figure 57.** New orders – inventories and recessions

Source: Authors' calculations; data from Quandl and NBER.

Dependent Variable: REAL_GDP_CONTRACTION(1)
Method: ML - Binary Probit (Quadratic hill climbing)
Date: 12/28/19 Time: 09:08
Sample (adjusted): 1954Q3 2019Q2
Included observations: 260 after adjustments
Convergence achieved after 5 iterations
Covariance matrix computed using second derivatives

| Variable | Coefficient | Std. Error | z-Statistic | Prob. |
|---|---|---|---|---|
| C | -0.455949 | 0.146818 | -3.105541 | 0.0019 |
| NEW_ORDERS_INVENTORIES_Q | -0.117577 | 0.020451 | -5.749207 | 0.0000 |

| | | | |
|---|---|---|---|
| McFadden R-squared | 0.227237 | Mean dependent var | 0.126923 |
| S.D. dependent var | 0.333529 | S.E. of regression | 0.298177 |
| Akaike info criterion | 0.603450 | Sum squared resid | 22.93868 |
| Schwarz criterion | 0.630840 | Log likelihood | -76.44854 |
| Hannan-Quinn criter. | 0.614461 | Deviance | 152.8971 |
| Restr. deviance | 197.8576 | Restr. log likelihood | -98.92882 |
| LR statistic | 44.96056 | Avg. log likelihood | -0.294033 |
| Prob(LR statistic) | 0.000000 | | |

| | | | |
|---|---|---|---|
| Obs with Dep=0 | 227 | Total obs | 260 |
| Obs with Dep=1 | 33 | | |

**Figure 58.** New orders – inventories and real GDP contractions

Source: Authors' computations; data from Quandl and BEA.

Dependent Variable: REAL_GDP_CONTRACTION(4)
Method: ML - Binary Probit (Quadratic hill climbing)
Date: 12/28/19 Time: 09:33
Sample (adjusted): 1954Q3 2018Q3
Included observations: 257 after adjustments
Convergence achieved after 5 iterations
Covariance matrix computed using second derivatives

| Variable | Coefficient | Std. Error | z-Statistic | Prob. |
|---|---|---|---|---|
| C | -0.689968 | 0.131384 | -5.251556 | 0.0000 |
| S_10Y_3M | -43.81004 | 9.170659 | -4.777197 | 0.0000 |

| | | | |
|---|---|---|---|
| McFadden R-squared | 0.131782 | Mean dependent var | 0.128405 |
| S.D. dependent var | 0.335193 | S.E. of regression | 0.313561 |
| Akaike info criterion | 0.681215 | Sum squared resid | 25.07181 |
| Schwarz criterion | 0.708834 | Log likelihood | -85.53608 |
| Hannan-Quinn criter. | 0.692322 | Deviance | 171.0722 |
| Restr. deviance | 197.0382 | Restr. log likelihood | -98.51909 |
| LR statistic | 25.96601 | Avg. log likelihood | -0.332825 |
| Prob(LR statistic) | 0.000000 | | |

| | | | |
|---|---|---|---|
| Obs with Dep=0 | 224 | Total obs | 257 |
| Obs with Dep=1 | 33 | | |

**Figure 59.** 10Y-3M, probit regression
Source: Authors' computations.

Dependent Variable: REAL_GDP_CONTRACTION(2)
Method: ML - Binary Probit (Quadratic hill climbing)
Date: 12/28/19 Time: 09:32
Sample (adjusted): 1954Q3 2019Q1
Included observations: 259 after adjustments
Convergence achieved after 5 iterations
Covariance matrix computed using second derivatives

| Variable | Coefficient | Std. Error | z-Statistic | Prob. |
|---|---|---|---|---|
| S_10Y_FEDFUNDS | -35.14493 | 6.706998 | -5.240039 | 0.0000 |
| C | -0.909958 | 0.112615 | -8.080287 | 0.0000 |

| | | | |
|---|---|---|---|
| McFadden R-squared | 0.157612 | Mean dependent var | 0.127413 |
| S.D. dependent var | 0.334081 | S.E. of regression | 0.302299 |
| Akaike info criterion | 0.658084 | Sum squared resid | 23.48580 |
| Schwarz criterion | 0.685550 | Log likelihood | -83.22191 |
| Hannan-Quinn criter. | 0.669127 | Deviance | 166.4438 |
| Restr. deviance | 197.5856 | Restr. log likelihood | -98.79281 |
| LR statistic | 31.14179 | Avg. log likelihood | -0.321320 |
| Prob(LR statistic) | 0.000000 | | |

| | | | |
|---|---|---|---|
| Obs with Dep=0 | 226 | Total obs | 259 |
| Obs with Dep=1 | 33 | | |

**Figure 60.** 10Y – Fed Funds, probit model, dependent variable: Real GDP contraction

Dependent Variable: RECESSION(3)
Method: ML - Binary Probit (Quadratic hill climbing)
Date: 12/28/19 Time: 11:28
Sample (adjusted): 1954Q3 2018Q4
Included observations: 258 after adjustments
Convergence achieved after 5 iterations
Covariance matrix computed using second derivatives

| Variable | Coefficient | Std. Error | z-Statistic | Prob. |
|---|---|---|---|---|
| C | -0.271979 | 0.135214 | -2.011475 | 0.0443 |
| S_10Y_3M | -81.81386 | 12.04533 | -6.792162 | 0.0000 |

| | | | |
|---|---|---|---|
| McFadden R-squared | 0.308354 | Mean dependent var | 0.162791 |
| S.D. dependent var | 0.369892 | S.E. of regression | 0.305100 |
| Akaike info criterion | 0.630057 | Sum squared resid | 23.83002 |
| Schwarz criterion | 0.657599 | Log likelihood | -79.27732 |
| Hannan-Quinn criter. | 0.641132 | Deviance | 158.5546 |
| Restr. deviance | 229.2426 | Restr. log likelihood | -114.6213 |
| LR statistic | 70.68798 | Avg. log likelihood | -0.307276 |
| Prob(LR statistic) | 0.000000 | | |

| | | | |
|---|---|---|---|
| Obs with Dep=0 | 216 | Total obs | 258 |
| Obs with Dep=1 | 42 | | |

**Figure 61.** 10-year – 3-month Treasury, probit model, dependent variable: Recession

Dependent Variable: RECESSION(3)
Method: ML - Binary Probit (Quadratic hill climbing)
Date: 12/28/19 Time: 09:36
Sample: 1954Q3 2018Q2
Included observations: 256
Convergence achieved after 5 iterations
Covariance matrix computed using second derivatives

| Variable | Coefficient | Std. Error | z-Statistic | Prob. |
|---|---|---|---|---|
| C | -0.667079 | 0.115878 | -5.756728 | 0.0000 |
| S_10Y_FEDFUNDS | -60.65471 | 8.375121 | -7.242248 | 0.0000 |

| | | | |
|---|---|---|---|
| McFadden R-squared | 0.330684 | Mean dependent var | 0.164063 |
| S.D. dependent var | 0.371058 | S.E. of regression | 0.304442 |
| Akaike info criterion | 0.613117 | Sum squared resid | 23.54197 |
| Schwarz criterion | 0.640814 | Log likelihood | -76.47904 |
| Hannan-Quinn criter. | 0.624257 | Deviance | 152.9581 |
| Restr. deviance | 228.5289 | Restr. log likelihood | -114.2644 |
| LR statistic | 75.57079 | Avg. log likelihood | -0.298746 |
| Prob(LR statistic) | 0.000000 | | |

| | | | |
|---|---|---|---|
| Obs with Dep=0 | 214 | Total obs | 256 |
| Obs with Dep=1 | 42 | | |

**Figure 62.** 10-year Treasury – Fed Funds, probit model, dependent variable: Recession

The last assertion is also supported by the relationship between recessions and New Private Housing Units Authorized by Building Permits (see Appendix 17), Privately Owned Housing Starts: 1-Unit Structures (see Appendix 18), monthly supply of houses (see Appendix 19), initial claims (see Appendix 20), ADS Index (see Appendix 21), and CFNAI (see Appendix 22).

ADS contains weekly initial claims; monthly payroll employment, manufacturing sales, industrial production data, and quarterly real GDP. This index mixes high- and low-frequency data in order to obtain a clear picture of the economic environment. It has an average value of 0. Positive values imply conditions above average, and negative values imply conditions below average.

CFNAI is an indicator calculated as the weighted average of 85 monthly macroeconomic indicators. It has an average value of 0, and the standard deviation is 1. When the index value is above 0, it means that growth is above trend, and when its values are negative it means that growth is below trend.

The 85 economic indicators that are included in the CFNAI can be divided into four categories: employment, unemployment, and hours; sales, orders, and inventories; consumption; and housing and income.

Periods of analysis and data transformation:

- New Housing Units Authorized by Building Permits: 1961M01–2019M10, current value minus the average of the last 12 months
- Privately Owned Housing Starts: 1-Unit Structures: 1959M12–2019M09, average of the last 3 months minus the average of the last 12 months
- Monthly supply of houses: 1963M01–2019M09, no data transformation
- Initial claims: 1968M01–2019M10, current value minus the average of the last 12 months
- ADS Index: 1960M03–2019M10 (average of daily values)
- CFNAI: 1967M03–2019M10, no data transformation

All the indicators, except for initial claims, ADS Index, and CFNAI, lead the recessions by two months. The initial claims and the two economic activity indexes are the most suitable indicators for recession nowcasting. We can conclude that the financial indicators, especially yield spreads, are better recession forecasters, whereas real variables are better for recession nowcasting. One FEDS note reached the same conclusion after using Bayesian Model averaging method on financial variables (slope of yield curve, curvature of the yield curve, GZ Index, TED spread, BBB corporate spread, trade-weighted dollar, and VIX) and on real variables (Real personal consumption expenditure, Real Disposable Income, Industrial production, housing permits, Initial claims, Purchasing Managers' Index, etc.).

## 2.4.2. Instances where inverted yield curve and credit variables may fail to predict crisis

There are two instances where the yield curve may fail to predict recessions – first, a gold standard system with low or no central bank intervention in a highly deflationary environment, and, second, when the central bank is capping both short- and long-term interest rates.

The first case was present in the United States during 1871–1933. Counting recessions with annual data gave us the figure of 71.43% of time spent into recessions and a monthly frequency of 48.30% of time into recession. Because most of the times there was a high recession risk, the yield spread was negative the majority of time. Therefore, the yield spread was negative both before and during recessions, becoming an ineffective indicator. The problem with a gold standard or a recession-prone regime is not that the yield spread will invert even in case of inflation shock, and not just output shocks, but that the inversions would happen frequently and the yield curve would lose effectiveness as recession predictor.

Figure 63 shows that the yield spread between long-term government bonds and commercial paper is typically negative between 1871 and 1933. Because this was the interest rate at the time, we used New York commercial paper rates instead of short-term interest rates (Officer, 2008).

Even under these conditions, the negative yield spread has predictive content and precedes recessions although its predictive content is diminished because McFadden $R^2$ is under 0.2 as illustrated in Figure 64. This result was obtained due to frequent recession occurrence as well as the low data frequency. Money supply contractions are the greatest forecasters in this scenario because (see Figure 65) bank credit has not been separated from money. Even in these situations, though, the yield spread remains a strong predictor (see Appendixes 23 and 24).

Even if an expected inflation shock (not an output shock) would produce a yield spread inversion, this event would reduce the profitability of the financial system, which will reduce the credit availability and credit standards and lead to a recession.

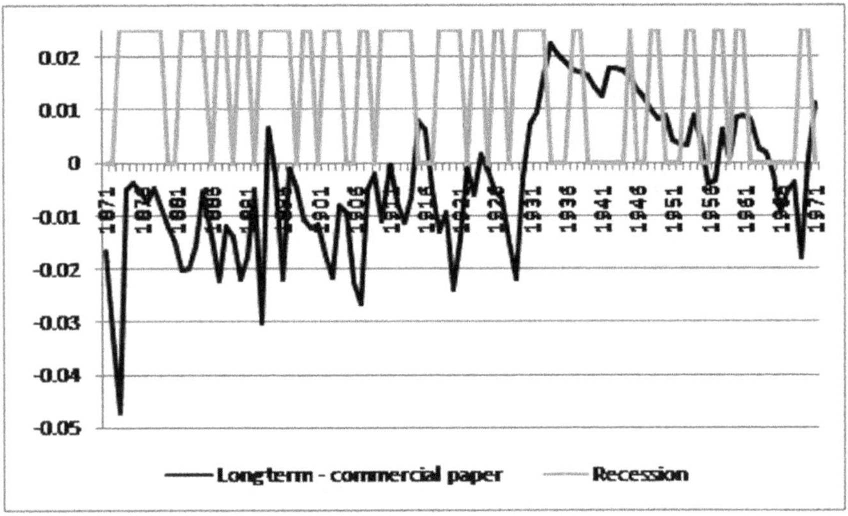


**Figure 63.** Long-term minus commercial paper

Source: Authors' computations; long-term government bond – Updated time series from Chapter 26 from Shiller, Robert, Market Volatility, 1989, http://www.econ.yale.edu/~shiller/data.htm, commercial paper from St. Louis Fed.

However, because of irregular issuance, short- and long-term interest rates on government bonds were not the best indicators of the yield market. Because the spread was almost always negative, it did not record periods when banks' profits declined. As a result, for this period with a high risk of recession, we should select private yields reflective of the yield market that best capture. This is exactly what Gerlach and Stuart (2018) have done. They used the spread of high-quality railroad bonds minus the call money rate from January 1857 to November 1913 (pre-Fed). The probit models they used revealed that the yield spread can predict recession, with the best performance one month ahead, but the influence of the yield spread flattening is considerable for up to 13 months.

Dependent Variable: RECESSION(1)
Method: ML - Binary Probit (Quadratic hill climbing / EViews legacy)
Date: 01/09/22 Time: 18:58
Sample (adjusted): 1871 1933
Included observations: 63 after adjustments
Convergence achieved after 3 iterations
Coefficient covariance matrix computed using second derivatives

| Variable | Coefficient | Std. Error | z-Statistic | Prob. |
|---|---|---|---|---|
| C | 0.227588 | 0.229488 | 0.991720 | 0.3213 |
| LONG_TERM_CPAPER | -38.01627 | 18.50985 | -2.053840 | 0.0400 |

| | | | |
|---|---|---|---|
| McFadden R-squared | 0.063540 | Mean dependent var | 0.714286 |
| S.D. dependent var | 0.455383 | S.E. of regression | 0.444589 |
| Akaike info criterion | 1.184003 | Sum squared resid | 12.05722 |
| Schwarz criterion | 1.252039 | Log likelihood | -35.29609 |
| Hannan-Quinn criter. | 1.210762 | Deviance | 70.59217 |
| Restr. deviance | 75.38197 | Restr. log likelihood | -37.69098 |
| LR statistic | 4.789798 | Avg. log likelihood | -0.560255 |
| Prob(LR statistic) | 0.028629 | | |

| | | | |
|---|---|---|---|
| Obs with Dep=0 | 18 | Total obs | 63 |
| Obs with Dep=1 | 45 | | |

**Figure 64.** Long-term minus commercial paper predicting recessions
Source: Authors' computations.

The second case is connected to interest rate limits, which regulate the yield spread. Essentially, we have demonstrated that whether an inversion is caused by a production shock or an inflation shock, it will be followed by a recession. The question is whether recessions occur in the absence of a yield spread inversion. The answer is yes. The following are the facts of the case:

- An environment in which the yield spread is controlled (from April 1942 to March 1951) because the Fed reduced Treasury Bill yield at 0.375% and long-term government bond yield at 2.5%;
- Doubling the reserve requirements (raising to 19.5% from 13% in August 16, 1936, to 22.75% in March 1, 1937, and to 26% in May 1, 1937) in an already fragile economy without a malleable financial system (recession of 1937, United States);
- In an economy where the government consumption expenditures and gross investment represent 48.40% of GDP in 1944 and also due to the end of the World War II, its GDP deflator–adjusted value has decreased by 65.81% in 2 years (see Figure 66 in Appendix 37).

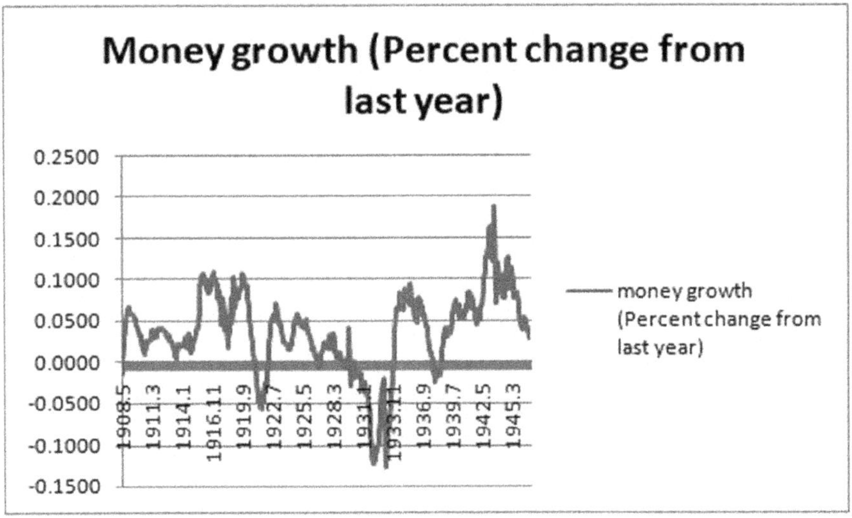


**Figure 65.** Money growth

Source: Authors' computations; data from NBER Macrohistory: XIV. Money and Banking U.S. Money Stock, Commercial Banks Plus Currency Held By Public, SA 05/1907-12/1946.

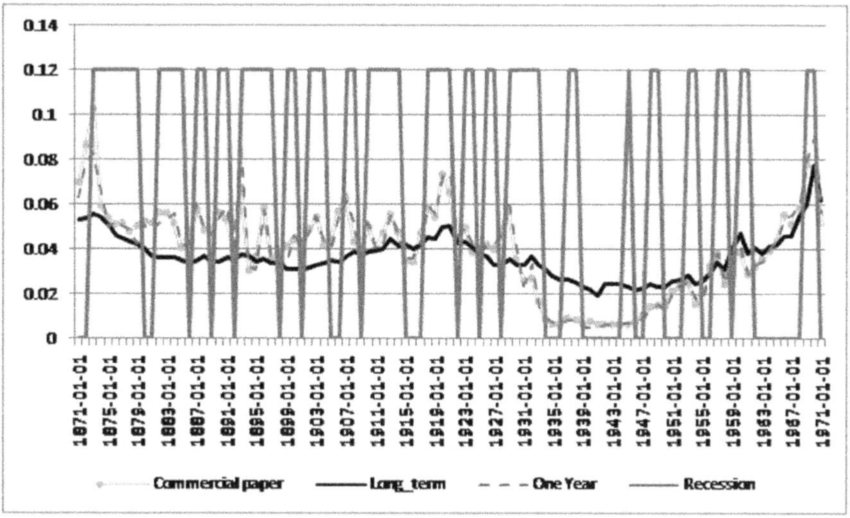


**Figure 67.** Recessions, commercial paper, long-term, and one-year yields
Source: Data from Shiller Database and NBER (Recessions).

We can observe in Figure 67 the evolution of the commercial paper rates – 1 year and long-term rates. Before the period 1948–1949, the short-term interest rates were catching up with the long-term interest rates signaling a recession.

The yield spread is not a reliable predictor of recessions in the United States alone. In the following sections, we will look into cases where the yield spread and credit factors failed to predict recessions.

Although the yield curve is an effective recession predictor, it was negative in 2002–2003 and despite the absence of a recession. Some analysts believed that the yield spread's forecasting capacity had diminished (Aziakpono & Khomo, 2007, p. 208). South Africa's Reserve Bank did not consider it a recession despite the fact that GDP fell in the fourth quarter of 2002, durable goods production fell from 2002Q2 to 2003Q4, and manufacturing production fell in two quarters (2002Q4 and 2003Q1). As a result, according to the definition, a recession occurred, but it was not as severe as the previous recessions.

Another noteworthy situation is Japan, where monetary easing appears to have reduced the yield spread's forecasting powers (see Figure 68 in Appendix 37).

However, if we consider the Japan Interbank Rate instead of governmental bonds with a maturity of 2 years (see Figure 69 in Appendix 37), we can conclude that the forecasting power of yield spreads has remained stable and that most inversions precede recessions as identified by the Business Cycle Chronologies from the Economic Cycle Research Institute (ECRI).

The ECRI use the same methodology as the National Bureau of Economic Research (NBER).

For 2000–2016, the identified recessions are as follows: 2000M08–2003M04, 2008M02–2009M03, 2010M08–2011M04, 2012M01–2013M01, and 2014M03–2014M08.

Germany is the next situation we'll look at. According to Sungki (2019), the yield spread is a very excellent predicting signal for German recessions; however, the credit variables do not perform well. This procedure is being carried out for a variety of reasons.

Germany is an exception because it is an export-led country, a member of the monetary union, and has higher productivity and smaller wage increases than the rest of the Eurozone. As a result, Germany's currency is depreciated in comparison to pre-Eurozone levels. German exports are being financed by consumption credit granted in other countries.

When credit in the other countries contract, German companies can no longer rely on retained profits which are actually the foreign credit to foreign nonfinancial enterprises, and this is the main reason why the flow of private credit leads to lags in economic growth (see Figure 70).

We used the following formula (32) to calculate private credit flow:

$$\Delta Credit = (Private\ Bank\ Credit_{t4} - Private\ Bank\ Credit_{t}) / Private\ Bank\ Credit_{t} \quad (32)$$

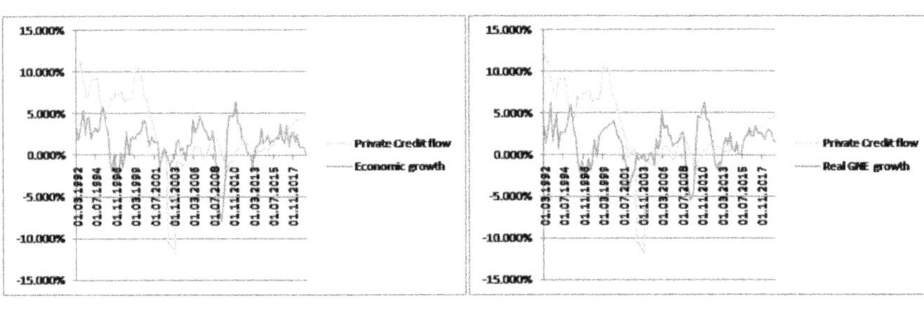


**Figure 70.** Credit flow, Germany

Source: Authors' computations; data from BIS database (long series on credit to nonfinancial sector). Credit to private nonfinancial sector from banks; total at market value – domestic currency – unadjusted; GDP; GDP Deflator; and trade balance from Eurostat database, quarterly data.

In this circumstance, the factories must borrow money to purchase equipment. However, while most economic research on the German economy focuses on credit stock and credit flow, we should pay special attention to credit distribution, especially that which prevailed during the Great Recession. Unlike small banks, which were only hit by the yield spread inversion, large banks were also affected by their foreign toxic assets. Small- and medium-sized nonfinancial firms had easier access to credit from small banks, primary cooperatives, and savings banks than large export-oriented enterprises, which were impacted by the big banks' tougher credit rules (Detzer et al., 2014).

Also, in terms of magnitude (rather than distribution), we may have looked into the wrong credit variables. According to Biggs, Mayer, and Pick (2009), GDP is income, which is a flow and thus should be connected with credit flow, whereas economic growth is a change in the flow, which should be correlated with credit impulse.

Credit impulse is defined as a shift in credit flow (see Equation 33):

$$\text{Credit Impulse} = [(\text{Private Bank Credit}_{t5} - \text{Private Bank Credit}_{t1}) - (\text{Private Bank Credit}_{t4} - \text{Private Bank Credit}_{t})] / GDP_{t4} \quad (33)$$

When comparing credit impulse to economic growth, the credit variable continues to lag behind economic activity; however, when accounting for the rise of internal demand (Real Gross National Expenditure), credit impulse outpaces economic activity (see Figure 71).

The conclusion is that credit increased SME productive capacity, while household credit increased internal demand and aided the economic recovery following the Great Recession.

Australia is the final scenario we will look at. Although Karunaratne's (2002) study demonstrates a strong link between inverted yield curves and recessions from 1972Q2 to 1997Q3, the association has since collapsed. The last recessionary month in Australia was 1991M12, despite many yield spread inversions. Inversions, on the other hand, anticipated economic downturns (see Appendix 25). For the other countries, the rule was that yield spread inversions could only anticipate recessions, whereas industrial output indicators such as the New Orders–Inventories Index are better suited to economic downturns. The impacts of yield spread inversions were mitigated by the country's rising population, wealth in natural resources such as iron and other minerals, significant trading ties with China, and fiscal policies. Barrett (2011) demonstrates that Australia would not have avoided the Great Recession if fiscal stimulus had not been implemented. According to the IMF (series GGGDTAAUA188N), central government debt/GDP was 9.687% of GDP in 2007 and has since risen to 41.369% of GDP in 2018.

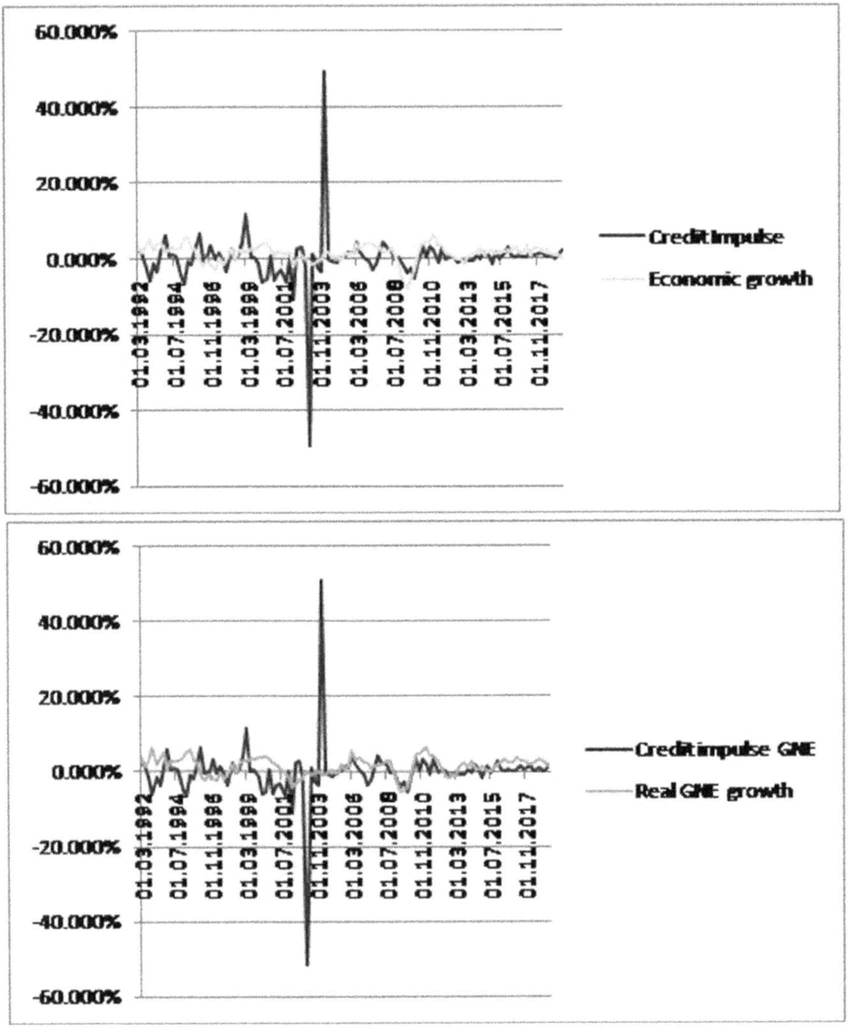


**Figure 71.** Credit impulse, Germany

Source: Authors' computations, data from BIS database (long series on credit to the nonfinancial sector). Credit to private nonfinancial sector from banks; total at market value – domestic currency – unadjusted; GDP; GDP deflator; and trade balance from Eurostat database, quarterly data.

Other circumstances, such as disease, could cause a recession due to high mortality rates, affecting labor inputs. That was a hypothetical situation. The second point is that, even with modest fatality rates, a sickness might induce a recession by stopping shipments. It could have a negative impact on the whole supply chain and on the carriers, although factories have safety stocks and the sea shipments are long-time travels. Tourism may be impacted as well. All these events happened recently due to Corona virus; however, all financial indicators signaled recession before the outbreak of the virus, and, also, this event has inverted the yield curve again and the stock market collapsed.

Wars could also be an influence. However, there are other examples of countries, such as the United States and Switzerland, that have profited economically from wars.

Finally, recessions can be caused by supply-side shocks such as oil shocks. Nonetheless, yield curve inversions occurred prior to the recessions attributed to oil shocks.

### 2.4.3. Other suitable indicators for predicting crises

Other appropriate indicators for predicting recessions, in our opinion, are the 30-year fixed-rate mortgage average minus Fed Funds, Moody's Seasoned AAA Corporate Bond Yield minus Fed Funds, 7 years minus Federal Funds, 5 years minus Federal Funds, 2 years minus Federal Funds, Margin Debit Change in report to the average of the last 12 months, and commercial paper rate minus bill rate spread. Following that, we attempted to assess whether these indicators are useful for forecasting the crisis.

## Research methodology and data

The 30-year fixed-rate mortgage average and Moody's Seasoned AAA Corporate Bond Yield perfectly illustrates the explanation of how the inversion of the yield spread affects the financial institutions' profitability and why we should pay more attention to the effect side of the yield spread inversion rather than the expectation side of it.

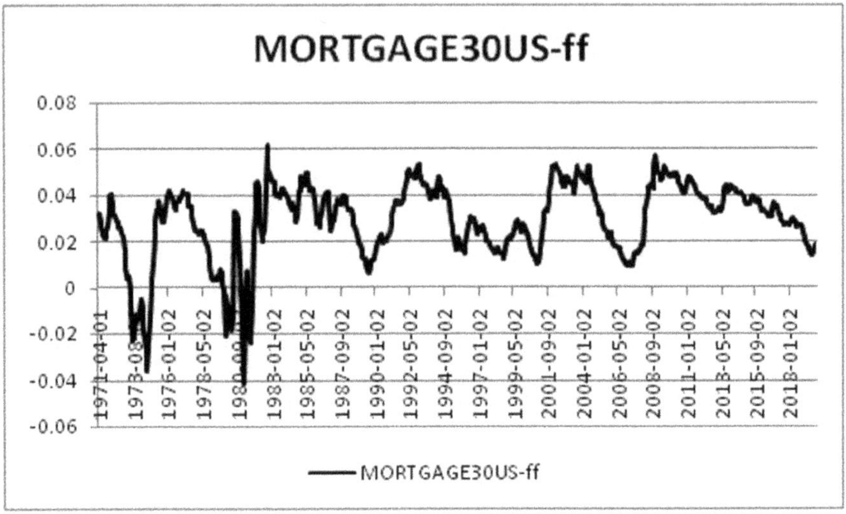


**Figure 72.** 30-year fixed-rate mortgage average

Source: Data from Freddie Mac, Primary Mortgage Market Survey, and H15, FRB.

Figures 72 and 76 show that MORTGAGE30US – Fed Funds and AAA – Fed Funds follow the same patterns as 10Y – Fed Funds. The same trend can be seen in Figure 73, where the 30-year fixed-rate mortgage average follows the 10-year Treasury rate. The long-term rates at which banks provide credit and long-term corporate bond yields are based on the 10-year Treasury rate, whereas short-term interest rates are based on the Federal funds rate. When long-term interest rates do not follow short-term interest rates, the financial system is in trouble, and it will tighten credit standards while decreasing credit supply availability.

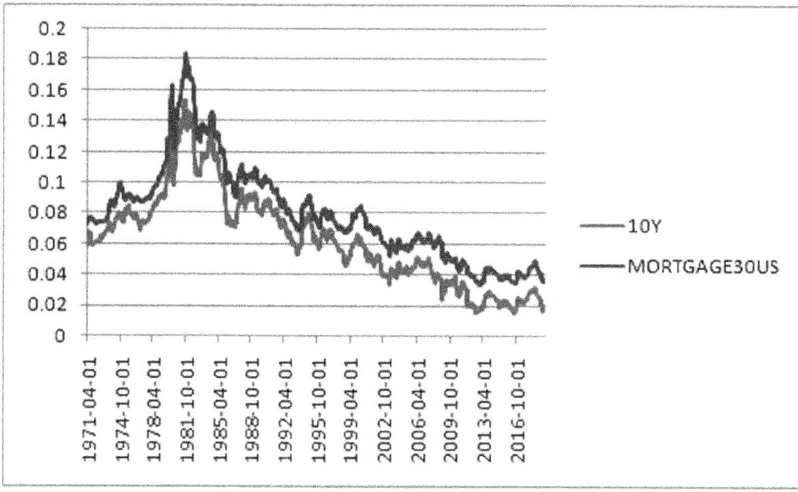


**Figure 73.** 10-year Treasury yield and 30-year fixed-rate mortgage average
Source: Data from Freddie Mac, Primary Mortgage Market Survey, and H15, FRB.

Dependent Variable: RECESSION
Method: ML - Binary Probit (Quadratic hill climbing / EViews legacy)
Date: 12/29/19 Time: 12:16
Sample (adjusted): 1972M07 2019M10
Included observations: 568 after adjustments
Convergence achieved after 5 iterations
Covariance matrix computed using second derivatives

| Variable | Coefficient | Std. Error | z-Statistic | Prob. |
|---|---|---|---|---|
| C | -0.040452 | 0.117168 | -0.345244 | 0.7299 |
| MORTGAGE30US_F(-15) | -47.01731 | 4.597355 | -10.22703 | 0.0000 |

| | | | |
|---|---|---|---|
| McFadden R-squared | 0.290998 | Mean dependent var | 0.137324 |
| S.D. dependent var | 0.344492 | S.E. of regression | 0.299951 |
| Akaike info criterion | 0.574351 | Sum squared resid | 50.92323 |
| Schwarz criterion | 0.589640 | Log likelihood | -161.1157 |
| Hannan-Quinn criter. | 0.580317 | Deviance | 322.2314 |
| Restr. deviance | 454.4861 | Restr. log likelihood | -227.2430 |
| LR statistic | 132.2547 | Avg. log likelihood | -0.283654 |
| Prob(LR statistic) | 0.000000 | | |

| | | | |
|---|---|---|---|
| Obs with Dep=0 | 490 | Total obs | 568 |
| Obs with Dep=1 | 78 | | |

**Figure 74.** 30-year fixed-rate mortgage average – Fed Funds, probit regression
Source: Authors' calculation, using data from Freddie Mac, Primary Mortgage Market Survey.

This is why the yield spreads of the MORTGAGE30US – Fed Funds rate and the AAA – Fed Funds rate are good recession predictors (see Figures 74 and 77).

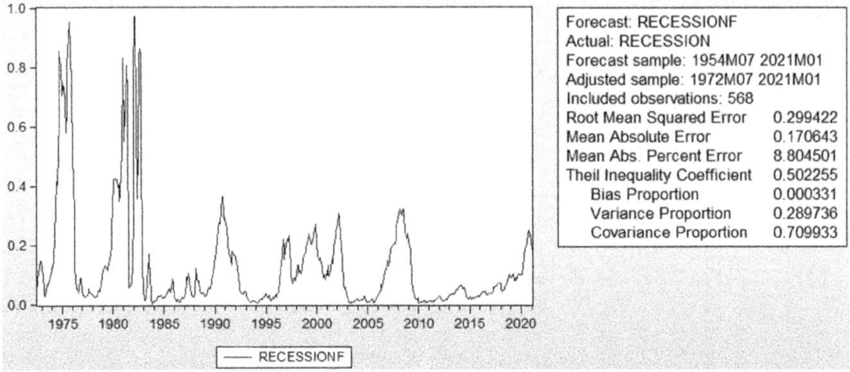


**Figure 75.** Recession prediction by using the 30-year fixed-rate mortgage average – Fed Funds

Source: Data from Freddie Mac, Primary Mortgage Market Survey.

Figure 75 depicts a spike in the probability of a recession, which reaches 25% in 2020M10.

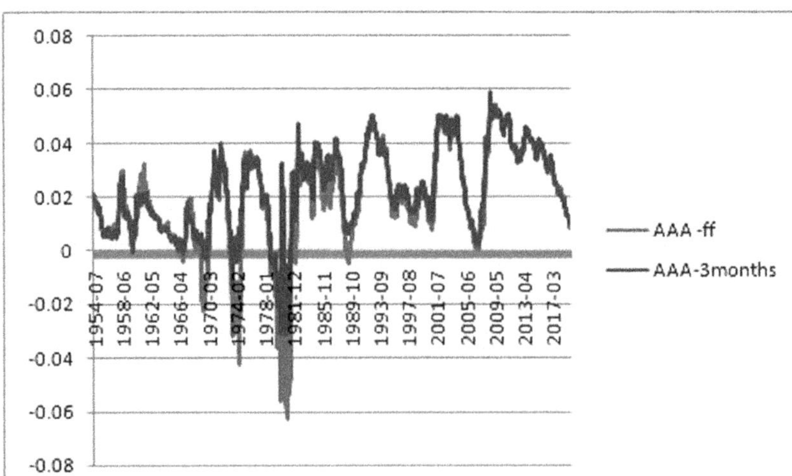


**Figure 76.** AAA – Federal Funds rate

Source: Authors' computations; data from St. Louis Fed.

Dependent Variable: RECESSION(9)
Method: ML - Binary Probit (Quadratic hill climbing)
Date: 12/29/19 Time: 16:53
Sample (adjusted): 1954M07 2019M01
Included observations: 775 after adjustments
Convergence achieved after 5 iterations
Covariance matrix computed using second derivatives

| Variable | Coefficient | Std. Error | z-Statistic | Prob. |
|---|---|---|---|---|
| C | -0.504533 | 0.075517 | -6.681023 | 0.0000 |
| AAA_FF | -43.80514 | 3.910015 | -11.20332 | 0.0000 |

| | | | |
|---|---|---|---|
| McFadden R-squared | 0.273196 | Mean dependent var | 0.141935 |
| S.D. dependent var | 0.349209 | S.E. of regression | 0.298195 |
| Akaike info criterion | 0.598904 | Sum squared resid | 68.73552 |
| Schwarz criterion | 0.610912 | Log likelihood | -230.0754 |
| Hannan-Quinn criter. | 0.603524 | Deviance | 460.1508 |
| Restr. deviance | 633.1153 | Restr. log likelihood | -316.5576 |
| LR statistic | 172.9645 | Avg. log likelihood | -0.296871 |
| Prob(LR statistic) | 0.000000 | | |

| | | | |
|---|---|---|---|
| Obs with Dep=0 | 665 | Total obs | 775 |
| Obs with Dep=1 | 110 | | |

**Figure 77.** AAA – FF

Source: Authors' computations, data from St. Louis Fed.

The period 1976M06–2019M10 is analyzed for the 7-year Treasury rate – Federal Funds, 5-year Treasury rate – Federal Funds, and 2 years – Federal Funds rate.

## Results and discussion

Even when compared to 10Y – FF and 10Y – 3MO, the McFadden coefficient is very high (compare Figures 78, 79, and 80 with Figures 87 and 88). The highest predictive power for all yield spreads is around 15–16 leads. We had the highest predictive power at 8 and 10 months lead for 1954M07–2019M10 yield spreads at the highest end of the curve (10 years). The lengthening of the period between yield curve inversions and the onset of recessions is a result of aggressive monetary policy aimed at avoiding cycles.

Although the predictive power is highest at 16 leads for 7Y-FF and 15 leads for 5-FF, we could find significant information at lower leads.

Dependent Variable: RECESSION(16)
Method: ML - Binary Probit (Quadratic hill climbing)
Date: 12/31/19 Time: 18:21
Sample (adjusted): 1976M06 2018M06
Included observations: 505 after adjustments
Convergence achieved after 5 iterations
Covariance matrix computed using second derivatives

| Variable | Coefficient | Std. Error | z-Statistic | Prob. |
|---|---|---|---|---|
| C | -0.834075 | 0.092859 | -8.982187 | 0.0000 |
| GS7_FF | -70.93736 | 7.712927 | -9.197204 | 0.0000 |

| | | | |
|---|---|---|---|
| McFadden R-squared | 0.380027 | Mean dependent var | 0.120792 |
| S.D. dependent var | 0.326209 | S.E. of regression | 0.269249 |
| Akaike info criterion | 0.464841 | Sum squared resid | 36.46496 |
| Schwarz criterion | 0.481572 | Log likelihood | -115.3725 |
| Hannan-Quinn criter. | 0.471404 | Deviance | 230.7449 |
| Restr. deviance | 372.1852 | Restr. log likelihood | -186.0926 |
| LR statistic | 141.4403 | Avg. log likelihood | -0.228460 |
| Prob(LR statistic) | 0.000000 | | |
| Obs with Dep=0 | 444 | Total obs | 505 |
| Obs with Dep=1 | 61 | | |

**Figure 78.** 7-Year Treasury minus Fed Funds
Source: Authors' computations; data from St Louis Fed.

According to Kşnbay and Baba's (2011) research, the 5Y-FF outperforms the 10YY-FF at 6 leads. At such low leads, 7Y-FF is even better. At 8 leads, the McFadden $R^2$ coefficient is 0.281500 for 7Y-FF, 0.277717 for 5Y-FF, and 0.274227 for 10Y-FF. Even at 9 (0.297456 vs. 0.292786 McFadden $R^2$) and 10 (0.293067 vs. 0.292008) month leads, 7Y-FF outperforms 10Y-FF. The closer we get to the recession, the more important 5Y-FF and 7Y-FF forecasting will become.

Dependent Variable: RECESSION(15)
Method: ML - Binary Probit (Quadratic hill climbing)
Date: 02/03/20 Time: 13:09
Sample (adjusted): 1976M06 2018M07
Included observations: 506 after adjustments
Convergence achieved after 5 iterations
Covariance matrix computed using second derivatives

| Variable | Coefficient | Std. Error | z-Statistic | Prob. |
|---|---|---|---|---|
| C | -0.940949 | 0.090769 | -10.36644 | 0.0000 |
| GS5_FF | -75.03765 | 8.018116 | -9.358514 | 0.0000 |

| | | | |
|---|---|---|---|
| McFadden R-squared | 0.365074 | Mean dependent var | 0.120553 |
| S.D. dependent var | 0.325930 | S.E. of regression | 0.270007 |
| Akaike info criterion | 0.475244 | Sum squared resid | 36.74339 |
| Schwarz criterion | 0.491950 | Log likelihood | -118.2367 |
| Hannan-Quinn criter. | 0.481796 | Deviance | 236.4735 |
| Restr. deviance | 372.4424 | Restr. log likelihood | -186.2212 |
| LR statistic | 135.9689 | Avg. log likelihood | -0.233669 |
| Prob(LR statistic) | 0.000000 | | |

| | | | |
|---|---|---|---|
| Obs with Dep=0 | 445 | Total obs | 506 |
| Obs with Dep=1 | 61 | | |

**Figure 79.** Yield spread, 5 years minus Fed Funds

Source: Authors' computations.

Dependent Variable: RECESSION(15)
Method: ML - Binary Probit (Quadratic hill climbing / EViews legacy)
Date: 12/28/19 Time: 13:31
Sample (adjusted): 1976M06 2018M07
Included observations: 506 after adjustments
Convergence achieved after 5 iterations
Covariance matrix computed using second derivatives

| Variable | Coefficient | Std. Error | z-Statistic | Prob. |
|---|---|---|---|---|
| C | -1.122664 | 0.087736 | -12.79596 | 0.0000 |
| S_2Y_FEDFUNDS | -102.0074 | 11.41131 | -8.939149 | 0.0000 |

| | | | |
|---|---|---|---|
| McFadden R-squared | 0.323475 | Mean dependent var | 0.120553 |
| S.D. dependent var | 0.325930 | S.E. of regression | 0.272068 |
| Akaike info criterion | 0.505863 | Sum squared resid | 37.30667 |
| Schwarz criterion | 0.522569 | Log likelihood | -125.9834 |
| Hannan-Quinn criter. | 0.512415 | Deviance | 251.9667 |
| Restr. deviance | 372.4424 | Restr. log likelihood | -186.2212 |
| LR statistic | 120.4756 | Avg. log likelihood | -0.248979 |
| Prob(LR statistic) | 0.000000 | | |

| | | | |
|---|---|---|---|
| Obs with Dep=0 | 445 | Total obs | 506 |
| Obs with Dep=1 | 61 | | |

**Figure 80.** 2-year Treasury minus Federal Funds rate
Source: Authors' computations; data from St. Louis Fed.

The margin debit represents the money borrowed from the broker to buy more shares. Margin debit is procyclical, as illustrated in Figure 81.

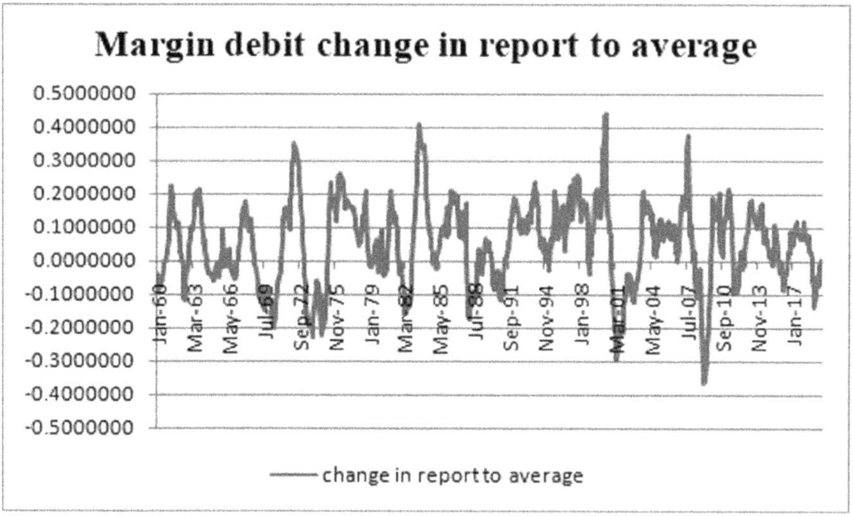


**Figure 81.** Margin debit

Source: Authors' computations; change in report to the previous 12 months, data from NYSE (January 1959–November 2017) and FINRA (December 2017–September 2019).

Although the 2001 recession is widely regarded as the end of a business cycle (in the technology sector), it occurred as a result of the 1997 Asian Crisis and the 1998 Russian Crisis, both of which caused financial turbulences around the world. Many investors increased margin debit (increased their debt to brokers and dealers) and speculated on the equity market, fueled by the dotcom bubble and irrational exuberance. When the stock market crashed, investors were required to keep the required margin. The investment losses sparked panic and a drop in consumer spending.

Margin debit indicator was built using NYSE data (January 1959–November 2017) and FINRA data (December 2017–September 2019), and the change report to the previous 12 months was calculated.

Figure 82 shows that the margin debit has the greatest predictive power, with no lead or lag. Margin debit is an excellent fit for the next 5 months until the current month of the recession and even for the next 6 months after the recession.

Dependent Variable: RECESSION
Method: ML - Binary Probit (Quadratic hill climbing)
Date: 12/30/19 Time: 02:37
Sample: 1960M01 2019M09
Included observations: 717
Convergence achieved after 5 iterations
Covariance matrix computed using second derivatives

| Variable | Coefficient | Std. Error | z-Statistic | Prob. |
|---|---|---|---|---|
| C | -1.188567 | 0.083117 | -14.29994 | 0.0000 |
| MARGIN_DEBIT | -9.584549 | 0.853926 | -11.22410 | 0.0000 |

| | | | |
|---|---|---|---|
| McFadden R-squared | 0.383751 | Mean dependent var | 0.140865 |
| S.D. dependent var | 0.348125 | S.E. of regression | 0.281005 |
| Akaike info criterion | 0.506627 | Sum squared resid | 56.45917 |
| Schwarz criterion | 0.519388 | Log likelihood | -179.6257 |
| Hannan-Quinn criter. | 0.511554 | Deviance | 359.2513 |
| Restr. deviance | 582.9642 | Restr. log likelihood | -291.4821 |
| LR statistic | 223.7128 | Avg. log likelihood | -0.250524 |
| Prob(LR statistic) | 0.000000 | | |

| | | | |
|---|---|---|---|
| Obs with Dep=0 | 616 | Total obs | 717 |
| Obs with Dep=1 | 101 | | |

**Figure 82.** Margin debit and recessions

Source: Authors' computations; change in report to the previous 12 months, data from NYSE (January 1959–November 2017) and FINRA (December 2017–September 2019).

Gilchrist and Zakrajek (2012) introduced a new corporate bond credit spread index calculated as the arithmetic average of credit spreads for each month (the difference between the yield on a corporate bond and the yield on a Treasury bond with the same maturity). Extraction of expected defaults from each credit spread yields the excess bond premium. In reality, the EBP reflects changes in credit market sentiment. Large credit spreads indicate a high level of risk. The excess bond premium is a powerful recession indicator, but it was deceptive in 2002, when EBP spiked as a result of accounting scandals that led to the bankruptcy of some large financial firms, but there was no recession. It was also deceptive about the possibility of a 2016 recession; however, as demonstrated, the McFadden $R^2$ can be a powerful recession predictor, particularly one month before the recession (see Figure 83).

Dependent Variable: RECESSION(1)
Method: ML - Binary Probit (Quadratic hill climbing)
Date: 12/29/19 Time: 16:11
Sample (adjusted): 1973M01 2019M09
Included observations: 561 after adjustments
Convergence achieved after 5 iterations
Covariance matrix computed using second derivatives

| Variable | Coefficient | Std. Error | z-Statistic | Prob. |
|---|---|---|---|---|
| C | -1.408809 | 0.088108 | -15.98955 | 0.0000 |
| EXCESS_BOND_PREMIUM | 1.509161 | 0.161200 | 9.362030 | 0.0000 |

| | | | |
|---|---|---|---|
| McFadden R-squared | 0.270471 | Mean dependent var | 0.139037 |
| S.D. dependent var | 0.346294 | S.E. of regression | 0.300239 |
| Akaike info criterion | 0.595440 | Sum squared resid | 50.39011 |
| Schwarz criterion | 0.610876 | Log likelihood | -165.0210 |
| Hannan-Quinn criter. | 0.601467 | Deviance | 330.0420 |
| Restr. deviance | 452.4042 | Restr. log likelihood | -226.2021 |
| LR statistic | 122.3622 | Avg. log likelihood | -0.294155 |
| Prob(LR statistic) | 0.000000 | | |
| Obs with Dep=0 | 483 | Total obs | 561 |
| Obs with Dep=1 | 78 | | |

**Figure 83.** Excess bond premium, probit regressions
Source: Authors' computations; EBP and Recession Risk time series, FRB.

The commercial paper rate minus bill rate spread is the final indicator that provides useful information, but it suffers from a lack of data continuity. However, we can extend the time series in the same way that Lown et al. (2000) did by combining the spread of 3-month maturity with the spread of 6-month maturity. For January 1970–August 1997, we use 6-month commercial paper minus 6-month Treasury bill, and, for September 1997–October 2019, we use 3-month commercial paper minus 3-month Treasury bill. Appendixes 26 and 27 present the results computed using the same methodology as the other tested indicators. We get an excellent fit for the period January 1970–October 2019 and a close-to-excellent fit for the period June 1976–October 2019. Monetary policy interventions are to blame for the drop in the McFadden coefficient.

### 2.4.4. Signals that are too weak or have lost their ability to add information

The Purchasing Managers' Index (PMI) is a difficult recession predictor. It is a diffusion index based on 400 supply and purchasing managers' expectations for new orders, production, inventories, and employment. A value greater than 50 indicates expansion, and a value less than 50 indicates contraction. As shown in Figure 84, the highest McFadden $R^2$ is obtained for a model with 2 lags, implying that PMI-50 actually lags recessions. In fact, it has preceded recessions in some cases, matched recessions in others, lagged recessions in others, and in some cases it was a false alarm signaling economic downturns rather than recessions. Only after testing in the final recession model will we be able to assess its relevance, but, for the time being, there are reservations about this indicator, despite the fact that the Corona virus may increase its importance.

Dependent Variable: RECESSION(-2)
Method: ML - Binary Probit (Quadratic hill climbing)
Date: 12/28/19 Time: 03:52
Sample (adjusted): 1954M09 2019M10
Included observations: 782 after adjustments
Convergence achieved after 5 iterations
Covariance matrix computed using second derivatives

| Variable | Coefficient | Std. Error | z-Statistic | Prob. |
|---|---|---|---|---|
| C | -1.070128 | 0.075943 | -14.09121 | 0.0000 |
| PMI_50 | -0.187151 | 0.014742 | -12.69474 | 0.0000 |

| | | | |
|---|---|---|---|
| McFadden R-squared | 0.455435 | Mean dependent var | 0.140665 |
| S.D. dependent var | 0.347898 | S.E. of regression | 0.239585 |
| Akaike info criterion | 0.447485 | Sum squared resid | 44.77292 |
| Schwarz criterion | 0.459408 | Log likelihood | -172.9668 |
| Hannan-Quinn criter. | 0.452070 | Deviance | 345.9335 |
| Restr. deviance | 635.2479 | Restr. log likelihood | -317.6240 |
| LR statistic | 289.3144 | Avg. log likelihood | -0.221185 |
| Prob(LR statistic) | 0.000000 | | |
| Obs with Dep=0 | 672 | Total obs | 782 |
| Obs with Dep=1 | 110 | | |

**Figure 84.** Purchasing Manager's Index, probit regressions

Source: Authors' computations; data from Quandl.

The 10-year Treasury – 2-year yield spread is a very good recession predictor, but it is weaker than other yield spreads such as the 10-year-3-month, 10-year-FF, 7-year-FF, 5-year-FF, and 2-year-FF (see Figures 85 and 86).

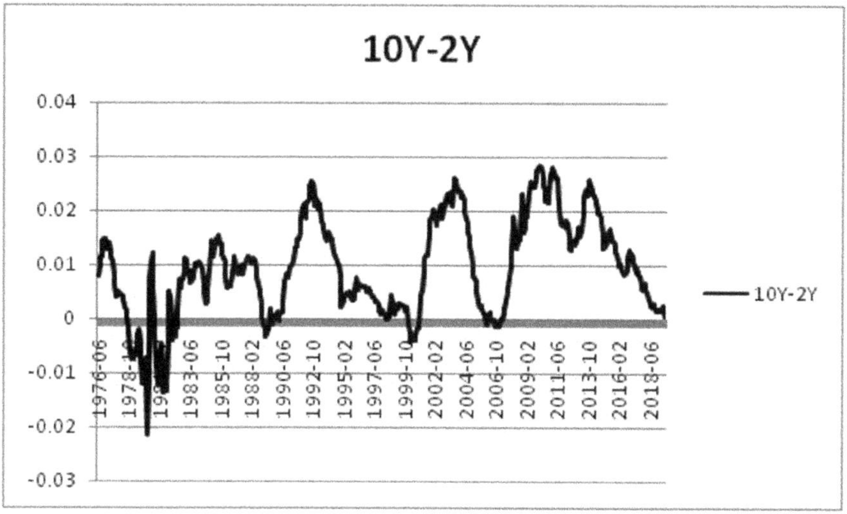


**Figure 85.** 10Y – 2Y

Source: Authors' computations; data from Table H15, FRB.

Dependent Variable: RECESSION(17)
Method: ML - Binary Probit (Quadratic hill climbing)
Date: 12/28/19 Time: 03:29
Sample (adjusted): 1976M06 2018M05
Included observations: 504 after adjustments
Convergence achieved after 5 iterations
Covariance matrix computed using second derivatives

| Variable | Coefficient | Std. Error | z-Statistic | Prob. |
|---|---|---|---|---|
| C | -0.610086 | 0.093619 | -6.516679 | 0.0000 |
| S_10Y_2Y | -116.9786 | 13.86049 | -8.439722 | 0.0000 |

| | | | |
|---|---|---|---|
| McFadden R-squared | 0.317044 | Mean dependent var | 0.121032 |
| S.D. dependent var | 0.326488 | S.E. of regression | 0.280825 |
| Akaike info criterion | 0.511924 | Sum squared resid | 39.58917 |
| Schwarz criterion | 0.528681 | Log likelihood | -127.0050 |
| Hannan-Quinn criter. | 0.518497 | Deviance | 254.0099 |
| Restr. deviance | 371.9275 | Restr. log likelihood | -185.9637 |
| LR statistic | 117.9175 | Avg. log likelihood | -0.251994 |
| Prob(LR statistic) | 0.000000 | | |
| Obs with Dep=0 | 443 | Total obs | 504 |
| Obs with Dep=1 | 61 | | |

**Figure 86.** 10Y – 2Y, probit model

Source: Authors' computations; data from Table H15, FRB.

When Figure 86 is compared to Figures 78, 79, 80, 87, and 88, we can see that the 10Y–2Y yield spread has the lowest predictive power of all yield spreads.

Dependent Variable: RECESSION(16)
Method: ML - Binary Probit (Quadratic hill climbing)
Date: 12/28/19 Time: 11:22
Sample (adjusted): 1976M06 2018M06
Included observations: 505 after adjustments
Convergence achieved after 5 iterations
Covariance matrix computed using second derivatives

| Variable | Coefficient | Std. Error | z-Statistic | Prob. |
|---|---|---|---|---|
| C | -0.423869 | 0.105084 | -4.033607 | 0.0001 |
| S_10Y_3M | -75.07027 | 8.212962 | -9.140463 | 0.0000 |

| | | | |
|---|---|---|---|
| McFadden R-squared | 0.354675 | Mean dependent var | 0.120792 |
| S.D. dependent var | 0.326209 | S.E. of regression | 0.274108 |
| Akaike info criterion | 0.483525 | Sum squared resid | 37.79311 |
| Schwarz criterion | 0.500256 | Log likelihood | -120.0902 |
| Hannan-Quinn criter. | 0.490088 | Deviance | 240.1803 |
| Restr. deviance | 372.1852 | Restr. log likelihood | -186.0926 |
| LR statistic | 132.0049 | Avg. log likelihood | -0.237802 |
| Prob(LR statistic) | 0.000000 | | |

| | | | |
|---|---|---|---|
| Obs with Dep=0 | 444 | Total obs | 505 |
| Obs with Dep=1 | 61 | | |

**Figure 87.** 10Y – 3M, probit model.

Source: Authors' computations; data from Table H15, FRB.

Dependent Variable: RECESSION(16)
Method: ML - Binary Probit (Quadratic hill climbing)
Date: 12/28/19 Time: 03:30
Sample (adjusted): 1976M06 2018M06
Included observations: 505 after adjustments
Convergence achieved after 5 iterations
Covariance matrix computed using second derivatives

| Variable | Coefficient | Std. Error | z-Statistic | Prob. |
|---|---|---|---|---|
| C | -0.796371 | 0.093502 | -8.517126 | 0.0000 |
| S_10Y_FEDFUNDS | -65.93889 | 7.254325 | -9.089597 | 0.0000 |

| | | | |
|---|---|---|---|
| McFadden R-squared | 0.382522 | Mean dependent var | 0.120792 |
| S.D. dependent var | 0.326209 | S.E. of regression | 0.270601 |
| Akaike info criterion | 0.463002 | Sum squared resid | 36.83208 |
| Schwarz criterion | 0.479733 | Log likelihood | -114.9080 |
| Hannan-Quinn criter. | 0.469565 | Deviance | 229.8161 |
| Restr. deviance | 372.1852 | Restr. log likelihood | -186.0926 |
| LR statistic | 142.3691 | Avg. log likelihood | -0.227541 |
| Prob(LR statistic) | 0.000000 | | |

| | | | |
|---|---|---|---|
| Obs with Dep=0 | 444 | Total obs | 505 |
| Obs with Dep=1 | 61 | | |

**Figure 88.** Yield spread, 10 Y – FF, probit model
Source: Authors' computations; data from Table H15, FRB.

Other weak indicators include the two-year swap spread; credit impulse; change in money stock – Federal Funds, change in loan stock; prime loan rate; and the Taylor Rule rate – Federal Funds rate and the output gap.

A derivative contract in which two parties exchange interest rates is what an interest rate swap is. The most common is the conversion of an adjustable rate to a fixed rate. It is used for both hedging and speculation. The fixed rate is the swap rate. The swap spread is the difference in interest rates between the swap rate and the Treasury rate for the same maturity. Prior to the GFC, the swap spread was a very good recession indicator, and its value would have increased prior to a recession due to increased bank risk versus government risk. In order for the broker/dealer to achieve a high ROE, post-crisis regulation (particularly capital requirements) has rendered swap spreads with long maturities and even the two-year spread swap negative. The reason is the limited availability of data in comparison to the yield curve and, more importantly, the regulatory distortions imposed on both brokers/dealers and investors.

Credit impulse is failing as a recession predictor because it is better suited to detect real GDP changes rather than recessions, and it is very volatile when calculated at a higher frequency (monthly). For bank credit (which is not seasonally adjusted), the following formula is used:

$$Credit\ impulse = [(Cr_{t0} - Cr_{t-12}) - (Cr_{t-12} - Cr_{t-24})] / Cr_{t-12} \tag{34}$$

Appendixes 28 and 29 demonstrate that credit impulse (monthly frequency) does not provide useful information for recession prediction.

The change in money supply–interest rates (Federal Funds rate) and change in loan stock–bank prime loan rate are a combination of Austrian and Hyman Minsky theories. According to the Austrian Business Cycle Theory, when interest rates rise above the change in money stock, misinvestments default. This is consistent with Minsky's hypothesis of financial instability. If interest rates rise faster than the change in money supply, speculative units (those who can't pay the principle) will become Ponzi units because they can't roll over the debt in these circumstances. The change in loan stock minus the bank prime loan rate improves the change in money supply–Federal Funds rate. However, these are not reliable indicators of a coming recession (see Appendixes 30 and 31). These indicators are more closely linked to the rate of delinquency (–0.575 correlation coefficient of Delinquency Rate on Commercial and Industrial Loans–DRBLACBN with change in loan stock minus bank prime loan rate) and subsequent bank crashes.

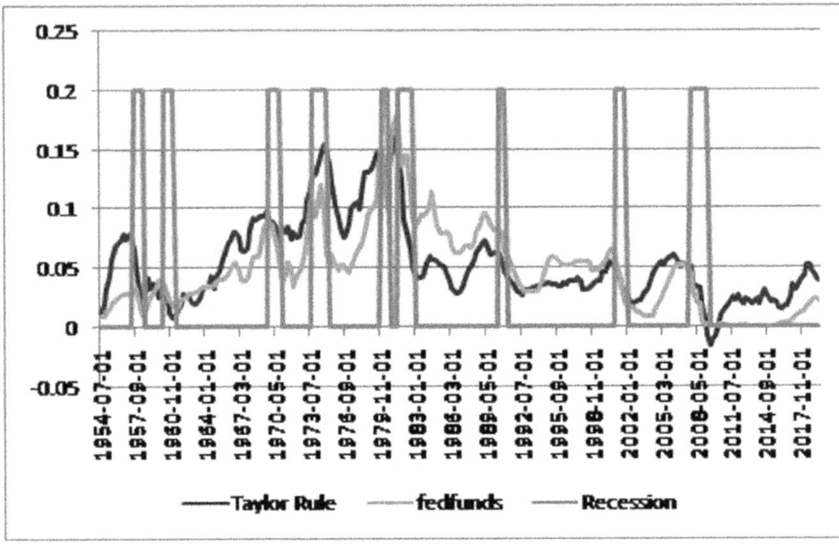


**Figure 89.** Taylor Rule and Federal Fed Funds
Source: St. Louis Fed.

The Taylor Rule is a tool used by policymakers to control inflation. St. Fed Louis employs the following formula:

$$GDP\ Deflator + 0.02 + 0.5 * (GDP\ Deflator - 0.02) + 0.5 * \frac{Real\ Gross\ Domestic\ Product - Real\ Potential\ GDP}{Real\ Potential\ GDP} \quad (35)$$

According to John B. Taylor (2009), policymakers who did not follow the Taylor Rule inflated housing bubbles. This mechanical view of economics is not shared by us. There were numerous additional complications, such as deregulation and securitization. Although it can provide useful information, such as the liquidity trap between 2009Q2 and 2010Q1 (negative Taylor Rule rates) and how extremely low interest rates can lead to bubbles, economics is a very complex organism. If low interest rates had been combined with higher capital requirements, the housing boom would not have occurred. Long-term interest rates must also be taken into account. Different measures may produce the same result, and similar policies may produce different outcome.

Figures 89 and 90 show that the deviations between the Taylor Rule and the actual Fed Funds rate are not a good predictor of recessions. Large positive deviations indicate a higher likelihood of a recession (see Figure 91), but recessions take a long time to manifest.

Dependent Variable: RECESSION(16)
Method: ML - Binary Probit (Quadratic hill climbing)
Date: 12/28/19 Time: 03:30
Sample (adjusted): 1976M06 2018M06
Included observations: 505 after adjustments
Convergence achieved after 5 iterations
Covariance matrix computed using second derivatives

| Variable | Coefficient | Std. Error | z-Statistic | Prob. |
|---|---|---|---|---|
| C | -0.796371 | 0.093502 | -8.517126 | 0.0000 |
| S_10Y_FEDFUNDS | -65.93889 | 7.254325 | -9.089597 | 0.0000 |

| | | | |
|---|---|---|---|
| McFadden R-squared | 0.382522 | Mean dependent var | 0.120792 |
| S.D. dependent var | 0.326209 | S.E. of regression | 0.270601 |
| Akaike info criterion | 0.463002 | Sum squared resid | 36.83208 |
| Schwarz criterion | 0.479733 | Log likelihood | -114.9080 |
| Hannan-Quinn criter. | 0.469565 | Deviance | 229.8161 |
| Restr. deviance | 372.1852 | Restr. log likelihood | -186.0926 |
| LR statistic | 142.3691 | Avg. log likelihood | -0.227541 |
| Prob(LR statistic) | 0.000000 | | |

| | | | |
|---|---|---|---|
| Obs with Dep=0 | 444 | Total obs | 505 |
| Obs with Dep=1 | 61 | | |

**Figure 90.** Taylor Rule – Fed Funds rate, probit equation
Source: Authors' computations.

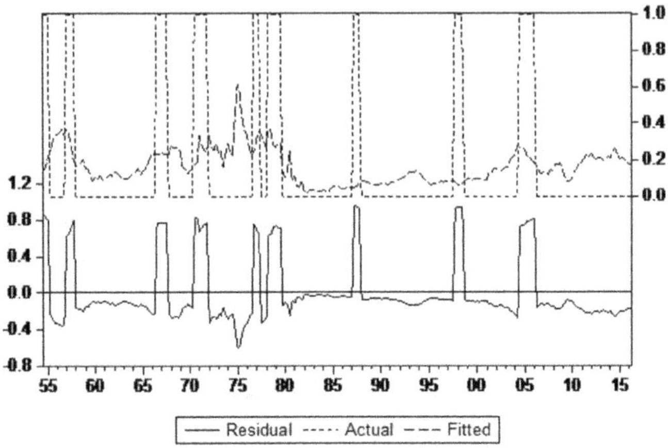


**Figure 91.** Recession probabilities based on a probit model with Taylor Rule – Fed Funds rate

Source: Authors' calculations.

The output gap ((Real GDP – Real Potential GDP) / Real Potential GDP) is the final indicator. We see no mechanism in which the output gap could predict recessions based solely on Figure 92. We could argue that supraproduction (Actual Real GDP > Real Potential GDP) exists, but there has been no positive output gap during the 1983Q1–1990Q2 expansion. Furthermore, the expansion period from 1961Q2 to 1969Q3 was quite long despite very large positive deviations, and the current expansion is the longest U.S. expansion despite the fact that the U.S. economy has experienced a large negative output gap for a very long time. Figure 93 depicts the reason for this. The Real Potential GDP growth rate in the United States from 1949Q1 to 2019Q3 was never negative. If the actual Real GDP had matched the Real Potential GDP, there would have been no recession in the United States during the studied period. Is this, however, feasible over long periods of time? No, it is not. A 0 output gap does not show the imbalances that were created to fill the gap. It does not reveal the debt accumulation and financial resource misallocation required to equalize Real Potential GDP with Actual Real GDP.

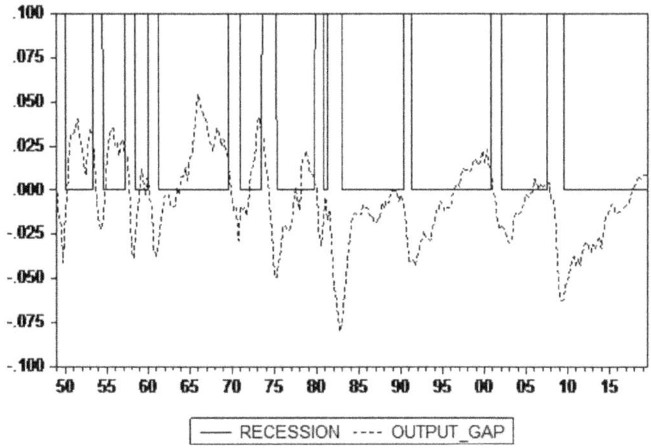


**Figure 92.** Recession and Output Gap, United States
Source: Authors' computations; U.S. Congressional Budget Office (CBO).

In a Talebian (from Taleb) framework, achieved stability will merely conceal the risks and long periods of prosperity will lead to deeper economic crises. According to Minsky, "stability is destabilizing." An economy with no output gap is analogous to a human who cannot experience the effects of gravity, such as a NASA pilot in space. The pilots will believe they are invincible if they are not subjected to stressors such as gravity. When they return to Earth, even a short walk will break their bones. The economy is the same way; without stressors, the economy will become fragile.

We propose a complementary theory: Not only can this policy lead to longer expansion phases, it can also contribute to a state of stagnation by undermining risks and causing a larger crisis. Economic growth rates will generally be lower in the long run. New technologies replace old technologies, but they do not create as many jobs. Poor policy will also contribute to the stagnation trend. When the output gap exceeds zero, policymakers will attempt to close the gap by raising interest rates and reducing the budget deficit, preventing businesses from taking advantage of opportunities. When the output gap is negative, central bankers especially will stimulate the economy, creating bubbles in the process. Smaller differences result in a lower average. Funds will increasingly flow to bubbles rather than to the real economy. It is not a good idea to limit volatility. Until a certain point, organisms benefit from volatility (Hormesis).

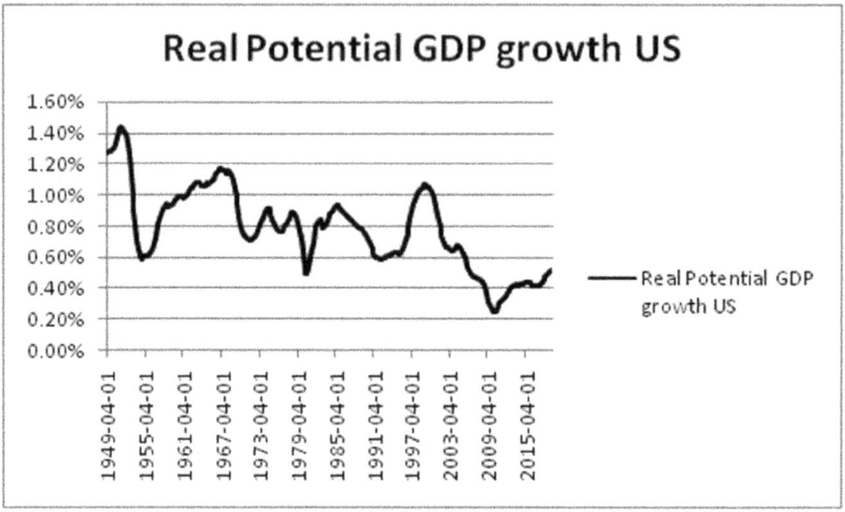


**Figure 93.** Real potential GDP growth, United States
Source: Authors' computations, U.S. CBO.

If we exclude the potential GDP frame, a smaller or no output gap could lead to lower Real Potential GDP growth or a lower long-term growth rate. Intervention may be used in the event of extremely large downside deviations that could result in long-term chronic aggregate demand.

There is no study that can demonstrate that Real Potential GDP is constantly increasing. According to Kawamoto, Ozaki, Kato, and Maehashi (2017) calculations, Japan experienced negative potential GDP growth rates for 1 year between 1983 and 2016. Negative potential GDP growth rates can be caused by highly reduced labor units, weak institutions, an indebted economy, and a damaged financial system.

Dependent Variable: RECESSION(-2)
Method: ML - Binary Probit (Quadratic hill climbing)
Date: 08/15/20 Time: 20:42
Sample (adjusted): 1949Q3 2019Q3
Included observations: 281 after adjustments
Convergence achieved after 5 iterations
Covariance matrix computed using second derivatives

| Variable | Coefficient | Std. Error | z-Statistic | Prob. |
|---|---|---|---|---|
| C | -1.531298 | 0.154295 | -9.924483 | 0.0000 |
| OUTPUT_GAP | -41.91675 | 6.091843 | -6.880799 | 0.0000 |

| | | | |
|---|---|---|---|
| McFadden R-squared | 0.281710 | Mean dependent var | 0.177936 |
| S.D. dependent var | 0.383141 | S.E. of regression | 0.328195 |
| Akaike info criterion | 0.686912 | Sum squared resid | 30.05167 |
| Schwarz criterion | 0.712808 | Log likelihood | -94.51119 |
| Hannan-Quinn criter. | 0.697298 | Deviance | 189.0224 |
| Restr. deviance | 263.1560 | Restr. log likelihood | -131.5780 |
| LR statistic | 74.13367 | Avg. log likelihood | -0.336339 |
| Prob(LR statistic) | 0.000000 | | |

| | | | |
|---|---|---|---|
| Obs with Dep=0 | 231 | Total obs | 281 |
| Obs with Dep=1 | 50 | | |

**Figure 94.** Output gap, probit regression
Source: Authors' computations; CBO and BEA.

The output gap, as shown in Figures 94 and 95, is not a good predictor. The highest McFadden $R^2$ is obtained for a model with 2 lags, implying that negative output gaps will persist for an additional two quarters after the recession ends. Lead 6 has the highest McFadden coefficient for leads (see Figure 95), but the coefficient is low.

Dependent Variable: RECESSION(6)
Method: ML - Binary Probit (Quadratic hill climbing)
Date: 08/15/20 Time: 20:40
Sample (adjusted): 1949Q1 2018Q1
Included observations: 277 after adjustments
Convergence achieved after 5 iterations
Covariance matrix computed using second derivatives

| Variable | Coefficient | Std. Error | z-Statistic | Prob. |
|---|---|---|---|---|
| C | -0.991192 | 0.099243 | -9.987523 | 0.0000 |
| OUTPUT_GAP | 24.77101 | 4.538365 | 5.458135 | 0.0000 |

| | | | |
|---|---|---|---|
| McFadden R-squared | 0.139070 | Mean dependent var | 0.166065 |
| S.D. dependent var | 0.372813 | S.E. of regression | 0.353865 |
| Akaike info criterion | 0.788574 | Sum squared resid | 34.43561 |
| Schwarz criterion | 0.814740 | Log likelihood | -107.2175 |
| Hannan-Quinn criter. | 0.799073 | Deviance | 214.4350 |
| Restr. deviance | 249.0737 | Restr. log likelihood | -124.5369 |
| LR statistic | 34.63868 | Avg. log likelihood | -0.387067 |
| Prob(LR statistic) | 0.000000 | | |

| | | | |
|---|---|---|---|
| Obs with Dep=0 | 231 | Total obs | 277 |
| Obs with Dep=1 | 46 | | |

**Figure 95.** Output gap, probit regression with 6 leads

Source: Authors' computations, CBO and BEA.

## 2.5. Preliminary conclusions

We are always trapped in the equilibrium framework during the expansion phase. Although the economy is growing at the moment, imbalances are accumulating and the economy is in disequilibrium. As we demonstrated in this chapter, real GDP growth and financial variables do not follow a normal distribution, so equilibrium is a mirage. The use of money for both goods and speculation contributes to the mismatch between demand and supply. Instead of accepting Say's law, we should embrace its inverse: Demand generates its own supply.

Recessions are typically caused by a sharp drop in aggregate demand. These decreases are the result of financial institutions experiencing income losses as a result of increased risk aversion, which has resulted in a reduction in credit availability and an increase in credit standards. The inverted yield spread indicates growing risk aversion and a decline in financial enterprise profitability.

The inverted yield spread proved to be a very good recession indicator 12 months in advance, in contrast to real variables, which are only good at forecasting recessions 2 months in advance and, in some cases, can only be used for recession nowcasting. Furthermore, the yield spread is far more effective in predicting recessions than economic downturns, whereas industrial indicators are the opposite. As a result, economic and financial cycles are indistinguishable. With the exception of pandemics, wars and supply shocks, they are all financial recessions.

There were some instances where the yield spread failed to predict recessions, particularly when long-term interest rates were controlled and when World War II ended with a dramatic reduction in government spending. The yield spread has remained a very good recession predictor for countries such as Japan and South Africa, whereas the yield spread's predictive capacity in Australia has diminished due to its growing population, strong commercial relationship with China, and fiscal policy.

Other recession-relevant financial variables, according to our research, are margin debit, excess bond premium, and the commercial paper rate minus bill rate spread, whereas indicators like change in M2 minus the interbank rate and change in loans minus prime loan rate are more associated with increases in the rate of delinquency rather than recessions.

# 3 Coordinates and Determinants of Financial Instability

**Abstract:** The financial instability can be linked to significant asset price changes and over-indebtedness, both of which can lead to an economic crisis. Obviously, we will focus on the most important and common determinants. Although nonfinancial black swans such as epidemics and great wars, as well as green swans, have a greater impact at times, they are very difficult to predict and the cumulative effects on financial instability are less than the conventional causes due to their low frequency. In this chapter, we look at the main causes of financial instability, such as capital mobility and capital size, declining profitability for financial institutions, economic inequality, and low and constant inflation. Higher capital mobility has always been associated with banking crises, while due to the inverted yield curve, declining profitability for financial institutions is typically followed by a recession. Economic inequality has more channels that lead to financial fragility like higher propensity for loans due to low incomes. The Global Savings Glut could have been a result of increasing inequality as the corporate sector became net holders of financial assets before the Great Recession. The last channel is the riskiness channel – the wealthy hold riskier assets. Last, low and constant inflation just guarantees price stability, not financial stability, as with a low and stable inflation targeting we can't avoid deflation.

**Keywords:** financial instability, capital mobility, capital size, inflation

## 3.1. Evidence from the literature

Financial instability is characterized by significant changes in asset prices and, in some cases, crises. These periods are distinguished by high volatility in asset prices, with an increase in asset prices (boom) typically followed by a significant decline in the prices of financial and real assets, resulting in liquidity/solvency issues in financial systems (Eschenback & Schuknecht, 2002).

Capital-to-Asset ratio, Regulatory Capital-to-Risk-Weighted Assets ratio, Regulatory Tier 1 Capital-to-Risk-Weighted Assets ratio, Return on Equity, share of nonperforming loans (NPL) in total loans, and Household Debt-to-GDP ratio are the coordinates of financial instability identified in the literature. These are among the financial soundness indicators for which the IMF collects data. Financial soundness indicators (NPL, Capital-to-Asset ratio, and Return on Equity) can foretell a banking crisis (Navajas & Thegeya, 2013). The financial sector has a strong influence on economic activity because nonfinancial sectors rely on the money created by banks and the intermediation provided by nonbanking financial institutions to carry out their operations. Furthermore, the wealth invested by nonfinancial sectors in the financial sector is at risk in the event of a financial crisis (IMF, 2003). However, almost all crises, in our opinion, are financial in nature because they are preceded (and caused) by the inversion of the yield spread and the resulting tightening of credit standards.

According to Minsky's Financial Instability Hypothesis, an economy's proclivity to crisis is derived from its financial structures, specifically depending on which among the following units dominates: hedge unit, covers both interest and principal; speculative unit, pays the interest but not the principal and must roll over on a regular basis; and the Ponzi unit can cover neither the interest nor the principal. When financial structures are weak, a large exogenous shock is not required to destabilize economic activity. Small endogenous variations can have the same effect as exogenous variations. Minsky, on the other hand, did not investigate these endogenous variations beyond the initial stage of euphoria and that an expected decline in expected income and an increase in cost financing would change the mix of financial structures. Kindelberger delved deeper into these disequilibrating forces. Kindleberger and Aliber (2005) demonstrated how deviations from rationality, herding behavior (p. 41), and hysteria can result in bubbles and manias (p. 42). Credit expansion and speculation can be viewed as the initial causes, whereas the detonators that undermine system confidence and lead to distressed sales are reversal of expectations, bankruptcy, or tightening of credit standards (p. 104).

For this phase, we disagree with Kindleberger's theory because, while selling real estate, stocks, and other assets can jolt the economy, a crisis is unlikely to occur unless credit standards are strengthened as a result of the negative yield spread. As long as credit flows to the speculative and Ponzi units, the financial structure's quality can continue to deteriorate without causing a recession. Even if a hypothetical economic system with a strong financial structure is unaffected by tightening credit standards, aggregate demand will fall and a moderate recession will emerge. As a result, all crises occur as a result of tighter credit standards caused by profitability losses caused by yield spread inversion.

## 3.2. Main determinants of financial instability

The most important factors should cause the greatest variations in credit supply and demand. Obviously, capital mobility will always account for the greatest fluctuations in credit supply. Many bubbles and subsequent banking and currency crises were caused by high capital mobility. Another supply factor is bank profitability, which is especially important when preceded by negative yield spreads.

High economic inequality is a significant demand-side variable. The increased proclivity of borrowers to avail loans in order to maintain or achieve their desired lifestyle is one of the channels through which financial stability is affected. Three theories dominate consumption research in mainstream economics: absolute income, permanent income, and the lifecycle hypothesis.

According to the absolute income hypothesis, as income grows, so does consumption. What Keynes failed to recognize is that the economy does not behave like a person. When a person's income rises, their consumption rises as well, but not as much as their income. As a person's income rises, so does their proclivity to consume. Keynes did not scale it properly because he believed that as national income increased, the consumption/national income ratio would decrease, resulting in stagnation.

We encounter the same problem with the permanent-income and lifecycle hypotheses, both of which ignore income distribution. The permanent-income and lifecycle hypotheses account for the effects of age on consumption because, in general, as we get older (and continue to work), we become more productive and earn more money. While these two theories outperform the absolute-income hypothesis, income inequality is a more important factor than age, so the relative-income hypothesis is a better choice. Despite rising inequality, the consumption/national income ratio will remain stable as long as credit availability remains stable and credit standards remain tight.

The other two channels are the riskiness channel, which occurs when the wealthy invest in riskier assets, and the corporate savings glut.

Finally, a low and stable inflation rate is a critical factor. Low and stable inflation can give economic agents a false sense of security, causing them to take on too many risks. This process will result in debt deflation because the debt accumulated during euphoric times will become unsustainable and the debt service ratio will become too large to pay. As the economy deflates, the debt will become even more difficult to repay. Low and stable inflation will not prevent deflation because expectations based on past values are important (the inflation rate is autocorrelated).

### 3.2.1. Capital mobility and the size of capital

Countries that experience large capital inflows are more likely to experience debt crises. Reinhart and Roggoff (2009) demonstrated the strong correlation between capital mobility and banking crises by updating Obstfeld and Taylor's

(2003) capital mobility index (see Figure 96). On the right-hand scale, a three-year moving average of the weight of all nations that have experienced banking crises is plotted. On the left-hand scale, we used Obstfeld and Taylor's (2003) capital mobility index. International banking crises have resulted from high global capital mobility. The Obstfeld–Taylor index is not perfect, but it is based on actual flows and sheds light on the significance of capital mobility as a factor in banking crises. Although domestic banking crises are not ruled out, currency crises have been added to the banking crises caused by large swings in capital inflows and outflows. Currency crises not only drive away investors but also increase the amount of debt denominated in foreign currency. Even in the case of 100% domestic capital, not only capital mobility, but also capital size, is an important factor in financial instability. Rising leverage implies a lower capital level in relation to total assets. Although debt/GDP ratio can rise, bank capital/bank assets ratio remain stable. Despite the fact that increasing leverage can result in a banking crisis, raising capital serves as a buffer.

According to Berger and Bouwman (2013), capital increases the survival probability of smaller banks not only during normal times but also during banking and market crises. Higher capital improves market share during normal times, helps profitability during market downturns, and improves survival during banking downturns for medium and large banks.

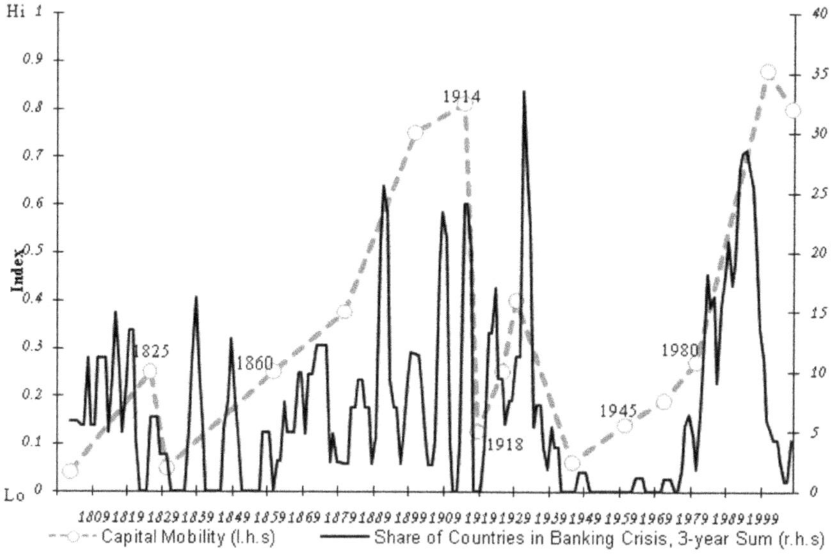


**Figure 96.** Capital mobility index and occurrence of banking crises: All nations, 1800–2008

Source: Reinhart and Rogoff (2009).

### 3.2.2. Decreasing profitability for financial institutions

We might expect credit availability to decrease and credit standards to tighten after a significant decrease in profitability for financial institutions or banks in this case study. However, this is not the case; only profitability decreases caused by yield curve inversions result in credit supply shortages and credit standard increases. Figure 97 shows that only when drops in net interest margins for all U.S. banks (quarterly, not seasonally adjusted) are associated with negative yield spreads do we see a higher net percentage of domestic banks tightening their standards. Because maturity conversion is the primary activity of banks, yield curve inversion has a significant impact on their profits. The explanation for declining profitability (not associated with negative yield spreads) that is not accompanied by tightening credit standards is that banks voluntarily reduce net interest margin to either stimulate bank credit demand or increase savings.

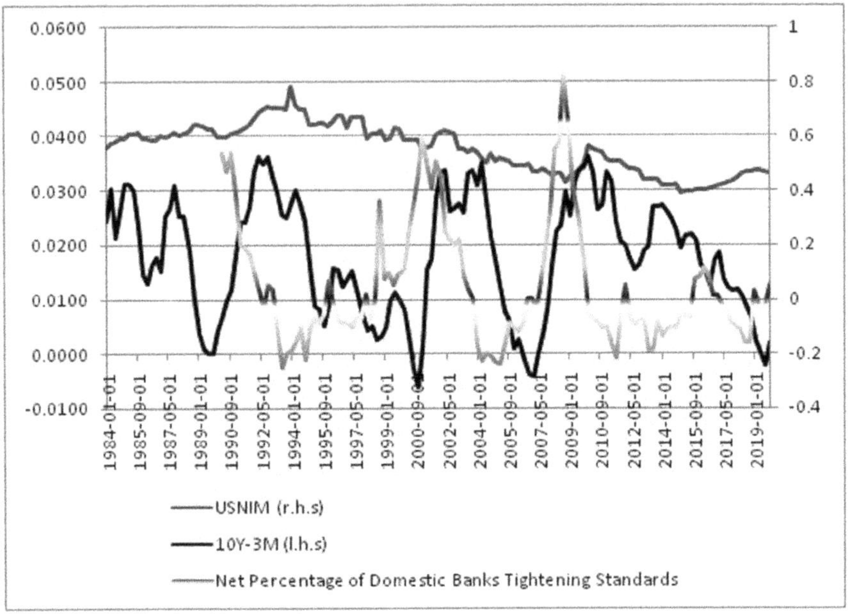


**Figure 97.** Yield spread, net interest margin, and credit standards
Source: Authors' computations; data from H15 Table, FRB, and St. Louis Fed.

Smaller banks are the most affected by the flattening of the yield spread in terms of distribution (Kapinos & Musatov, 2018). Although smaller banks always have a higher net interest rate margin, during the time the yield curve stays flat and even 12 quarters after of period of flat yield curve, the net interest rate margin will fall more for banks with average earning assets less than US$1 billion and between US$1 billion and US$15 billion than for banks with assets greater than US$15 billion and for all banks in general. The reason for this occurrence is that large banks have more diverse portfolios which are less impacted by this process. This does not, however, imply that smaller banks will lend less than larger banks. Due to the bank consolidation process, an analysis of the response of the change in loans due to yield curve flattening or inversion is no longer applicable. Basically, it depends on the strategy adopted by small- and medium-sized banks – how tight are the credit standards and credit availability – but it also depends on credit demand, because even though the net interest margin of small banks will decrease more, it will still be higher than the net interest margin of large banks and economic agents' income will stagnate or decrease during the recession (which follows yield curve inversions). Another important factor is the big banks' strategy, which determines whether he big banks will focus more on the portfolio's other assets.

### 3.2.3. Economic inequality

Following that, we examined how economic inequality affects financial stability.

## Research methodology and data

Is Piketty correct? Is r-g increasing over time (*r* being the asset return and *g* the income growth)? A stationarity test can be used to determine whether a household's net worth/disposable income is relatively stable. Figures 98 and 99 show that the net worth/income ratio is nonstationary from 1952Q1 to 2019Q3.

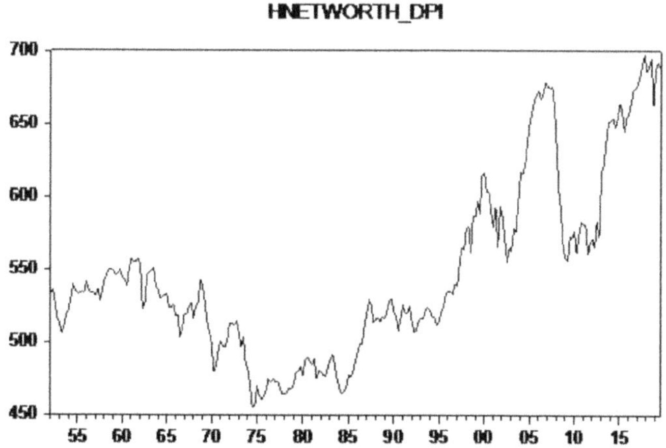


**Figure 98.** Household net worth/disposable income

Source: Authors' computations; data from Federal Reserve Board.

Null Hypothesis: HNETWORTH_DPI has a unit root
Exogenous: Constant
Lag Length: 0 (Automatic - based on SIC, maxlag=15)

| | | t-Statistic | Prob.* |
|---|---|---|---|
| Augmented Dickey-Fuller test statistic | | -0.278116 | 0.9248 |
| Test critical values: | 1% level | -3.454443 | |
| | 5% level | -2.872041 | |
| | 10% level | -2.572439 | |

*MacKinnon (1996) one-sided p-values.

**Figure 99.** ADF test of household net worth/disposable income ratio
Source: Authors' computations; data from Federal Reserve Board.

## Results and discussion

The results show an explosive process, which means that the mean and variance of wealth/income ration are not constant over time, resulting in constant changes in the wealth/income ratio. This implies that the concentration of wealth at the top is not stationary but rather explosive.

We would expect a decrease in aggregate demand and the consumption/disposable income ratio as economic inequality increased during the Great Moderation. Instead, low-income households maintained their standard of living by becoming indebted. Furthermore, rising inequality resulted in bubbles and a greater wealth effect, resulting in a greater proclivity for consumption (see Figure 100).

**Figure 100.** Consumption/disposable income ratio and income inequality
Source: Authors' computations; data from BEA and Tax Policy Center (TPC).

To emphasize the link between consumption proclivity and income inequality, we proposed a new inequality indicator. Gini (coefficient with values ranging from 0 to 1) is defined as the mean expected deviation between any two random variables divided by the mean (Taleb, 2015). As a result, the Gini Index does not place a premium on extremes. At the other end of the spectrum, quintiles, deciles, and percentiles only show a portion of the picture (only the extremes), whereas the Palma ratio (the share of the richest 10% divided by the bottom 40%) excludes the middle class.

Our index is the standard deviation of household income quintiles (quintiles are calculated as percentage of household mean income divided by total of mean quintile incomes). As a result, it emphasizes extreme quintiles while also taking into account the middle class. The lack of measurement for intra-quintile inequality is a weakness of this new index. Possible improvements include replacing quintiles with percentiles and calculating the variation coefficient for all income levels. This new index, on the other hand, still contains useful information.

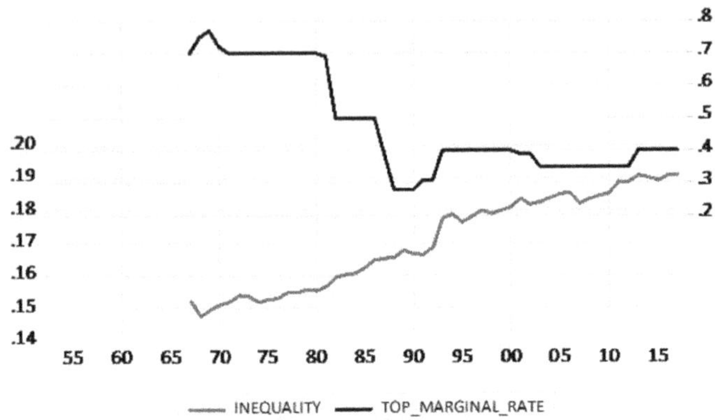


**Figure 101.** Top marginal rate and income inequality

Source: Authors' computations; data from Tax Policy Center Urban Institute and TPC.

Figures 101, 102, and 103 show that while fiscal policy played a role in rising inequalities (Tănăsescu & Oprean, 2016), the market (globalization, demographics, migration, etc.) played a larger role.

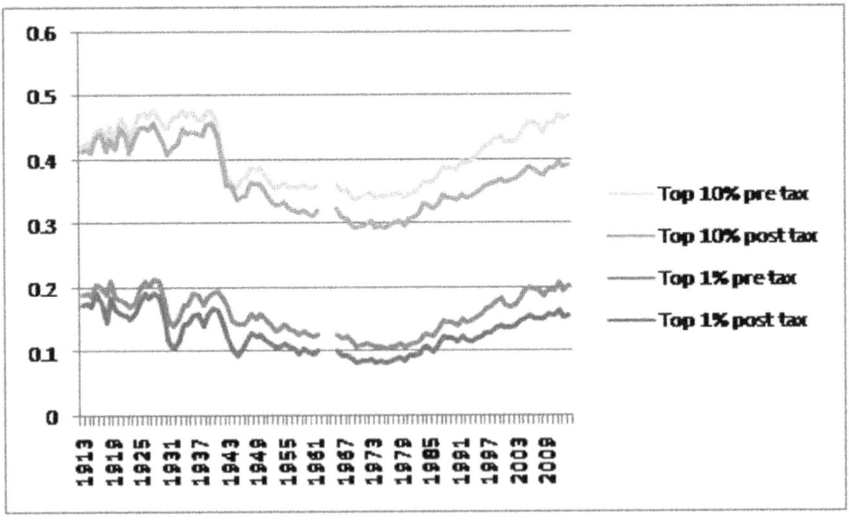


**Figure 102.** Top income percentile and decile, pre-tax and post-tax

Source: World Inequality Database.

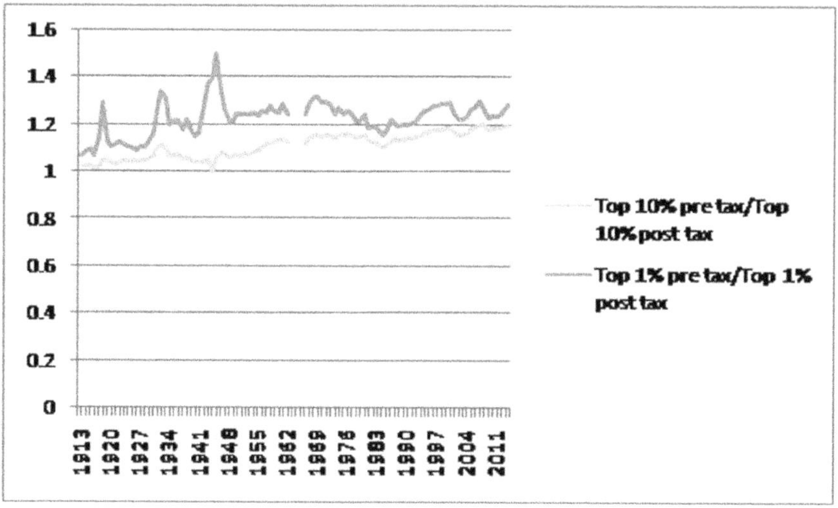


**Figure 103.** Top income percentile and decile, pre-tax and post-tax
Source: Authors' computations; data from World Inequality Database.

Capitalism, by definition, is based on inequality. Large-scale production is only possible with massive wealth accumulation, and the prospect of becoming wealthy motivates us to become more productive. However, extreme inequality can have a number of negative consequences, including bubbles, poor education and health for low-income families, and a lack of human capital development. As the Laffer curve indicates, the relationship between inequality and economic growth is most likely parabolic (tax rate with tax revenue). In capitalist systems, income quality would make large-scale production impossible and productivity gains would be rare because there would be no incentive to work harder. At the other end of the spectrum, extreme inequality would result in lower economic growth due to financial fragility, lower social mobility (the Great Gatsby Curve shows a positive correlation between income inequality and lack of social mobility), and, thus, lower productivity gains due to a lack of worker incentives. Correlations and regressions are not appropriate methods for highlighting the lack of shared prosperity for the top income shares. As a result, we have created indexes that will decompose the income of the top shares into contributions of inequality and economic growth.

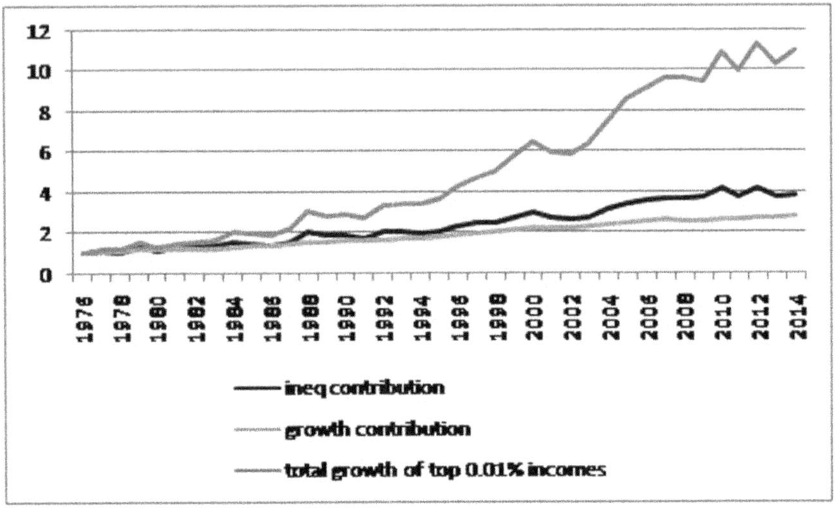


**Figure 104.** Inequality and growth contributions to top 0.01% Incomes

Source: Authors' computations; data from BEA and World Inequality Database (pre-tax national income share adult sequal split USA).

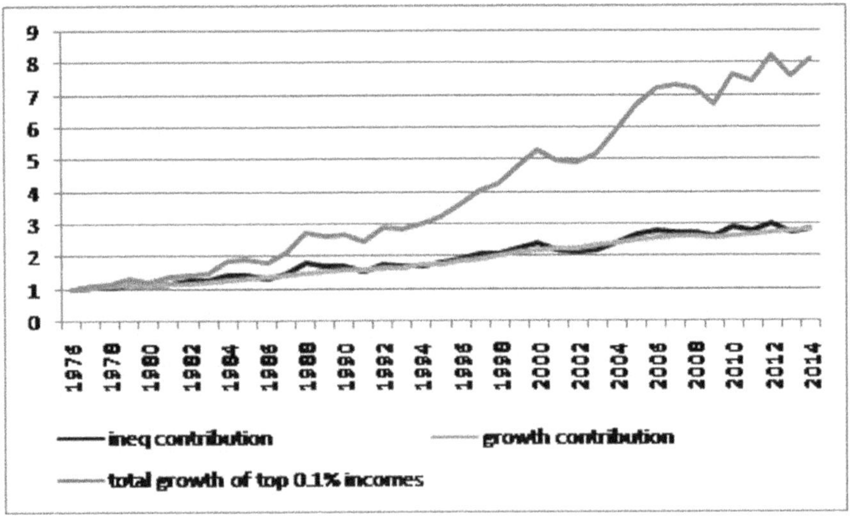


**Figure 105.** Inequality and growth contributions to top 0.1% Incomes

Source: Authors' computations; data from BEA and World Inequality Database (pre-tax national income share adult sequal split USA).

$$Income\ of\ Top\ Income\ Shares_{t+1} = Income\ of\ Top\ Income\ Shares_t * (1+g_{inequality}) * (1 + g_{GDP}) \quad (36)$$

Current income equals past income multiplied by changes in economic growth and inequality (change in the top income shares).

$$Inequality\ contribution = (1 + g_{inequality})^q,\ where\ q = 1,2..,38 \quad (37)$$

$$Economic\ growth\ contribution = (1 + g_{gdp})^q \quad (38)$$

As shown in Figures 104 and 105, the 0.1% top incomes are derived almost equally from real GDP growth and income inequality increases, whereas the 0.01% top incomes are derived primarily from income inequality, implying that the prosperity created by the richest 0.01% is not shared.

Economic inequality affects financial stability via four channels: riskiness, greater proclivity to borrow, savings glut, and current account deficits (Dragoe, 2016). According to the riskiness channel, wealthy households have a higher proportion of their holdings invested in riskier assets, a theory confirmed by Carroll (2000). The problem arises when the risky assets are stocks rather than entrepreneurial investments, which results in stock market bubbles and Minsky moments.

The second channel, proclivity to borrow, also contributes to financial insecurity. As shown in Figure 106, the leverage ratio is higher not only in the bottom percentiles but also in the bottom decile and decreases in the top decile as economic inequality increases.

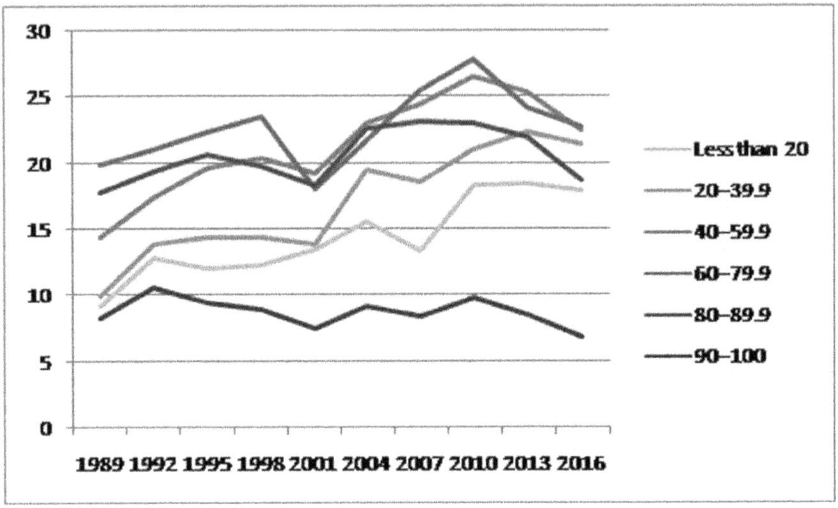


**Figure 106.** Leverage ratio for income deciles
Source: Survey of Consumer Finances 2016.

The lowest-income households used leverage to offset the rise in income inequality. According to Kumhof et al. (2013), an increase in household debt is associated with an increase in the share of income for the high-income groups. Capitalists reduced the wage cost/revenue ratio due to greed, expected lower profitability, immigration, globalization, and so on. Low-income households reacted by becoming overindebted. The poor's debt became the income of entrepreneurs and investors, and the poor's debt repayment became the income of financiers. As shown in Figure 107, the top 1%'s share of income is positively correlated with the evolution of household debt during the Great Moderation.

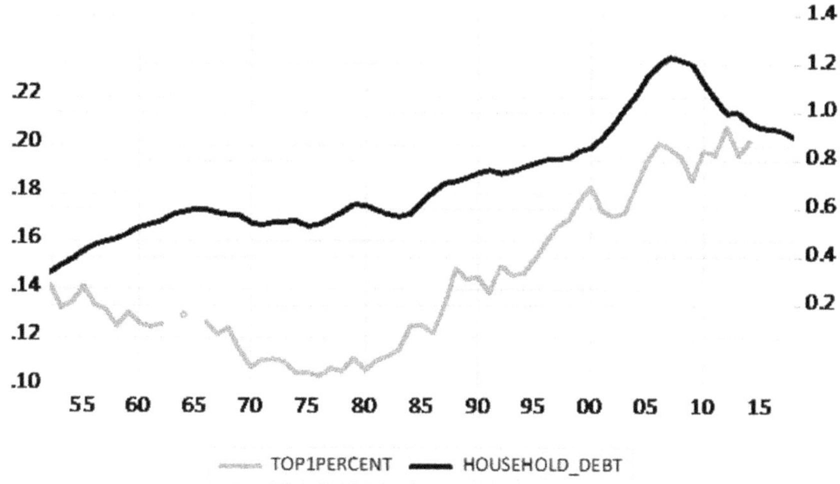


**Figure 107.** Leverage ratio for households (household debt/disposable personal income)

Source: Authors' computations; World Inequality Database and St. Louis Fed.

With the onset of the Great Recession, this vicious circle came to an end. Growing income inequality contributed to unsustainable household debt and, implicitly, the Great Recession, as well as the subsequent slow recovery by acting as a drag on aggregate demand growth (Cynamon & Fazzari, 2014). Essentially, the poor spent more than they earned. All of the mainstream consumption theories were disproved. According to the absolute-income theory (see Equation (39) and Figure 108), the permanent-income hypothesis and the lifecycle model, income is the most important factor in consumption. According to the permanent-income theory, changes in permanent income influence consumption behavior, so the current level of consumption is determined by both income and past consumption (see Equation (40) and Figure 109). According to the lifecycle hypothesis, consumption is planned based on life stages. As a result, consumption is influenced by both income and wealth (see Equation (41) and Figure 110). After applying logarithms to the time series, we used the first difference.

$$\Delta C = \alpha + \beta * \Delta Y \quad (39)$$

$$\Delta C = \gamma + \theta_1 * \Delta Y + \theta_2 * \Delta C(-1) \quad (40)$$

$$\Delta C = \nu + \rho_1 * \Delta Y + \rho_1 * \Delta W \quad (41)$$

Although income appears to be the main determinant of consumption at the macro level in each case (see Figures 108, 109, 110), debt was essential for

Dependent Variable: DL_REAL_CONSUMPTION
Method: Least Squares
Date: 04/02/20 Time: 20:37
Sample (adjusted): 1953 2018
Included observations: 66 after adjustments

| Variable | Coefficient | Std. Error | t-Statistic | Prob. |
|---|---|---|---|---|
| C | 0.010150 | 0.001467 | 6.918245 | 0.0000 |
| DL_REAL_INCOME | 0.727429 | 0.040120 | 18.13112 | 0.0000 |

| | | | |
|---|---|---|---|
| R-squared | 0.837041 | Mean dependent var | 0.031968 |
| Adjusted R-squared | 0.834495 | S.D. dependent var | 0.016764 |
| S.E. of regression | 0.006820 | Akaike info criterion | -7.108115 |
| Sum squared resid | 0.002977 | Schwarz criterion | -7.041762 |
| Log likelihood | 236.5678 | Hannan-Quinn criter. | -7.081895 |
| F-statistic | 328.7373 | Durbin-Watson stat | 1.830055 |
| Prob(F-statistic) | 0.000000 | | |

**Figure 108.** Absolute-income hypothesis applied

Source: Authors' computations.

Dependent Variable: DL_REAL_CONSUMPTION
Method: Least Squares
Date: 04/02/20 Time: 20:38
Sample (adjusted): 1954 2018
Included observations: 65 after adjustments

| Variable | Coefficient | Std. Error | t-Statistic | Prob. |
|---|---|---|---|---|
| C | 0.008505 | 0.001988 | 4.278219 | 0.0001 |
| DL_REAL_INCOME | 0.710849 | 0.042027 | 16.91394 | 0.0000 |
| DL_REAL_CONSUMPTION(-1) | 0.064923 | 0.052673 | 1.232575 | 0.2224 |

| | | | |
|---|---|---|---|
| R-squared | 0.839623 | Mean dependent var | 0.031732 |
| Adjusted R-squared | 0.834449 | S.D. dependent var | 0.016784 |
| S.E. of regression | 0.006829 | Akaike info criterion | -7.090192 |
| Sum squared resid | 0.002891 | Schwarz criterion | -6.989836 |
| Log likelihood | 233.4313 | Hannan-Quinn criter. | -7.050595 |
| F-statistic | 162.2945 | Durbin-Watson stat | 1.920053 |
| Prob(F-statistic) | 0.000000 | | |

**Figure 109.** Permanent-income hypothesis applied

Source: Authors' computations.

Dependent Variable: DL_REAL_CONSUMPTION
Method: Least Squares
Date: 04/02/20 Time: 11:22
Sample (adjusted): 1953 2018
Included observations: 66 after adjustments

| Variable | Coefficient | Std. Error | t-Statistic | Prob. |
|---|---|---|---|---|
| C | 0.009720 | 0.001497 | 6.491557 | 0.0000 |
| DL_REAL_INCOME | 0.698271 | 0.045858 | 15.22689 | 0.0000 |
| DL_REAL_NET_WORTH | 0.036626 | 0.028365 | 1.291251 | 0.2013 |

| | | | |
|---|---|---|---|
| R-squared | 0.841243 | Mean dependent var | 0.031968 |
| Adjusted R-squared | 0.836203 | S.D. dependent var | 0.016764 |
| S.E. of regression | 0.006785 | Akaike info criterion | -7.103933 |
| Sum squared resid | 0.002900 | Schwarz criterion | -7.004403 |
| Log likelihood | 237.4298 | Hannan-Quinn criter. | -7.064604 |
| F-statistic | 166.9162 | Durbin-Watson stat | 1.795587 |
| Prob(F-statistic) | 0.000000 | | |

**Figure 110.** Lifecycle hypothesis applied
Source: Authors' computations.

low-income families. Consumption is always dependent on income in aggregate because the debt used for consumption becomes the income of the rich.

According to Duesenberry's (1949) relative-income hypothesis, the percentage of one's income spent depends on one's income percentile position. Individuals with low incomes are more likely to save less. However, if the income distribution improves, the meetings with individuals with higher consumption (in nominal terms) will decrease, resulting in a lower propensity to consume (Duesenberry, 1949, pp. 44–45).

As capitalists save a higher proportion of their incomes and the corporate sector can maintain higher liquidity rates, the decreases in savings glut and long-term wage share contribute to higher ex ante savings than desired investment. Prior to the GFC, nonfinancial corporations were amassing large sums of cash and had become net savers (IMF, 2006), putting downward pressure on real interest rates and buying back their own stock, resulting in asset price bubbles (Dragoe, 2016).

The final channel, namely, current account deficit, has been present not only in the United States (due to the dollar being the main reserve currency and due to savings glut) but also globally as income inequalities have grown. Increasing income and wealth inequality around the world, combined with high corporate savings, resulted in a savings glut in the United States and, as a result, a massive current account deficit prior to the Great Recession (see Figure 111 in Appendix 37). The United States was not the only country with a growing current account deficit. Between 1988 and 2006, the standard deviation of OECD countries' current account deficits/GDP ratio increased (Blanchard, 2007). Credit demand exploded as a result of high income inequality, and many states resorted to financial liberalization to smoothen the consumption of low-income families (Kumhof et al., 2012).

What role can monetary policy play in improving income distribution? The most important policy goal is to reduce unemployment without creating bubbles. Because unemployment will be low, the labor market supply will be low as well, driving up wages and, thus, the wage share.

It is simply incorrect to assert that the level of distribution has no bearing on economy. The cash flows that validate household and business debts are determined by the growth and distribution of nominal income (Minsky, 1980).

### 3.2.4. Low and stable inflation

Financial stability is jeopardized by the low and consistent inflation targeting policy (Stevanović & Milenković, 2020). The autocorrelation test for GDP deflator using the data sample 1959Q2–2019Q1 (Appendix 11) revealed that the GDP deflator rate is dependent on previous values, implying that expectations based on previous values matter for future inflation rates. We tested the autocorrelation of the PCE inflation rate because the Federal Open Market Committee targets inflation using the price index for personal consumption expenditures. The autocorrelation for PCE inflation rate is also valid for the data sample 1947Q2–2019Q4, seasonally adjusted data (data expressed in logs and the first difference is applied; see Appendix 32), though the values are lower than for GDP deflator.

According to Keen (2011), if inflation rate is high when a crisis occurs, increasing cash flows allow for repayment of debt contracted during economic expansion. As a result, economy will experience low growth and high inflation but will avoid falling into a liquidity trap.

Although the Fed's monetary policy objectives, as mandated by Congress through the Federal Reserve Act, are to achieve maximum employment and stable prices (2% change in the PCE index), the main aim of Fed is to establish to ensure financial stability. Financial stability does not imply a low and stable inflation rate. In our opinion, Federal Reserve should prioritize financial stability over inflation targeting and transform monetary policy into a financial stability tool alongside macroprudential policy.

## 3.3. Preliminary conclusions

In this chapter, we looked at some of the main causes of financial insecurity, such as capital mobility and capital size, declining profitability for financial institutions, economic inequality, and low and stable inflation. Banking crises are frequently preceded by high capital mobility and high leverage, which equates to small capital size. A recession usually follows a decline in financial institution profitability due to an inverted yield spread. Economic inequality contributes to financial fragility through a variety of channels, including a higher proclivity for loans as a result of low income. Higher corporate savings are also a result of high inequality and contribute to global savings glut. The last channel is riskiness; because the wealthy own riskier assets, an increase in inequality will result in bubbles and a decrease in safe assets. In addition, low and consistent inflation does not provide financial stability because it cannot prevent deflation and the economy's entry into the liquidity trap.

# 4 Potential Solutions for Financial Stability

**Abstract:** In this chapter, we will look at possible solutions for ensuring financial stability. We discuss the benefits and drawbacks of the Chicago Plan, as well as the advantages and disadvantages of a cashless society. Cashless society is an important project with many benefits, but if it is adopted just to allow negative interest rates, it will be destructive for the economy because money creation will be slowed, causing, in turn, stock market bubbles. We also investigate whether capital requirements management can be used to control credit supply. We compare various monetary strategies such as inflation targeting with price-level targeting, inflation channel without a target, and nominal GDP targeting. We also discuss the limitations of yield curve management and look into ways to improve the helicopter money-drop solution. Finally, our analysis revealed that helicopter money would be more successful as people's Quantitative Easing (QE) than quantitative easing, which ultimately reflects a transfer of capital to banks. We believe that central banks should place greater emphasis on financial stability to avoid large economic contractions.

**Keywords:** financial stability, Chicago Plan, cashless society, inflation targeting, yield curve management

## 4.1. Advantages of Chicago Plan

Following the Great Depression, many leading U.S. economists (primarily from the University of Chicago) advocated for a monetary revolution, which became known as the Chicago Plan. Fisher (1936) expounded the Chicago Plan, being a firm believer in the project. It entails separating credit and money. Money is created not by saving but by extending bank credit and purchasing government bonds by banks. Under the Chicago Plan regime, money is only created through government debt and banks are only financial intermediaries and not money creators. Banks would have 100% reserves and would only lend after acquiring Treasury credit or new equity. Despite initial interest, the Roosevelt administration chose to separate commercial banks from investment banks, establish the FDIC, and eliminate double liability.

Kumhof and Benes (2012) reintroduced the Chicago Plan and agreed with the benefits identified by Fisher (1936). Fisher (1936) outlined four benefits of this proposal: no runs, better control of credit growth, government issuing money at 0% interest, and lowering public and private debt.

The first argument is self-evident; even when banks are subject to a full-reserve regime, they may still incur credit losses that could threaten their existence and may not be able to fund their way out of insolvency, as Credit Suisse did in October 2008.

The second advantage has a drawback. Credit expansion would be solely dependent on customer deposits and equity. In order to have 100% reserve backing, banks would obtain treasury credit for deposits at a 1:1 ratio. Within this financial system, private savings would exceed government currency investment, resulting in a deflationary economy (Kregel, 2012). To avoid deflation and stagnation, government would need to intervene with large deficits. This brings us to the third argument: Government should print money with no interest. This is feasible not only within the framework of the Chicago Plan. Fears of inflation prompted the implementation of the act prohibiting direct government financing, such as Articles 123 and 125 of the Lisbon Treaty (for European Union). Until 1935, the Federal Reserve occasionally purchased short-term Treasury securities directly from the U.S. Treasury. Direct financing was prohibited by Congress in 1935, but exemptions were granted. The previous one expired in 1981 (Garbade, 2014). Direct government financing at 0% interest rates is possible; all that is required is an agreement between governments and central banks.

Fisher (1936) suggests that the final advantage is reduced public and private debt. Treasury credit, according to the framework developed by Kumhof and Benes (2012), will cancel public debt as well as a portion of private debt. Furthermore, public debt will be issued at no interest rate, so even with large deficits, public debt/GDP ratio will not rise as much as it does now. The dynamics of private debt are more complicated. The treasury credit will not pay 0% interest because it must protect against credit losses. This, combined with the fact that banks will not create their own funds and that government issuance of money will not generate the necessary savings for banks to extend credit at the desired rate, will result in higher funding and lending rates. Banks could also acquire nonmonetary liabilities in order to increase lending.

The amount of reintermediation would rise. Another possibility is that domestic banks in a country that has implemented the Chicago Plan will increase their borrowings from the rest of the world. This system would neither guarantee real-economy stability nor financial stability. Sectoral overinvestment and underinvestment, as well as financial bubbles, would continue to exist (Kregel, 2012).

These types of proposals were recommended in Iceland (Sigurjónsson, 2015) and Switzerland's Sovereign Money Initiative, and both were rejected and the latter by vote. According to Sigurjónsson (2015), domestic banks may be at a competitive disadvantage when compared to foreign banks due to a lack of money creation capability.

## 4.2. The benefits of a cashless society

A cashless society would have numerous advantages. One primary benefit would be reduced tax evasion because transactions would be easier to track. Another significant benefit would be the reduced impact of bank runs. Bank runs are still possible because customers will transfer funds between banks. This means, as a result of technological advances, a bank's bankruptcy will be more rapid; however, the good news is that money will still remain in the banking system and banks' ability to make loans will not be as severely harmed as it was during previous bank runs. Also, because people and businesses will not have cash, money will no longer leave the banking system through this channel and banks will be better equipped to make loans in general.

There are some drawbacks, such as the fact that this could be a small boost for fintech, which would mean that some money would leave the banking system. However, because fintech is intertwined with banks, it would only be a temporary exit of money, as opposed to crypto-assets, where the exit time can be very long. One example is Revolut, which is primarily used for exchanges and is thus closely linked to bank accounts. However, Revolut and other apps are also used for peer-to-peer lending. Although it is a transfer of purchasing power rather than an addition of purchasing power, it contributes to economic growth by increasing the propensity for consumption and allowing enterprises that are considered too risky by banks to be financed and create added value. This is one of the reasons, along with speculation, securitization, and regulatory avoidance, why the nonbank sector grew so rapidly prior to the Great Recession.

The greatest disadvantage would be if a cashless society were implemented solely to allow negative interest rates in order to stimulate demand. Long term, more and more funds would be directed to housing, stock market, gold, and crypto-assets in order to earn a yield, causing bubbles in the process. Also, during times of financial distress, banks may be discouraged from resuming lending if current accounts, savings deposits, and even term deposits pay negative interest rates.

Higher current account fees and available purchase data for the largest banks and corporations could also be significant disadvantages.

## 4.3. Capital requirements management

Are capital adequacy ratios the best instrument for taming both bank and nonbank credit bubbles? One channel that financial institutions can use in order for eluding the imposed capital adequacy ratios is the securitization channel.

Through securitization, assets (credit) will no longer be part of the balance sheet and the capital/assets ratio will improve without constraining credit. However, if capital requirements for special purpose vehicles increase, the process will be hampered and financial institutions will find it harder to circumvent regulations.

Banks, according to Werner (2016), can generate their own capital. This is likewise true for Credit Suisse. The bank did not want public assistance for its declining capital, and, in 2008, by lending to Gulf investors, it created the funds utilized by them to purchase newly issued shares. Of course, in nations such as the United Kingdom, such operations are banned (Section 678 of the Companies Act 2006 – the prohibition of assistance for acquisition of shares in public company). Even if regulations forbid these practices, banks can still evade them in some cases by employing complex methods. Although laws can strengthen this mechanism, the act of banks creating their own capital enhances their solvency during recessions. It is also more difficult for smaller banks to get new capital.

Despite obvious drawbacks, we feel that in some cases it can be a valuable tool and that it would have been effective in Romania prior to the Global Financial Crisis (GFC).

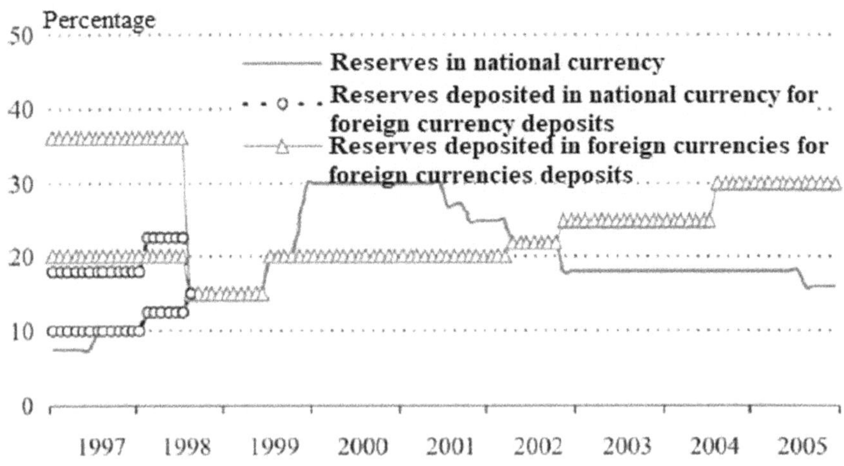


**Figure 112.** Evolution of reserve requirement ratio

Source: Isarescu (2006), p. 85.

Reserves for foreign currency deposits were permitted to be deposited in Lei (Romanian National Currency) at the National Bank of Romania from January

1997 to July 1998 (see Figure 112). This policy meant that lending in national currency was subject to additional liquidity limits, but lending in foreign currencies was not subject to additional liquidity constraints.

As capital inflows increased rapidly prior to GFC, the banking system became inundated with subordinated debt. Subordinated debt is not subject to the minimum reserve requirement, and the minimum reserve requirement ratio was higher for national currency than for foreign currency between 1999 and 2002 (see Figure 113). The interest rate gap was also very large, and, with the introduction of the Euro, people and businesses were drawn to borrowing in foreign currency, while foreign financial institutions were ready to invest in Romania. Borrowers were hurt by the evolution of the Leu/Eur exchange rate. Lower monetary policy rates, along with a near-zero reserve requirement ratio for national currency and a higher Tier 1 capital ratio requirement, would have restrained credit expansion in foreign currency.

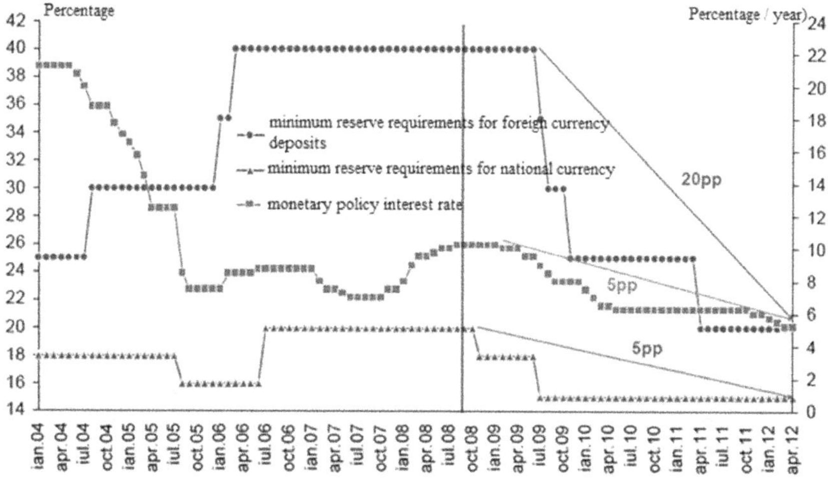


**Figure 113.** Reserve requirement ratio and monetary policy evolution

Source: Isarescu (2012), p. 85.

## 4.4. Inflation targeting versus price-level targeting, inflation channel, and nominal GDP

As low and stable inflation has failed to prevent a liquidity trap during the Great Recession, policymakers and the academy are searching for alternatives. The most popular proposals are price-level targeting, moderate inflation targeting, using an inflation channel without an explicit target, nominal GDP targeting, and nominal GDP–level targeting.

Price-level targeting is actually average inflation targeting. For example, if during one period inflation is 3%, the inflation in the next period needs to be 1% so that in average inflation will be 2% – the targeted inflation. This policy has many drawbacks but has two big disadvantages. The most frequent disadvantages would be the useless interventions under this regime. Even if inflation goes up due to increasing prices of raw materials or the rise of indirect taxes like VAT, according to this rule, the central banks should lower inflation in the next period. Likewise, if inflation is decreasing due to higher productivity, central bankers will have to increase the inflation during the next period. Under inflation targeting regime, central banks can ignore these nonmonetary temporary deviations from target.

The most important disadvantage is its volatile nature. If inflation overshoots constantly or suddenly hits a peak, deflation might be required to bring back prices to the established path, which in turn would induce financial instability. Another big drawback is the magnitude of the investment required in communication (Bernanke, 2017) and explaining the compensation of the past deviations from the target.

The benefits include improved methods for calculating the zero lower bound (ZLB) and counterbalancing monetary hawks. Targeting a price level is better suited to avoiding the ZLB because it creates expectations of "lower-for-longer" interest rates during the ZLB (Bernanke, 2017). Price-level targeting, on the other hand, cannot prevent ZLB. The other major advantage is that it prevents monetary hawks and doves from constantly deviating from targets. A monetary hawk is an FOMC member who is obsessed with keeping inflation low, whereas doves are concerned with keeping unemployment low. In the case of inflation targeting, monetary hawks may generate a positive gap between the suggested price-level path and the actual price level, whereas doves may develop a negative gap.

Due to the issues faced by price level in the case of supply shocks, Bernanke (2017) recommends a temporary price-level targeting which should be implemented only during ZLB. The Fed Chair Jerome Powell adopted the target of 2% inflation rate on average due to benefits listed above.

The most valuable insight about avoiding depressions is provided by Minsky's analysis. In Minsky's view (2016), a depression can be avoided with rising cash flows (which enable debt repayment) due to high inflation. According to Croitoru (2012, p. 36), cash flows depend on investments and inflation. The level of investment falls during recessions, so the only solution that can be adopted to prevent liquidity traps is to target a higher inflation rate. As prices and wages grow, the debt (both debt accumulated during boom and new debt) with fixed interest rate is easier to pay. Also, the variable interest rate debt (both old and new) will be easier to pay but will remain so only temporarily until the point at which the interest rates include rising inflation expectations and start to grow.

Laurence Ball (2013) contends that a 4% inflation rate is preferable to avoiding the ZLB. In addition, nominal interest rates would be higher in a moderate-inflation regime, giving central banks more power to combat recessions.

Entering a recession with moderate inflation would avoid debt deflation and liquidity trap, as inflation won't decline sharply due to inflation expectations.

The inflation channel without a specific target is a personal proposal. Its main advantage is letting the economy to function freely. The central bank's primary concern would be that inflation does not leave the inflation channel. In order to avoid liquidity trap, the lower bound should be 3% and the upper band should be 5.5%. It would be important for the upper band to be under 6% for avoiding build-up of inflationary expectations; in 1976, the inflation rate was 6.08% and rose during the following years. Although monetary policy was a big factor, inflation expectations played a very important role as well.

Constraining inflation won't bring long-term prosperity. Disinflation can enhance GDP growth when it is caused by technological improvements that scale production, not when aggregate demand is constrained by monetary policy in order to prevent wage increases and inflationary pressures. Moderate inflation does not have inflation costs (menu costs, shoe leather costs); however, it does pose a higher level of risk.

Cogley and Sargent (2002) and Stock and Watson (2007) concluded that a decline in inflation persistence took place from the early 1980s onwards. Hirose, Kurozumi, and Van Zandweghe (2018) found out that the source of decline in inflation persistence that started with Volcker's disinflation is not only the aggressive reaction of monetary policy to inflation but also the average or trend level of inflation. Therefore, a higher average inflation rate implies a higher level of inflation persistence and more time to return to the average or targeted inflation rate. However, it is a small price to pay in order to avoid liquidity trap. When compared to moderate inflation targeting, the inflation channel is inferior in one case: Intervention may be too late, causing inflation to rise.

Other policies could be nominal GDP targeting and nominal GDP–level targeting (NGLT). NGLT is impractical due to constant ex post revisions (Wessel, 2018). Nominal GDP targeting would have some advantages over inflation targeting and Taylor Rule. In the case of supply-side shocks, nominal GDP targeting would be superior to inflation targeting as the implied monetary policy won't be contractionary.

The nonstationary behavior of real interest rates (see Appendix 34) is not only the consequence of changing monetary regimes; it also implies that nominal interest rates have long-term effects on real economic growth and asset prices. However, the cross-correlations coefficients are higher between Federal funds and PCE core inflation than cross-correlation coefficients for Fed Funds and changes in nominal GDP from previous quarter (see Appendixes 35 and 36).

The advantages over Taylor Rule are the simplicity and avoiding the task of estimating values based on a theoretical concept that doesn't exist and which can be only derived from data.

Nominal GDP targeting without adjusting for Reinhart–Rogoff effect (slower economic growth after financial crises) is a bad idea (Bullard, 2012) and could lead to high inflation or asset price bubbles. Also, policymakers could over- or under-estimate the potential of economy even during booms.

The current monetary policy strategy of targeting a low and stable inflation and caring more for the inflation rate to not surpass the target (lower inflation than the target was acceptable while inflation over the target was actively constrained) has made the economies prone to debt deflation. Targeting a moderate inflation rate, reducing the short-term interest rate and increasing the monetary base before and during the yield inversion will ease the pain of debtors and protect the profits of financial institutions from further harm. The following recession would likely be soft. However, the goal is not to prevent cycles but, rather, to avoid large contractions, which can only be achieved with greater focus on financial stability.

## 4.5. Yield curve and interest rates management

During the monetary policy meeting that took place between September 20 and September 21, 2016, Bank of Japan decided to extend quantitative and qualitative monetary easing and to adopt yield curve control. The plan was to apply an interest rate of –0.1% to the open market operations and the long-term interest rate, more specifically 10-year Japan Government Bond, yields made to remain around 0% with changes in the targets when needed (see Figure 114).

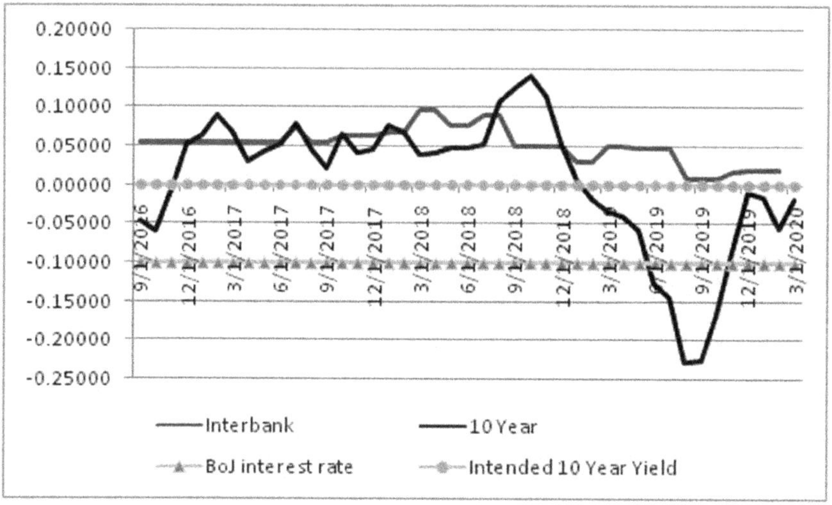


**Figure 114.** Japan Interest rates
Source: Bank of Japan (2016).

Obviously, this policy was introduced to reduce Japan's massive fiscal debt. But the difference between the intended 10-year yield and the Bank of Japan's interest rate is very narrow. This makes the system very prone to yield curve inversions.

Between early 1942 and 1951, the yield on long-term Treasury bonds in the United States was regulated at 2.5%, for 7- to 9-year yields at 2%, and for 1-year yield at 0.875%. In addition, until July 1947, the yield on short-term Treasury bills was regulated at 0.375%. This policy was successful for a variety of reasons. Along with interventions, the key factors were the high spread and low bill rates (Chaurushiya & Kuttner, 2003).

Because a 0.375% bill rate would have meant a lower yield on long-term government bonds, investors preferred the latter, forcing the Federal Reserve to intervene and buy the abandoned bill rates. In July 1947, the bill rate was raised due to inflationary pressures. Investors were once again drawn to Treasury bills and began to replace long-term government bonds with the former. To keep the cap, the Federal Reserve had to act and accumulate long-term government bonds. As the Korean War began, inflation began to rise once more.

Aside from the reasons stated above for keeping long-term interest rates regulated, we need to also explain why this benefited the entire economy and not just the public finances. Interest rates were not as close to 0% as they are now (May, 2020), and measures were implemented during World War II and the Korean War resulting in less speculation in the property and stock markets. Furthermore, credit was not decoupled from money, implying less reintermediation and overtrading.

This suggests that more money is still in the production–consumption system. Although reintermediation has marginally declined during the Great Recession, money velocity has been declining (see Figure 115), implying that more money is going into the speculative system.

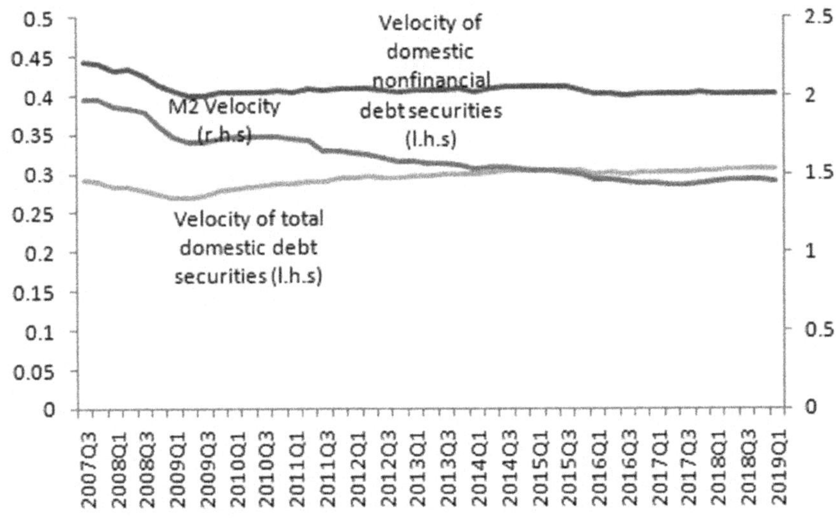


**Figure 115.** Money and debt securities velocities

Source: Authors' computations; data from Federal Reserve.

The low-spread target also increases the likelihood of yield spread inversions, increasing the probability of a recession. It is doubtful whether central banks will ever attempt to pursue positive yield curves in order to avoid recessions. Simply put, central banks cannot function as central planners. Long-term interest rates are determined by short-term interest rates and investor sentiment. Unexpected and powerful occurrences, such as the COVID-19 shutdown, will always invert the yield spread. Central bankers, on the other hand, can prevent the negative yield spread from reaching a very high absolute value and can regulate the duration of the yield spread inversion. But the question is, will it help or hurt the economy? We believe that it would be detrimental to the economy in the long run. Central banks would incentivize banks to increase resource misallocation, to invest more in proprietary trading, and more business owners would invest in banks and other financial institutions instead of manufacturing, resulting in long-term stagnation.

## 4.6. Considerations on "helicopter money drop" solution

The United States has been caught in a Krugman-style liquidity trap. Hicks (1937) and Krugman's liquidity trap is related to the impotency of the monetary policy to stimulate economy at very low interest rates, whereas Keynes' liquidity trap states that central banks lose their control over interest rate because of the substitution between bonds and cash at the zero interest rate.

The estimated negative Taylor Rule rate for 2009Q2–2010Q1 provides evidence for Krugman's liquidity trap. Following Japan's lost decade, several macroeconomists proposed that extending the monetary base would help Japan escape the liquidity trap. According to Krugman (1998), the central bank must steer clear of committing itself to help the economy escape the liquidity trap. Anticipated increased inflation rates will result in negative interest rates, which will encourage spending. Bernanke (2000) went as far as describing Japan's liquidity trap as a self-induced paralysis by the Bank of Japan, arguing that central banks have many tools even at ZLB.

In 2008, in order to avoid a depression, central banks applied three types of unconventional monetary policies:

- Qualitative easing, which implies that the quality of bank's assets will increase as the central bank purchases toxic assets without increasing its balance sheet;
- Quantitative easing – involves expanding the monetary base;
- Credit easing – the term coined by Bernanke (2009) – involves both the expansion of its balance sheet and altering the composition to improve credit conditions.

According to Loisel (2019), aggregate demand depends on the future trend of the general level of interest rates and also on the expected credit spread. Despite 0% short-term interest rate and despite using credit easing and multiplying the monetary base by almost 5 times, the economic performance of United States was not at a high level. As seen in Figure 116, increasing the monetary base had little influence on the money supply and nominal GDP.

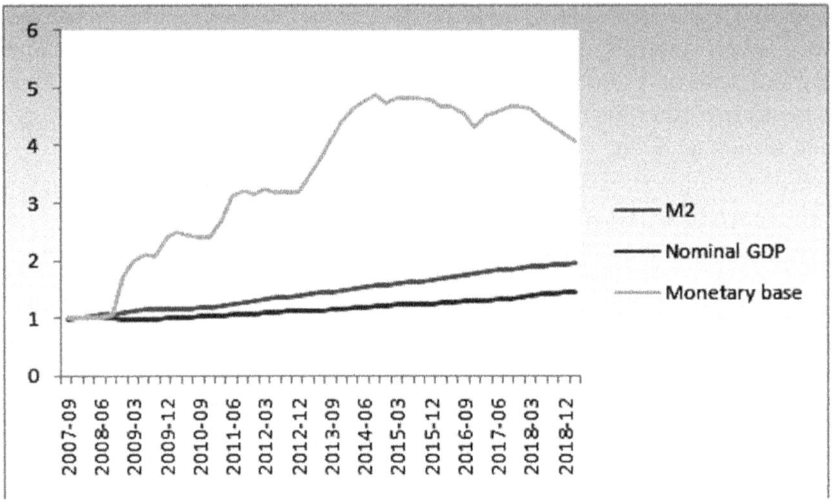


**Figure 116.** Monetary base, money supply, and nominal GDP evolution
Source: Dragoe and Oprean-Stan (2020).

Feldstein (2015) argued that the decision to pay interest for excess reserves is to be blamed as the causal factor behind such a situation. However, the BOJ nearly doubled the monetary base without paying interest on surplus reserves from 2001 to 2005, resulting in no major economic growth or inflation. The other mainstream economists who favor monetary intervention are using the updated form of liquidity trap as excuse for the low success of monetary policies. But the Krugman-style liquidity trap did not last as much as Quantitative Easing (QE)/credit easing. In fact, reducing corporate spreads and M0 expansion can't increase M2 if banks are risk-averse.

Credit-easing policies were ineffective due to banks' low-risk strategies. But in Figure 116, we can observe another process: Money supply growth outpaced nominal GDP growth. This implies a velocity decrease, which means more money is used for speculations. The speculation motive is highly sensitive to artificial low interest rates. When interest rates are close to 0%, investors can use leverage to invest in riskier assets. Besides overtrading, too much reliance on monetary policy can also lead to economic inequalities. The Fed's expansion of monetary base is not distributed uniformly "like water into a tank, but rather oozes like honey into a saucer, dolloping one area first and only then very slowly dribbling to the rest" (Spitznagel, 2012). Quantitative easing (QE) was converted into capital for the largest banks.

Instead of rewarding banks and big companies for lack of precaution, we propose peoples' QE (no reimbursement). The stimulus named Cares Act contains a similar policy. As these funds will be directed to low-income families, the effect will be stronger, as permanent-income theory states that temporary incomes will have little effect on consumption. Also, most likely, trade deficit would not expand drastically since during recessions the openness tends to decrease. Nonetheless, it is financed with public debt.

A better alternative to increasing governmental debt would be for Fed to assist households especially during difficult times like the previous full-scale COVID-19 lockdown. Of course, it could also finance budget deficits both at the Federal and state levels (e.g., infrastructure investments and subsidies), which would lead to more positive outcomes and improvements in the quality of life of the low-income population. However, it would still have the distribution issue, and money could flow into financial speculations in the form of share buybacks. People's QE can solve the distribution problem evocated by Hayek and will be more efficient due to lack of intermediaries in the money flow and, hence, unhindered flow of money into real economic activity. Paradoxically, helping individuals instead of helping financial institutions can ensure financial stability, as QE is frequently linked to asset price bubbles. The fact that people's QE is inflationary is not a flaw. Actually, stagflation is the price we pay for avoiding a depression (Minsky, 2016). Due to moderate or high inflation, cash flows rise and enable the repayment of debt contracted during boom periods in the economy (Keen, 2011).

## 4.7. Preliminary conclusions

We analyzed solutions like Chicago Plan, cashless society, inflation targeting, price-level targeting, nominal GDP, yield spread target, and helicopter money forms.

The Chicago Plan is deflationary and would require strong government intervention to promote growth. Cashless society is an important project with many benefits, but if it is adopted just to allow negative interest rates, it will prove destructive for the economy because money creation will be slowed, causing, in turn, stock market bubbles. We found that capital requirements can't temper bankers' euphoria and credit flow; however, they did limit the extreme credit growth in Romania before the 2008 U.S. economic crisis whose impacts were felt globally. Targeting a moderate inflation rate would avoid deflation and liquidity traps. The idea of targeting the yield spread in order to eliminate economic cycles is fascinating; however, it would fail as central banks can't control long-term interest rates to such a degree (Tănăsescu, Bucur, & Oprean-Stan, 2016). In the past, Federal Reserve has influenced long-term interest rates to reduce public debt, but central banks never attempted to maintain a positive yield spread.

Finally, our analysis revealed that helicopter money would be more successful as people's QE than bank's QE, which ultimately reflects a transfer of capital to banks.

# 5 Economic Crisis Forecast Model

**Abstract:** Although recessions can occur due to pandemics, wars, and supply-side shocks, common recessions have financial roots. The ordinary recession mechanism starts with the euphoria of financial institutions. Entrepreneurs are fooled by bankers' and other risk managers' euphoria and central bank's low interest rates. Investments in projects that otherwise would not be profitable will become attractive. This will lead to production misalignments and housing and stock market bubbles. The eventual adjustment will occur in the following three cases: reevaluation of risks by investors and migration to long-term bonds; monetary contraction due to rising interest rates by central bank in order to avoid high inflation or an overheated economy; a mix of the former two cases. In this chapter, we outline the regular recession mechanism and develop an econometric model for forecasting recessions in the United States. We'll see if this model might have forecasted the Great Recession. We will also examine how the COVID-19 recession differs from other recessions in relation to our suggested model.

**Keywords:** recession mechanism, forecasting recessions, model, COVID-19

## 5.1. The usual recession mechanism

In fact, the three situations described above correspond to a yield curve inversion. The inverted yield curve is not just a signal of impending recession (investors anticipate a drop in economic activity and/or monetary contraction); its consequences are equally significant. Because financial institutions borrow on the short term and lend on the long term, the yield curve inversion reduces their profitability. Financial institutions will tighten credit standards and reduce lending availability to reduce credit losses. Stricter credit criteria are even more essential than greater credit supply because the changes in bank credit began only after the onset of the Great Recession, whereas credit requirements grew prior to the crisis. Tightening credit standards has a greater impact than increasing credit availability since retaining the same supply of credit but imposing harsher conditions or refusing to extend loans to economic agents in need of refinancing could lead to bankruptcy. Following the yield curve inversion, banks will be impacted by the growing spread between the Federal funds rate and the bill rate, followed by the growing spread between the financial commercial paper interest rate and the Federal Funds rate (see Figure 117). Both spreads are signals, but they also have a negative impact on the banks' profitability and liquidity. Banks will have financing issues following the inversion. Banks will resort to interbank borrowing as a response. As interbank loans are viewed as riskier, demand for them will rise, as will the interbank interest rate (raising risk premium). Banks will issue financial commercial paper to finance their operations when the supply of interbank loans shrinks due to high risks.

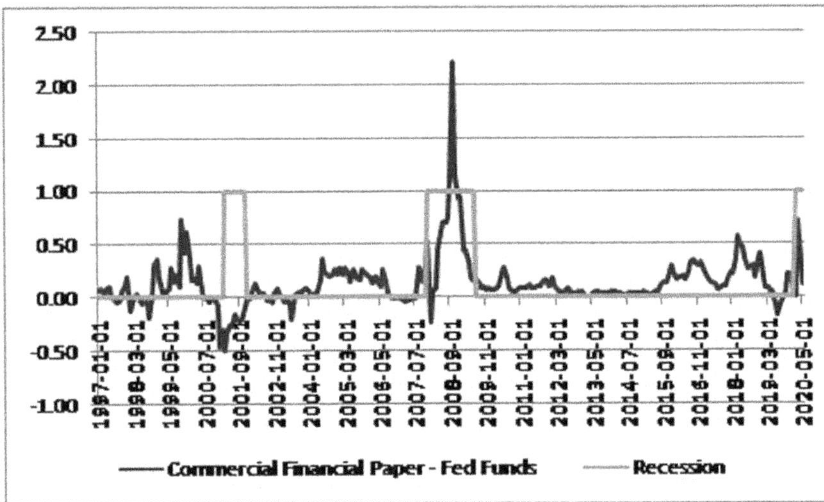


**Figure 117.** Commercial financial paper – Fed Funds rate spread
Source: Authors' computations; data from St. Louis Fed.

Meanwhile, as credit rules tighten, borrowing becomes more difficult for households and nonfinancial companies. As credit criteria tighten and loan availability shrinks, nonfinancial companies will replace loans with bonds and nonfinancial commercial paper. Credit spreads and the nonfinancial commercial paper rate minus bill rate gap will grow as demand and risks rise. As credit standards tighten for households and nonfinancial companies and rising spreads put additional pressure on nonfinancial entities, aggregate demand decreases. Businesses will see decreased levels of new orders and inventory build-up. Their reaction involves a reduction in output and an adjustment in inventory. These actions will have an impact on their employees as well as the service sector. Due to tighter credit standards, lower credit supply, and uncertainty, demand for new houses will fall, resulting in fewer new housing starts, but monthly supply of properties would grow in order for economic agents and households to pay their debts or due to executions. The factory adjustments, drop in house demand, negative swings in margin debit, and stock market's high volatility, all of these will all cut down the demand and precipitate a recession. As a result, firms will respond with enormous layoffs, further reducing spending. Another effect of inventory reduction and layoffs is that companies are unable to respond to large variations in demand. The economic forecast will be determined by expectations, debt ratios (to GDP), the capital adequacy of financial institutions, and fiscal and monetary policy.

## 5.2. The model proposal

## Research methodology and data

As we have previously described the mechanism for regular recessions and emphasized the impact of financial events (such as yield spread inversions, increasing financial market volatility, and decreasing margin debit) on the real economy, we design a model based primarily on financial indicators. If our model fits recessions and forecasts the Great Recession, it implies that most recessions have financial roots. The chosen independent variables are as follows: AAA bond yield minus Federal Funds rate (AAA_FF), commercial paper minus bill rate spread (commercial_paper_BR), excess bond premium, yield spreads at different maturities (10 years – 3 months equivalent bond basis Yield, 7 and 5 years – Federal Funds rate, and 30-year fixed mortgage rate – Federal Funds rate – MORTGAGE30US_F), margin debit, New Orders–Inventories Index, monthly supply of houses, New Private Housing Units Authorized by Building Permits (Permits), and Housing Starts.

We start with a probit regression with lagged independent variables. The dependent variable is a dummy variable in which the value is equal to 1 during recession periods (NBER definition) and 0 in case of no recession. We created this variable with the help of the Eviews add-in named RecDum. The model predicts recessions one month ahead as most indicators (with the exception of the yield spreads) signal recessions one month before occurring.

We will utilize the stepwise-forwards least squares regression in for shrinking the number of variables included in the model. We use lowest probability value (under 0.05) as the selection criteria for adding variables. The model starts introducing variables one by one by using the criterion of lowest *p* value. After each consecutive addition, the preceding variables are checked again against the selected *p* value of 0.05 in this case. After reducing the number of explanatory variables we will run again a probit model with the selected variables. Although the resulting probit model will be an improved model, it can still suffer from multicollinearity.

In order to minimize this weakness, we will employ a logistic regularized (lasso) regression. The logistic (logit) regression is similar to probit, and the difference between the two is that in the probit regression we use the cumulative standard normal distribution function for modelling the regression function and with the logit model we utilize a logistic distribution for regression. The variance of the logit model is higher than that of probit; its tails are heavier because its distribution curve is more spread out (Cakmakyapan & Goktas, 2013; Bilder & Loughin, 2015, p. 120), which can be an advantage.

The lasso method is used for both operator selection and avoidance of overfitting. It was introduced by Tibshirani (1996). Lasso is defined by the following Equation (Hastie et al., 2009, p. 42):

$$\hat{\beta}^{lasso} = argmin \sum_{i=1}^{N} (y_i - \beta_0 - \sum_{j=1}^{p} x_{ij}\beta_j)^2 \tag{42}$$

subject to $\sum_{j=1}^{p} |\beta_j| \leq t$

Lasso can also be defined as in Equation 43:

$$\hat{\beta}^{lasso} = argmin \sum_{i=1}^{N} (y_i - \beta_0 - \sum_{j=1}^{p} x_{ij}\beta_j)^2 + \lambda \sum_{j=1}^{p} |\beta_j|\} \tag{43}$$

The penalty has also the following form:

$$\lambda\,[(1-\alpha)\,||\beta||_2^2 + \alpha||\beta||_1] \tag{44}$$

When α =1 we have a lasso regression, and if α = 0 then the applied model is a ridge regression (Ekstrøm, 2017, p. 121).

We use RapidMiner Studio Educational 9.7.001 to compute the logistic equations with regularization (lasso).

We utilized the following formula for determining the recession probability:

$$Recession\ probability = \frac{\exp(\beta_0 + \sum_{j=1}^{p} x_{ij}\beta_j)}{1 + \exp(\beta_0 + \sum_{j=1}^{p} x_{ij}\beta_j)} \tag{45}$$

We use the Count $R^2$ to assess the model's accuracy. It converts the estimated probabilities into a binary variable (0 and 1). A 50% or a higher recession probability means that the model predicts recession (value 1), and an under-50% probability means no recession (value 0). The attached values are compared with NBER recession dates. We calculate Count $R^2$ by dividing the number of correct cases to total count (see Equation 46).

$$R^2 = \frac{\text{Correct}}{\text{Total Count}} \tag{46}$$

## Results and discussion

The Mc Fadden $R^2$ coefficient is very high at 0.831 (see Figure 118); however, there are two issues regarding this model. One of them is multicollinearity, and the other one is the false recessions indicated by the model as shown in Figure 119. We will start with fixing the second problem. The false recessions from February 1988 and January 2019 occurred due to falls in margin debit registered before the yield spread inversions, despite the fact that on average, margin debit contracts one month before recessions.

So we should always consider a recession only after yield spread inversions. We will eliminate false recessions by introducing Purchasing Managers' Index (PMI) – 50 in the model. Although in some cases this index can only nowcast but not forecast recessions, it is a strong indicator, and it lasts as long as the recession and can reduce the influence of margin debit on the dependent variable. After adding PMI – 50 in the model, EViews 7.2 could not compute consistent statistical results when using 1 lag for the independent variables (see Figure 120). However, when using current values, the McFadden $R^2$ is improved (see Figure 121) and false recessions disappeared (see Figure 122). The results could also indicate that PMI – 50 is better at nowcasting than forecasting recessions. In order to forecast, we need lags and we need to eliminate overfitting and multicollinearity by removing the weakest predictors.

Dependent Variable: RECESSION
Method: ML - Binary Probit (Quadratic hill climbing)
Date: 07/28/20 Time: 15:27
Sample (adjusted): 1976M07 2019M10
Included observations: 520 after adjustments
Convergence achieved after 7 iterations
Covariance matrix computed using second derivatives

| Variable | Coefficient | Std. Error | z-Statistic | Prob. |
|---|---|---|---|---|
| C | -8.759772 | 2.192864 | -3.994672 | 0.0001 |
| AAA_FF(-1) | 72.13060 | 91.06763 | 0.792055 | 0.4283 |
| COMMERCIAL_PAPER_BR(-1) | -261.0675 | 101.0468 | -2.583630 | 0.0098 |
| EXCESS_BOND_PREMIUM(-1) | 0.853073 | 0.711530 | 1.198928 | 0.2306 |
| GS5_FF(-1) | 271.6949 | 376.2521 | 0.722109 | 0.4702 |
| GS7_FF(-1) | 171.3257 | 638.9240 | 0.268147 | 0.7886 |
| HOUSING_STARTS(-1) | -14.84561 | 5.743646 | -2.584702 | 0.0097 |
| MARGIN_DEBIT(-1) | -15.45659 | 3.720379 | -4.154573 | 0.0000 |
| MONTHLY_SUPPLY_H(-1) | 60.28520 | 24.14476 | 2.496824 | 0.0125 |
| MORTGAGE30US_F(-1) | 101.6356 | 69.12188 | 1.470382 | 0.1415 |
| NEW_ORDERS_INVENTORIES(-1) | -0.041081 | 0.041440 | -0.991324 | 0.3215 |
| PERMITS(-1) | -1.388158 | 3.160429 | -0.439231 | 0.6605 |
| S10Y_3M(-1) | 269.3845 | 88.95951 | 3.028169 | 0.0025 |
| S10Y_FF(-1) | -849.5896 | 444.8059 | -1.910023 | 0.0561 |

| | | | |
|---|---|---|---|
| McFadden R-squared | 0.831031 | Mean dependent var | 0.117308 |
| S.D. dependent var | 0.322096 | S.E. of regression | 0.142323 |
| Akaike info criterion | 0.176020 | Sum squared resid | 10.24940 |
| Schwarz criterion | 0.290546 | Log likelihood | -31.76514 |
| Hannan-Quinn criter. | 0.220884 | Deviance | 63.53029 |
| Restr. deviance | 375.9873 | Restr. log likelihood | -187.9936 |
| LR statistic | 312.4570 | Avg. log likelihood | -0.061087 |
| Prob(LR statistic) | 0.000000 | | |
| Obs with Dep=0 | 459 | Total obs | 520 |
| Obs with Dep=1 | 61 | | |

**Figure 118.** Recession model without PMI_50

Source: Authors' computations; data from St. Louis Fed.

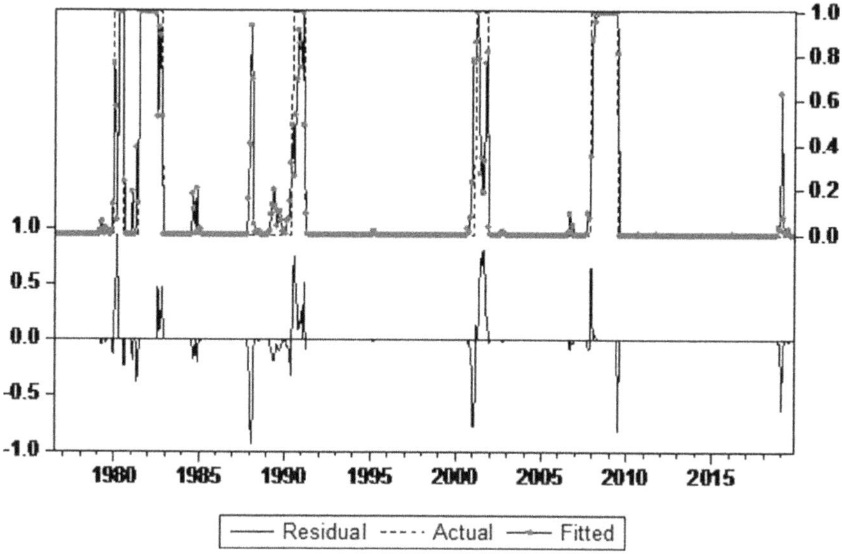


**Figure 119.** Recession model residuals actual data and fitted values

Source: Authors' computations; data from St. Louis Fed.

Dependent Variable: RECESSION
Method: ML - Binary Probit (Quadratic hill climbing)
Date: 07/28/20 Time: 15:30
Sample (adjusted): 1976M07 2019M10
Included observations: 520 after adjustments
Convergence achieved after 10 iterations
WARNING: Singular covariance - coefficients are not unique
Covariance matrix computed using second derivatives
WARNING: Complete separation detected at estimated parameters (results may not be valid)

| Variable | Coefficient | Std. Error | z-Statistic | Prob. |
|---|---|---|---|---|
| C | -2236.360 | NA | NA | NA |
| AAA_FF(-1) | 55961.98 | NA | NA | NA |
| COMMERCIAL_PAPER_BR(-1) | -88333.78 | NA | NA | NA |
| EXCESS_BOND_PREMIUM(-1) | 64.66746 | NA | NA | NA |
| GS5_FF(-1) | 232114.1 | NA | NA | NA |
| GS7_FF(-1) | -107027.5 | NA | NA | NA |
| HOUSING_STARTS(-1) | -2889.821 | NA | NA | NA |
| MARGIN_DEBIT(-1) | -1642.254 | NA | NA | NA |
| MONTHLY_SUPPLY_H(-1) | 6558.002 | NA | NA | NA |
| MORTGAGE30US_F(-1) | 30276.52 | NA | NA | NA |
| NEW_ORDERS_INVENTORIES(-1) | 4.022304 | NA | NA | NA |
| PERMITS | -3416.787 | NA | NA | NA |
| PMI_50(-1) | -66.56359 | NA | NA | NA |
| S10Y_3M(-1) | 100887.0 | NA | NA | NA |
| S10Y_FF(-1) | -286075.1 | NA | NA | NA |

| | | | |
|---|---|---|---|
| McFadden R-squared | 1.000000 | Mean dependent var | 0.117308 |
| S.D. dependent var | 0.322096 | S.E. of regression | 1.4E-145 |
| Akaike info criterion | 0.057692 | Sum squared resid | 1.0E-287 |
| Schwarz criterion | 0.180399 | Log likelihood | 0.000000 |
| Hannan-Quinn criter. | 0.105761 | Deviance | 0.000000 |
| Restr. deviance | 375.9873 | Restr. log likelihood | -187.9936 |
| LR statistic | 375.9873 | Avg. log likelihood | 0.000000 |
| Prob(LR statistic) | 0.000000 | | |

| | | | |
|---|---|---|---|
| Obs with Dep=0 | 459 | Total obs | 520 |
| Obs with Dep=1 | 61 | | |

**Figure 120.** Recession model including PMI_50 (1 lag)

Source: Authors' computations; data from St. Louis Fed.

Dependent Variable: RECESSION
Method: ML - Binary Probit (Quadratic hill climbing)
Date: 07/28/20 Time: 15:31
Sample (adjusted): 1976M06 2019M09
Included observations: 520 after adjustments
Convergence achieved after 9 iterations
Covariance matrix computed using second derivatives

| Variable | Coefficient | Std. Error | z-Statistic | Prob. |
|---|---|---|---|---|
| C | -33.70940 | 15.56896 | -2.165167 | 0.0304 |
| AAA_FF | 723.1179 | 416.3124 | 1.736960 | 0.0824 |
| COMMERCIAL_PAPER_BR | -784.8873 | 373.2002 | -2.103127 | 0.0355 |
| EXCESS_BOND_PREMIUM | -7.682347 | 4.119058 | -1.865074 | 0.0622 |
| GS5_FF | 654.9974 | 682.8320 | 0.959236 | 0.3374 |
| GS7_FF | 608.2226 | 1445.483 | 0.420775 | 0.6739 |
| HOUSING_STARTS | -60.36490 | 31.01285 | -1.946448 | 0.0516 |
| MARGIN_DEBIT | -38.34208 | 18.17467 | -2.109644 | 0.0349 |
| MONTHLY_SUPPLY_H | 291.1773 | 134.6045 | 2.163206 | 0.0305 |
| MORTGAGE30US_F | -14.43175 | 128.4769 | -0.112330 | 0.9106 |
| NEW_ORDERS_INVENTORIES | 0.266120 | 0.169185 | 1.572953 | 0.1157 |
| PERMITS | 17.84026 | 10.06526 | 1.772459 | 0.0763 |
| PMI_50 | -1.449155 | 0.657686 | -2.203415 | 0.0276 |
| S10Y_3M | 539.9157 | 261.3151 | 2.066148 | 0.0388 |
| S10Y_FF | -2426.341 | 1608.047 | -1.508875 | 0.1313 |

| | | | |
|---|---|---|---|
| McFadden R-squared | 0.937029 | Mean dependent var | 0.117308 |
| S.D. dependent var | 0.322096 | S.E. of regression | 0.086429 |
| Akaike info criterion | 0.103224 | Sum squared resid | 3.772320 |
| Schwarz criterion | 0.225930 | Log likelihood | -11.83815 |
| Hannan-Quinn criter. | 0.151293 | Deviance | 23.67631 |
| Restr. deviance | 375.9873 | Restr. log likelihood | -187.9936 |
| LR statistic | 352.3109 | Avg. log likelihood | -0.022766 |
| Prob(LR statistic) | 0.000000 | | |

| | | | |
|---|---|---|---|
| Obs with Dep=0 | 459 | Total obs | 520 |
| Obs with Dep=1 | 61 | | |

**Figure 121.** Recession model including PMI_50

Source: Authors' computations; data from St. Louis Fed.

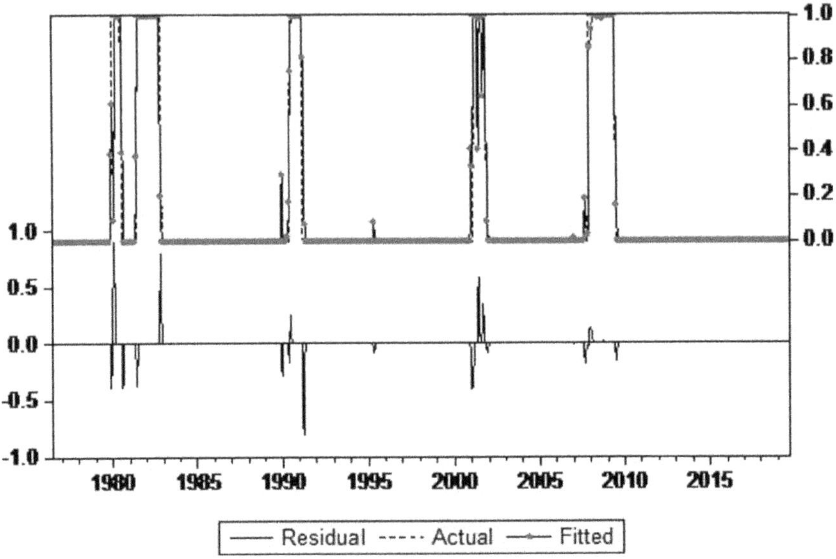


**Figure 122.** Recession model including PMI_50 – residuals, actual data, and fitted values

Source: Authors' computations; data from St. Louis Fed.

As the last probit regression reveals (Figure 121) that not all independent variables are statistically significant, we take the next step and use the stepwise regression for shrinking the number of factors. The variables indicated by the stepwise model (under 0.05 *p* value, see Figure 123) are as follows: excess bond premium, monthly supply of houses, housing starts, PMI – 50, margin debit, and yield spreads (10 years – 3 months, 10 years – Federal Funds rate; 30 years fixed-rate average mortgage – Federal Funds rate). The eliminated variables are commercial paper_BR, yields spreads (5 and 7 years – Federal Funds, AAA_FF), Permits and New Orders – Inventories. Although removing the indicator Permits is understandable because Housing Starts reacts faster to economic and financial conditions and the plans will be updated and the yield spreads (GS5_FF, GS7_FF and AAA_FF) are not as efficient as S10Y_3M and S10Y_FF, we think that some variables shouldn't have been removed. New Orders_Inventories Index shows the rise in inventories due to lower demand and, therefore, that Final Sales are contracting and the change in inventories will soon adjust, while Commercial_Paper_BR indicates stricter credit standards and replacement of loans with commercial paper.

Dependent Variable: RECESSION
Method: Stepwise Regression
Date: 07/11/20 Time: 08:46
Sample (adjusted): 1973M02 2019M10
Included observations: 561 after adjustments
No always included regressors
Number of search regressors: 15
Selection method: Stepwise forwards
Stopping criterion: p-value forwards/backwards = 0.05/0.05
Note: final equation sample is larger than stepwise sample (rejected regressors contain missing values)

| Variable | Coefficient | Std. Error | t-Statistic | Prob.* |
|---|---|---|---|---|
| EXCESS_BOND_PREMIUM(-1) | 0.070380 | 0.023492 | 2.995935 | 0.0029 |
| MONTHLY_SUPPLY_H(-1) | 4.283003 | 0.730664 | 5.861799 | 0.0000 |
| HOUSING_STARTS(-1) | -0.637754 | 0.138069 | -4.619100 | 0.0000 |
| PMI_50(-1) | -0.010405 | 0.001921 | -5.417334 | 0.0000 |
| MARGIN_DEBIT(-1) | -0.427874 | 0.092260 | -4.637685 | 0.0000 |
| C | -0.258094 | 0.064712 | -3.988350 | 0.0001 |
| S10Y_FF(-1) | -20.29881 | 2.568191 | -7.903933 | 0.0000 |
| S10Y_3M(-1) | 17.80386 | 2.483452 | 7.168997 | 0.0000 |
| MORTGAGE30US_F(-1) | 4.849064 | 2.462384 | 1.969256 | 0.0494 |

| | | | |
|---|---|---|---|
| R-squared | 0.612430 | Mean dependent var | 0.139037 |
| Adjusted R-squared | 0.606813 | S.D. dependent var | 0.346294 |
| S.E. of regression | 0.217142 | Akaike info criterion | -0.200613 |
| Sum squared resid | 26.02727 | Schwarz criterion | -0.131153 |
| Log likelihood | 65.27203 | Hannan-Quinn criter. | -0.173493 |
| F-statistic | 109.0325 | Durbin-Watson stat | 0.473177 |
| Prob(F-statistic) | 0.000000 | | |

Selection Summary

Added EXCESS_BOND_PREMIUM(-1)
Added COMMERCIAL_PAPER_BR(-1)
Added HOUSING_STARTS(-1)
Added PMI_50(-1)
Added MONTHLY_SUPPLY_H(-1)
Removed COMMERCIAL_PAPER_BR(-1)
Added MARGIN_DEBIT(-1)
Added C
Added COMMERCIAL_PAPER_BR(-1)
Added S10Y_3M(-1)
Added S10Y_FF(-1)
Removed COMMERCIAL_PAPER_BR(-1)
Added MORTGAGE30US_F(-1)

**Figure 123.** Stepwise regression

Source: Authors' computations; data from St. Louis Fed.

Dependent Variable: RECESSION
Method: ML - Binary Probit (Quadratic hill climbing)
Date: 07/11/20 Time: 08:42
Sample (adjusted): 1973M02 2019M10
Included observations: 561 after adjustments
Convergence achieved after 6 iterations
Covariance matrix computed using second derivatives

| Variable | Coefficient | Std. Error | z-Statistic | Prob. |
|---|---|---|---|---|
| C | -5.809631 | 1.133285 | -5.126362 | 0.0000 |
| EXCESS_BOND_PREMIUM(-1) | 0.707440 | 0.434887 | 1.626722 | 0.1038 |
| MONTHLY_SUPPLY_H(-1) | 32.41170 | 13.93064 | 2.326648 | 0.0200 |
| HOUSING_STARTS(-1) | -7.702293 | 3.002792 | -2.565044 | 0.0103 |
| PMI_50(-1) | -0.111605 | 0.027543 | -4.052063 | 0.0001 |
| MARGIN_DEBIT(-1) | -9.255339 | 1.873313 | -4.940625 | 0.0000 |
| S10Y_FF(-1) | -142.9855 | 42.08550 | -3.397499 | 0.0007 |
| S10Y_3M(-1) | 88.58946 | 42.80761 | 2.069479 | 0.0385 |
| MORTGAGE30US_F(-1) | 50.14932 | 39.82027 | 1.259392 | 0.2079 |

| | | | |
|---|---|---|---|
| McFadden R-squared | 0.815980 | Mean dependent var | 0.139037 |
| S.D. dependent var | 0.346294 | S.E. of regression | 0.154193 |
| Akaike info criterion | 0.180484 | Sum squared resid | 13.12398 |
| Schwarz criterion | 0.249945 | Log likelihood | -41.62580 |
| Hannan-Quinn criter. | 0.207605 | Deviance | 83.25159 |
| Restr. deviance | 452.4042 | Restr. log likelihood | -226.2021 |
| LR statistic | 369.1526 | Avg. log likelihood | -0.074199 |
| Prob(LR statistic) | 0.000000 | | |

| | | | |
|---|---|---|---|
| Obs with Dep=0 | 483 | Total obs | 561 |
| Obs with Dep=1 | 78 | | |

**Figure 124.** Probit regression with the variables recommended by stepwise regression
Source: Authors' computations; data from St. Louis Fed.

The probit regression computed with the variables recommended by the stepwise regression still contains coefficients with *p* value over 0.05 (see Figure 124). After excluding the independent variable with the highest *p* value (MORTGAGE30ES_F) we obtain a regression with statistically significant coefficients (see Figures 125 and 126). But we have doubts regarding removing COMMERCIAL_PAPER_BR and New Orders–Inventories Index, and multicollinearity is still a problem (see Table 10).

Dependent Variable: RECESSION
Method: ML - Binary Probit (Quadratic hill climbing)
Date: 07/11/20 Time: 18:48
Sample (adjusted): 1973M02 2019M10
Included observations: 561 after adjustments
Convergence achieved after 6 iterations
Covariance matrix computed using second derivatives

| Variable | Coefficient | Std. Error | z-Statistic | Prob. |
|---|---|---|---|---|
| C | -5.146017 | 0.962796 | -5.344868 | 0.0000 |
| EXCESS_BOND_PREMIUM(-1) | 0.921796 | 0.404786 | 2.277244 | 0.0228 |
| MONTHLY_SUPPLY_H(-1) | 33.22360 | 13.60230 | 2.442500 | 0.0146 |
| HOUSING_STARTS(-1) | -6.984755 | 2.851660 | -2.449365 | 0.0143 |
| PMI_50(-1) | -0.118996 | 0.026286 | -4.527026 | 0.0000 |
| MARGIN_DEBIT(-1) | -8.697200 | 1.786521 | -4.868232 | 0.0000 |
| S10Y_FF(-1) | -110.4747 | 31.73034 | -3.481674 | 0.0005 |
| S10Y_3M(-1) | 111.1336 | 40.09488 | 2.771765 | 0.0056 |

| | | | |
|---|---|---|---|
| McFadden R-squared | 0.812348 | Mean dependent var | 0.139037 |
| S.D. dependent var | 0.346294 | S.E. of regression | 0.155036 |
| Akaike info criterion | 0.179848 | Sum squared resid | 13.29207 |
| Schwarz criterion | 0.241591 | Log likelihood | -42.44734 |
| Hannan-Quinn criter. | 0.203955 | Deviance | 84.89468 |
| Restr. deviance | 452.4042 | Restr. log likelihood | -226.2021 |
| LR statistic | 367.5095 | Avg. log likelihood | -0.075664 |
| Prob(LR statistic) | 0.000000 | | |

| | | | |
|---|---|---|---|
| Obs with Dep=0 | 483 | Total obs | 561 |
| Obs with Dep=1 | 78 | | |

**Figure 125.** Probit regression

Source: Authors' computations; data from St. Louis Fed.

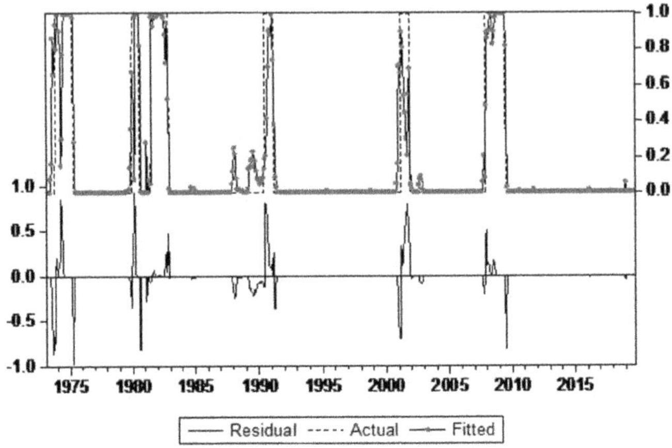


**Figure 126.** Probit regression – residuals, actual data, and fitted values

Source: Authors' computations; data from St. Louis Fed.

**Table 10.** Correlations

| | EXCESS_BOND_ PREMIUM(-1) | PMI_50(-1) | MARGIN_ DEBIT(-1) | S10Y_FF(-1) | S10Y_3M(-1) |
|---|---|---|---|---|---|
| EXCESS_BOND_ PREMIUM(-1) | 1 | −0.533869 | −0.527012 | −0.063787 | 0.009722 |
| MONTHLY_ SUPPLY_H(-1) | 0.352258 | −0.272277 | −0.383744 | −0.343511 | −0.233554 |
| HOUSING_ STARTS(-1) | −0.285152 | 0.326864 | 0.436937 | 0.357417 | 0.306335 |
| PMI_50(-1) | −0.533869 | 1 | 0.422591 | 0.114191 | 0.062406 |
| MARGIN_ DEBIT(-1) | −0.527012 | 0.422591 | 1 | 0.193587 | 0.114085 |
| S10Y_FF(-1) | −0.063787 | 0.114191 | 0.193587 | 1 | 0.950626 |
| S10Y_3M(-1) | 0.009722 | 0.062406 | 0.114085 | 0.950626 | 1 |

Source: Authors' computations

For removing multicollinearity, we use a logistic regularized (lasso) regression.

**Table 11.** Lasso Logistic regression

| Independent variables | Coefficient | Std. Coefficient |
|---|---|---|
| AAA_FF | 663.9275007 | 12.5514229 |
| COMMERCIAL_PAPER_BR | –874.523024 | –2.918120104 |
| EXCESS_BOND_PREMIUM | –7.61434507 | –4.085532456 |
| GS5_FF | 880.3821237 | 11.45481538 |
| GS7_FF | 0 | 0 |
| HOUSING_STARTS | –67.3198927 | –5.991936778 |
| MARGIN_DEBIT | –49.0814125 | –6.013182572 |
| MONTHLY_SUPPLY_H | 324.1519721 | 5.42836469 |
| MORTGAGE30US_F | 0.002913151 | 4.38E-05 |
| NEW_ORDERS_INVENTORIES | 0.305895463 | 1.961302891 |
| PERMITS | 18.91903145 | 2.341199533 |
| PMI_50 | –1.66543091 | –9.607093199 |
| S10Y_3M | 613.8798202 | 8.033296813 |
| S10Y_FF | –2062.18464 | –32.68022048 |
| Intercept | –37.7072042 | –18.60195291 |
| R^2: 0.994230769 | | |
| Lambda | 0.00002139 | |
| Alpha | 1 | |

Source: Authors' computations

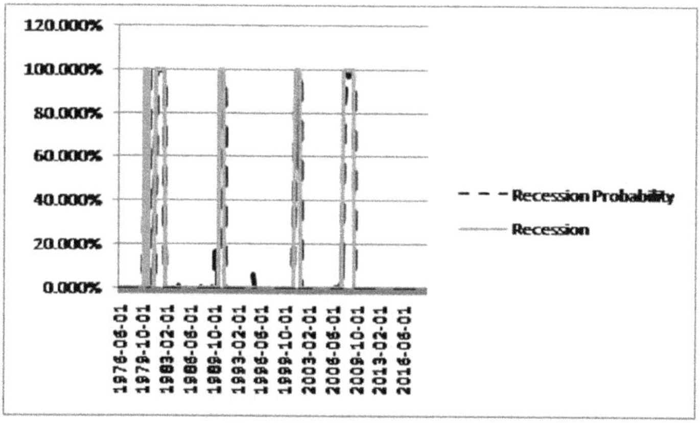


**Figure 127.** Recession and recession probability

Source: Authors' computations; data from St. Louis Fed.

**Table 12.** Lasso Logistic regression (with 1 lag)

| **Independent variables** | **Coefficient** | **Std. Coefficient** |
|---|---|---|
| AAA_FF(-1) | 802.716 | 15.17519283 |
| COMMERCIAL_PAPER_BR(-1) | -630.7776 | -2.104787008 |
| EXCESS_BOND_PREMIUM(-1) | -1.673146 | -0.897738872 |
| GS5_FF(-1) | 2452.433 | 31.90906631 |
| GS7_FF(-1) | -1179.743 | -17.12025965 |
| HOUSING_STARTS(-1) | -28.95165 | -2.576897147 |
| MARGIN_DEBIT(-1) | -35.33363 | -4.328880794 |
| MONTHLY_SUPPLY_H(-1) | 220.4292 | 3.691385419 |
| MORTGAGE30US_F(-1) | -99.29147 | -1.493112825 |
| NEW_ORDERS_INVENTORIES(-1) | 0.044292 | 0.28398452 |
| PERMITS(-1) | -12.46285 | -1.542257273 |
| PMI_50(-1) | -0.710502 | -4.098553733 |
| S10Y_3M(-1) | 825.4687 | 10.80217101 |
| S10Y_FF(-1) | -2687.8 | -42.59457648 |
| Intercept | -26.83611 | -16.25178239 |
| R^2: 0.978846154 | | |
| Lambda | 0.0000203 | |
| Alpha | 1 | |

Source: Authors' computations

The first applied logistic lasso model is rather a nowcast (see Figure 127 and Table 11). As Count $R^2$ is 0.994, the model fits the recessions very well. However, since the independent variables are not lagged, the model is useful for identifying instead of predicting recessions. The high value for Count $R^2$ could suggest that PMI_50 is a good indicator for determining whether the economy experiences a recession instead of forecasting recessions. Within this model, the regression coefficient for GS7_FF was forced to 0.

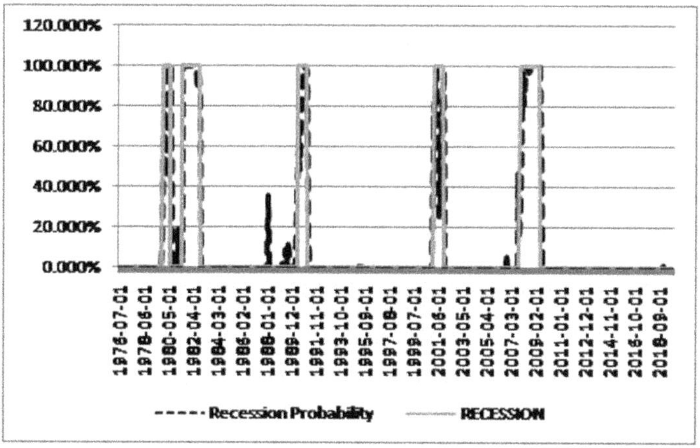


**Figure 128.** Recession and recession probability (model with 1 lag)
Source: Authors' computations; data from St. Louis Fed.

The next model is a regression with data during 1976M07–2019M10 and includes lagged independent variables and is therefore equipped for predictions (see Figure 128 and Table 12). As $R^2$ is very high, we can conclude that it is an efficient model for predicting recessions.

## 5.3. Testing the predictive power of the model based on financial indicators of the Great Recession

The next step was to apply the model to the July 1976–November 2007 period for the dependent variable and to the June 1976–October 2007 period for the independent variables for predicting recessions one month ahead. We use the computed coefficients (see Table 13) and update the forecast with the new values of the indicators (static forecast).

**Table 13.** Lasso Logistic regression (with 1 lag) for predicting the Great Recession

| **Independent variables** | **Coefficient** | **Std. Coefficient** |
|---|---|---|
| AAA_FF(-1) | 491.6285467 | 9.537839099 |
| COMMERCIAL_PAPER_BR(-1) | -1638.17366 | -5.528092169 |
| EXCESS_BOND_PREMIUM(-1) | -3.00070822 | -1.34999119 |
| GS5_FF(-1) | 0 | 0 |
| GS7_FF(-1) | 7107.042554 | 113.6567895 |
| HOUSING_STARTS(-1) | -61.9771886 | -5.308828417 |
| MARGIN_DEBIT(-1) | -75.3868627 | -9.220324437 |
| MONTHLY_SUPPLY_H(-1) | 172.7664251 | 2.638292607 |
| MORTGAGE30US_F(-1) | -44.3342647 | -0.715980606 |
| NEW_ORDERS_INVENTORIES(-1) | 0.624188907 | 3.791703212 |
| PERMITS(-1) | -42.7258212 | -5.209782056 |
| PMI_50(-1) | -1.64603861 | -9.747828348 |
| S10Y_3M(-1) | 2083.765843 | 29.23422902 |
| S10Y_FF(-1) | -9368.89037 | -160.469811 |
| Intercept | -39.1843007 | -32.52513307 |
| R^2: 0.965384615 | | |
| R^2 for out of sample predictions: 0.902097902 | | |
| Lambda | 0.00001956 | |
| Alpha | 1 | |

Source: Authors' computations.

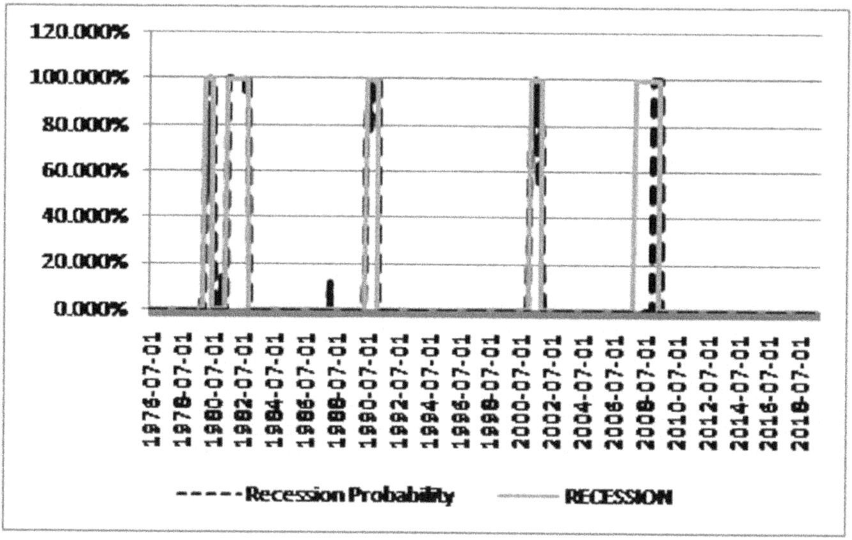


**Figure 129.** Recession and recession probability (model with 1 lag) for predicting the Great Recession

Source: Authors' computations; data from St. Louis Fed.

The model indicates recession only for January 2009–June 2009 (see Figure 129), whereas the Great Recession lasted between December 2007 and June 2009. We attempt to improve the model by removing PMI_50 (see Table 14).

**Table 14.** Lasso Logistic regression (1 lag, without PMI_50) for predicting the Great Recession

| **Independent variables** | **Coefficient** | **Std. Coefficient** |
|---|---|---|
| AAA_FF(-1) | 51.68578138 | 1.002729947 |
| COMMERCIAL_PAPER_BR(-1) | -742.439383 | -2.505395754 |
| EXCESS_BOND_PREMIUM(-1) | 1.239311029 | 0.5575547 |
| GS5_FF(-1) | -95.5993524 | -1.393695667 |
| GS7_FF(-1) | 1224.222858 | 19.57793818 |
| HOUSING_STARTS(-1) | -25.917545 | -2.22003938 |
| MARGIN_DEBIT(-1) | -36.4175209 | -4.454109722 |
| MONTHLY_SUPPLY_H(-1) | 175.5077685 | 2.680155289 |
| MORTGAGE30US_F(-1) | 275.2178236 | 4.444657545 |
| NEW_ORDERS_INVENTORIES(-1) | -0.05949973 | -0.361437564 |
| PERMITS(-1) | 2.539274128 | 0.309626928 |
| S10Y_3M(-1) | 390.6109671 | 5.480083336 |
| S10Y_FF(-1) | -1825.67168 | -31.26999866 |
| Intercept | -19.725573 | -9.946567298 |
| R^2: 0.0962264 | | |
| Out of sample R^2:0.9346405 | | |
| lambda | 0.00001516 | |
| alpha | 1 | |

Source: Authors' computations.

We compute the marginal effects (see Table 15) with Equations 47 and 48.

$$Marginal\,effect = \beta_k * \frac{1}{1+e^{-Z}} * \frac{e^{-Z}}{1+e^{-Z}} \tag{47}$$

$$\text{where} \quad Z = \beta_0 + \beta_1 * \overline{x_1} + \beta_2 * \overline{x_2} + \ldots + \beta_j * \overline{x_j} \tag{48}$$

**Table 15.** Marginal Effects

| Independent variables | Marginal effects |
|---|---|
| AAA_FF(-1) | 0.003920268 |
| COMMERCIAL_PAPER(-1) | –0.056312608 |
| EXCESS_BOND_PREMIUM(-1) | 0.000093999 |
| GS5_FF(-1) | –0.007251028 |
| GS7_FF(-1) | 0.092854964 |
| HOUSING_STARTS(-1) | –0.001965796 |
| MARGIN_DEBIT(-1) | –0.002762199 |
| MONTHLY_SUPPLY_H(-1) | 0.013311929 |
| MORTGAGE30US_F(-1) | 0.020874746 |
| NEW_ORDERS_INVENTORIES(-1) | –0.000004513 |
| PERMITS(-1) | 0.000192599 |
| S10Y_3M(-1) | 0.029627095 |
| S10Y_FF(-1) | –0.138473708 |

Source: Authors' computations.

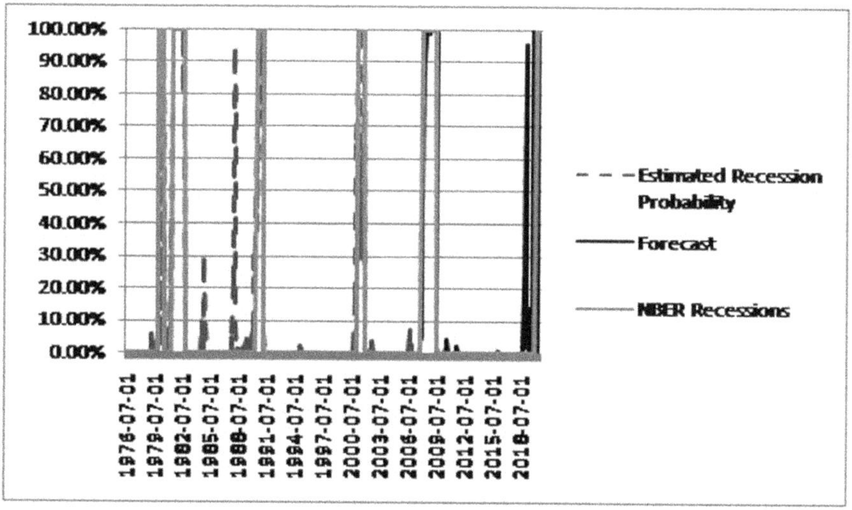


**Figure 130.** Recession and recession probability (1 lag, without PMI_50) for predicting the Great Recession

Source: Authors' computations; data from St. Louis Fed.

This time we forecast (pseudo-forecast) recessions for December 2007–August 2020. The new model forecasted 48.592% recession probability for January 2008 and 98.525% for February 2008 (see Figures 130 and 131). The Count $R^2$ for out-of-sample predictions is 93.46% for the entire sample period and 97.03% for December 2007–October 2019 meaning that the model made only 4 wrong predictions out of 143 months until October 2019. The high residual registered in February 1988 occurred because of the negative changes in margin debit, housing permits, and housing starts. We should always consider a recession only after an inversion of the yield spread (10 years constant maturity – 3 months secondary market bond equivalent rate). The error in prediction for January 2019 is also due to negative changes in margin debit in regards to the average of the previous 12 months and due to the registered decline in housing starts. Margin debit can't signal recession alone, but when it is accompanied by the yield spread inversion it is an important signal.

The model can be improved and extended to take into account recessions only after yield spread; however, experts can't be replaced by econometric models.

As the Great Recession could have been predicted by using this model which is based mainly on financial indicators, we can conclude that finance has a powerful effect on economic cycles.

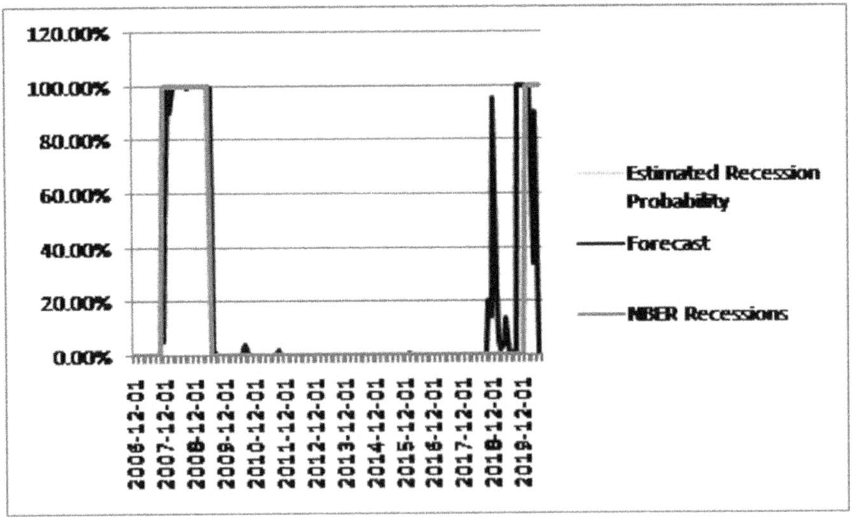


**Figure 131.** Recession probability and the Great Recession

Source: Authors' computations; data from St. Louis Fed.

For Romania it is much more difficult to design a similar model for predicting recessions due to lack of indicators and long time series. Also, except for Coronavirus recession, since 1995 only two recessions have been recorded in Romania (see Appendix 33) with a different, underperforming definition (two consecutive quarters of decrease of real GDP) when compared to NBER's.

Like in the case of United States, we should start considering a recession only after a yield spread inversion. As shown in Figure 132, yield spread inversions occurred before and during the economic crisis that started in 2008Q4 in Romania. The explanation for the delayed recession (when yield inversions are included) are significant capital inflows due to long-term interest rate differentials with the Eurozone. Capital inflows contributed to substantial increases in loan volume, which kept the economy booming until banks with foreign capital withdrew their capital as a result of the implications of negative yield spreads reported in origin countries and Romania.

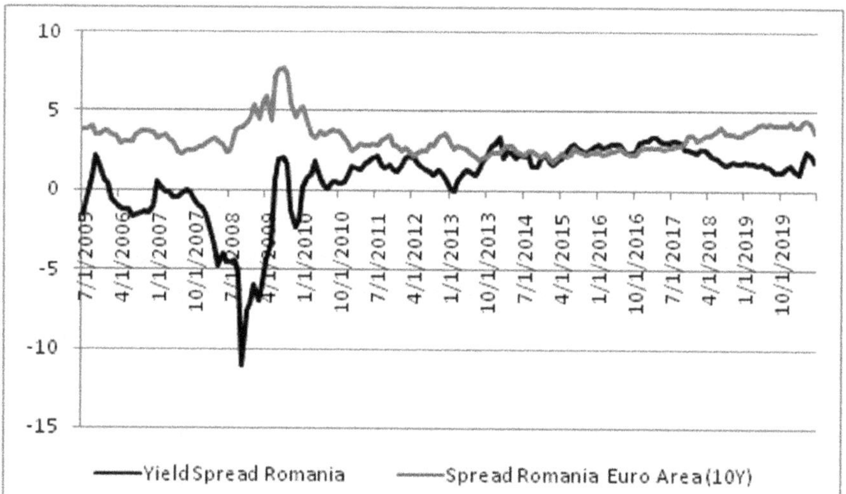


**Figure 132.** Yield spread – Romania and long-term interest rate differential between Romania and Eurozone

Source: Authors' computations; data from Eurostat.

## 5.4. Coronavirus recession in correlation with the proposed model

Although a recession was most likely already on its way due to the yield spread inversion which occurred in June 2019 (10Y-3MO), Coronavirus created its own recession. The U.S. recession started in February 2020 due to supply chain issues caused by COVID-19. Furthermore in March, the lockdown affected the wages. A supply-side crisis was converted into a demand crisis which in turn affected the supply again. A health crisis was turned into an economic crisis by politicians in order to isolate the virus, and the economic crisis metamorphosed into a financial crisis. Due to uncertainty, S&P 500 declined in February and March 2020 and the yield spread inverted (10 years – 3 months) in February, while housing starts registered significant negative changes in March and April. This time credit standards were tightened after the start of recession and not before the recession (see Figure 133). Fiscal deficits exploded due to high unemployment and low incomes.

Although this crisis does not follow the ordinary recession mechanism, the consequences are the same. Although some economists like Bullard (2020) named it a massive investment in health, it was expected to be the worst recession since the 1929 depression (IMF, 2020). Our model indicated the start of the recession prematurely in November 2019 due to market uncertainty reflected in margin debit and yield spreads (GS5_FF and GS7_FF).

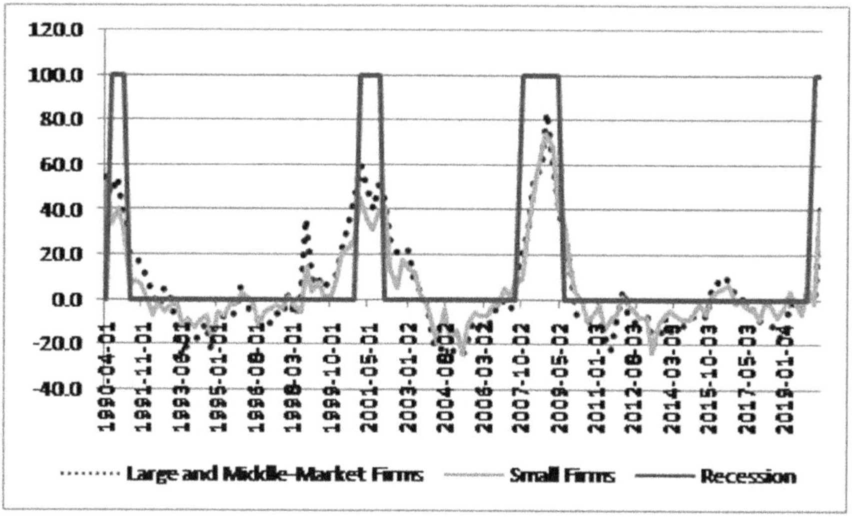


**Figure 133.** Net percentage of domestic banks tightening standards for commercial and industrial loans

Source: St. Louis Fed.

There was a documented precedent, namely the Spanish Flu. The Spanish Flu started in 1917. An estimated 40–50 million people died worldwide because of the Spanish Flu (Potter, 2001). Due to World War I, factories were not closed as the war needed the products. Government spending represented 38% of GDP. The war compensated the negative economic impact of influenza, although coal output was reduced and the textile industry was affected as well (Benmelech & Frydman, 2020). This shows that fiscal stimulus can offset the negative economic effects of pandemics (Dobrotă, Voda, & Dumitraşcu, 2021; Vodă, Dobrotă, & Cristea, 2020).

## 5.5. Preliminary conclusions

We presented the usual recession mechanism in the fifth chapter. It begins with a yield spread inversion caused by investors' reevaluation of risks and migration to long-term bonds or a monetary contraction caused by higher interest rates by central banks in order to avert high inflation or an overheating economy or a combination of the two. Financial institutions' profits will suffer as a result of the negative yield spread, as will credit conditions.

Tighter lending conditions will result in fewer new orders and an increase in inventory, as well as reduced house demand and fewer housing starts. After factory adjustments, production will fall and the unemployment rate will rise.

We suggested and estimated an econometric model predicting recessions in the United States using a regularized logistic regression mostly with financial indicators. With a one-month delay, this model would have forecast the Great Recession. We can conclude that finance has a significant role in economic cycles. In Romania, as in the United States, we should consider a recession only after the yield spread inverts. Yield spread inversions occurred both before and during Romania's economic crisis, which began in the fourth quarter of 2008. The explanation for the delayed recession (when yield inversions are included) are significant capital inflows due to long-term interest rate differentials with the Eurozone. Capital inflows contributed to substantial increases in loan volume, which kept the economy booming until banks with foreign capital withdrew their capital as a result of the implications of negative yield spreads reported in origin countries and Romania.

The Coronavirus recession had an inverse mechanism in that it began owing to restrictions and that financial institutions tightened credit conditions only after the restrictions were imposed.

# References


Arellano, C., Ramanarayanan, A., (2012), Default and the Maturity Structure in Sovereign Bonds, *Journal of Political Economy*, University of Chicago Press, 120(2), pp. 187–232.

Aziakpono, M. J., Khomo, M. M., (2007), Forecasting Recession in South Africa: A Comparison of the Yield Curve and other Economic Indicators, *South African Journal of Economics*, 75(2), pp. 194–212.

Ball, L., (2013), The Case for 4% Inflation, *Central Bank Review*, Central Bank of the Republic of Turkey.

Bank of Japan, (2016), New Framework for Strengthening Monetary Easing:"Quantitative and QualitativeMonetary Easing with Yield Curve Control", September 21, 2016, available online at: https://www.boj.or.jp/en/announcements/release_2016/k160921a.pdf, Acessed on 20th June 2020.

Barrett, C., (2011), Australia and the Great Recession, *Australian Scholar Woodrow Wilson International Center for Scholars.*

Barsky, R. B., Kilian, L., (2000), A Monetary Explanation of the Great Stagflation of the 1970s, *NBER Working Paper,* No. 7547, available online at: https://www.nber.org/papers/w7547.pdf [Accessed 1 March 2020].

Benmelech, E., Frydman, C., (2020), The 1918 influenza did not kill the US economy, available online at: https://voxeu.org/article/1918-influenza-did-not-kill-us-economy [Accessed 1 July 2020].

Berg, A. G., Ostry, J. D., (2011), Inequality and Unsustainable Growth: Two Sides of the Same Coin?, *IMF Staff Discussion Note*, (SDN/11/08).

Berger, A. N., Bouwman, C. H. S., (2013), How does capital affect bank performance during financial crises?, *Journal of Financial Economics*, 109(1), pp. 146–176.

Bernanke, B. S., (2000), Japan's Slump: A Case of Self-Induced Paralysis? Paper presented at *American Economic Association meetings*, available online at: http://www.princeton.edu/~pkrugman/bernanke_paralysis.pdf?, [Accessed 28 March 2020].

Bernanke, B. S., (2009), The Crisis and the Policy Response, At the Stamp Lecture, *London School of Economics*, London, England, available online at: https://www.federalreserve.gov/newsevents/speech/bernanke20090113a.htm [Accessed 15 April 2020].

Bernanke, B. S., (2017), Monetary Policy in a New Era, Rethinking Monetary Policy in a New Normal, PIIE, *Brookings Institution.*

Bernanke, Ben S. and Blinder, Alan S., (1992), The Federal Funds Rate and the Channels of Monetary Transmission, *American Economic Review, American Economic Association*, 82(4), pp. 901–921.

Bhatia, A. V., Bayoumi, T., (2012), Leverage? What Leverage? A Deep Dive into the U.S. Flow of Funds in Search of Clues to the Global Crisis, *IMF Working Paper12/162, Washington, DC: International Monetary Fund.*

Biggs, M., Mayer, T., Pick, A. (2009), Credit and Economic Recovery, De Nederlandsche Bank Working Paper No. 218/2009.

Bilder, C. R., Loughin, T. M., (2015), Analysis of Categorical Data with R. Boca Raton, FL: Chapman and Hall/CRC, *Biometrics*, 71, pp. 1198–1199. 10.1111/biom.12440.

Blanchard, O., (2007), Current Account Deficits in Rich Countries, *NBER Working Papers 12925*, 54(2), pp. 191–219, available online at: http://www.nber.org/papers/w12925 [Accessed 5 May 2020].

Blinder, Alan S., (1979), *Economic Policy and the Great Stagflation*. New York: Academic Press.

Blinder, Alan S., (1982), The Anatomy of Double-Digit Inflation in the 1970s, NBER Chapters, in: *Inflation: Causes and Effects*, pp. 261–82, National Bureau of Economic Research, Inc.

Blinder, A. S., Rudd, J. B., (2008), The Supply Shock Explanation of the Great Stagflation Revisited by Alan S. Blinder, Princeton University and Jeremy B. Rudd, Federal Reserve Board, *CEPS Working Paper No. 176*, available online at: https://www.princeton.edu/ceps/workingpapers/176blinder.pdf [Accessed 1 May 2020].

Bordo, M., Haubrich, J., (2004), The Yield Curve, Recession and the Credibility of the Monetary Regime: long run evidence 1875–1997, *Econometric Society 2004 North American Summer Meetings 165*, Econometric Society.

Borio, C., (2012), The Financial Cycle and Macroeconomics: What have we Learnt?, *BIS Working Papers No 395*.

Brătian, V., Bucur, A., Oprean, C., Tănăsescu, C. (2016), Discretionary vs Nondiscretionary in Fiscal Mechanism–Nonautomatic Fiscal Stabilisers vs Automatic Fiscal Stabilisers, *Economic research-Ekonomska istraživanja*, *29*(1), 1–17.

Broner, F. A., Lorenzoni, G., Schmukler, S. L., (2007), Why Do Emerging Economies Borrow Short Term?, *NBER Working Papers 13076, National Bureau of Economic Research*, Inc.

Bullard, James (2020), Expected US Macroeconomic Performance during the Pandemic Adjustment Period, VoxEU.org, 4 April, available at https://voxeu.org/article/expected-us-macroeconomic-performanceduring-pandemic-adjustment-period.

Bullard, J., (2012), Price Level Targeting: The Fed Has It About Right, *Speech 205, Federal Reserve Bank of St. Louis.*

Cakmakyapan, S., Goktas, A., (2013), A Comparison Of Binary Logit And Probit Models With A Simulation Study, *Journal of Social and Economic Statistics*, Bucharest University of Economic Studies, 2(1), pp. 1–17.

Campbell, R. H., (1988), The Real Term Structure and Consumption Growth, *Journal of Financial Economics*, 22(2), pp. 305–333.

Carroll, C. D., (2000), Portfolios of the Rich, *NBER Working Papers 7826, National Bureau of Economic Research*, Inc.

Cauwels, P., Sornette, D., (2012), The Illusion of the Perpetual Money Machine, *Swiss Finance Institute Research Paper Series*, Swiss Finance Institute, pp. 12–40,

Chaurushiya, R., Kuttner, K., (2003), Targeting the Yield Curve: The Experience of the Federal Reserve, pp. 1942–1951, Authorized for public release by the FOMC Secretariat on 04/15/2016.

Christiano, L. J., (2012), Christopher A. Sims and Vector Autoregressions, *Scand. J. of Economics*, 114(4), pp. 1082–1104, doi: 10.1111/j.1467-9442.2012.01737.x

Christiano, L. J., (2017), The Great Recession: A Macroeconomic Earthquake, *Economic Policy Paper 17-01*, Federal Reserve Bank of Minneapolis.

Codirlaşu, A., Moinescu, B., Chidesciuc, A. N., (2010), *Econometrie avansată*, The Academy of Economic Studies, Bucharest.

Cogley, T., Nason, J. M., (1995), Effects of the Hodrick-Prescott Filter on Trend and Difference Stationary Time Series. Implications for business cycle research, *Journal of Economic Dynamics and Control*, 19(1–2), pp. 253–278.

Cogley, T., Sargent, T. J., (2002), Evolving Post-World War II U.S. Inflation Dynamics, in Ben S. Bernanke and Kenneth Rogoff, eds., *NBER Macroeconomics Annual*, vol. 16, pp. 331–373.

Croitoru, L., (2012), *Politica monetara: Ipostaze neconventionale*, Curtea Veche Publising.

Croitoru, L., (2015), *„Stagnareaseculară", „Bulelesalvatoare" şicreştereaeconomicăînRomânia*, Preliminar, Bucureşti.

Cynamon, B. Z., Fazzari., S. M., (2014), Inequality, the Great Recession and Slow Recovery, *Working Papers Series 9, Institute for New Economic Thinking*.

De Grauwe, P., (2010), Booms and Busts: New Keynesian and Behavioral Explanations, *CESifo Working Paper Series 3293.*

Detzer, D., Creel, J., Labondance, F., et al., (2014), Financial Systems in Financial Crisis—An Analysis of Banking Systems in the EU, *Intereconomics*, 49, pp. 56–87, available online at: https://doi.org/10.1007/s10272-014-0489-8 [Accessed 4 April 2020].

Dobrotă, G., Voda, A. D., Dumitrașcu, D. D., (2021), The effects of fiscal policy shocks on the business environment. *Journal of Business Economics and Management, 22*(4), 1084–1103.

Dragoe, S. I., (2016), Inequality Fragility Hypothesis, *Expert Journal of Economics*, Sprint Investify, 4(2), pp. 34–52.

Dragoe, S. I., Oprean-Stan. C., (2018), A New International Monetary System on the Horizon, *Economic Computation and Economic Cybernetics Studies and Research*, 52(1), pp. 89–105.

Dragoe, S. I., Oprean-Stan. C., (2020), Bitcoin, the Mother of all Bubbles or the Future of Money?, *International conference Knowledge-Based Organization*, 26(2), pp. 13–18.

Duesenberry, J. S., (1949), *Income, Saving and the Theory of Consumer Behavior*, Cambridge, MA: Harvard University Press.

Ekstrøm, C. T., (2017), *The R Primer*, 2nd Edition, Chapman & Hall/CRC, The R Series, XVII + 408 pp., ISBN 9781138631977.

Ergungor, O. E., (2004), Market - vs. Bank-based Financial Systems: Do Rights and Regulations Really Matter?, *Journal of Banking and Finance*, 28(12), pp. 2869–2887.

Eschenbach, F., Schuknecht, L., (2002), The Fiscal Costs of Financial Instability Revisited, *Working Paper Series 191*, European Central Bank.

Estrella, A., (2002), Securitization and the Efficacy of Monetary Policy, *FRBNY Economic Policy Review*, 8(1), pp. 243–255.

Estrella, A., Hardouvelis, G. A., (1991), The Term Structure as a Predictor of Real Economic Activity, *The Journal of Finance*, 46(2), pp. 555–576.

Estrella, A., Trubin, M. R., (2006), The Yield Curve as a Leading Indicator: Some Practical Issues, *Current Issues in Economics and Finance*, Federal Reserve Bank of New York.

Feldstein, M. (2015), *The Inflation Puzzle*, Project Syndicate, available at: https://www.project-syndicate.org/commentary/low-inflation-quantitative-easing-by-martin-feldstein-2015-05?barrier=accesspaylog [Accessed 3 July 2020].

Fisher, I., (1933), The Debt-Deflation Theory of Great Depressions, *Econometrica*, 1, pp. 337–357.

Fisher, I., (1936), 100% Money and the Public Debt, *Economic Forum*, Spring Number, April-June, pp. 406–420.

Foresti, P., (2007), Testing for Granger Causality Between Stock Prices and Economic Growth, *MPRA Paper No. 2962*, available online at: http://mpra.ub.uni-muenchen.de/2962/. Accesed on 15th February 2020.

Garbade, K. D., (2014), Direct Purchases of U.S. Treasury Securities by Federal Reserve Banks, *Liberty Street Economics 20140929*, Federal Reserve Bank of New York.

Garber, P., (1989), Tulipmania, *Journal of Political Economy*, 97(3), pp. 535–560.

Garber, P., (2000), *Famous First Bubbles: The Fundamentals of Early Manias*, Cambridge, Mass., MIT Press.

Gerlach, S., Stuart, R., (2018), The Slope of the Term Structure and Recessions: The Pre-Fed Evidence, *CEPR Discussion Paper 13013*, pp. 1857–1913.

Gilchrist, S., Zakrajšek, E., (2012), Credit Spreads and Business Cycle Fluctuations, *American Economic Review*, 102(4), pp. 1692–1720.

Goldstein, D., Taleb, N., (2007), We Don't Quite Know What We Are Talking About, *The Journal of Portfolio Management*, (33), pp. 84–86. 10.3905/jpm.2007.690609.

Granger, C. W. J., (1969), Investigating Causal Relations by Econometric Models and Cross-spectral Methods, *Econometrica*, 37(3), pp. 424–438.

Gurley, J. G., (1961), Review of Milton Friedman, A program for Monetary Stability, Review of Monetary Stability, *Review of Economics Statistics*, 43, pp. 307–308.

Haldane, A. G., (2012), Tails of the Unexpected, Speech given at *The Credit Crisis Five Years On: Unpacking the Crisis*, conference held at the University of Edinburgh Business School.

Haldane, A. G., (2016), *The Dappled World,* GLS Shackle Biennial Memorial Lecture.

Hansen, A. H., (1939), Economic Progress and Declining Population Growth, *The American Economic Review*, 29(1), pp. 1–15.

Harvey, C. R., (1988), The Real Term Structure and Consumption Growth, *Journal of Financial Economics*, 22(2), pp. 305–333.

Hastie, T., Tibshirani, R., Friedman, J., (2009), *The Elements of Statistical Learning: Data Mining, Inference and Prediction*, 2nd Edition. Springer, New York.

Hayek, F. A., (1990), *Denationalisation of Money—The Argument Refined An Analysis of the Theory and Practice of Concurrent Currencies*, The Institute of Economic Affairs, London, pp. 130–131.

Herman, A., Igan, D., Solé, J., (2017), The Macroeconomic Relevance of Bank and Nonbank Credit: An Exploration of U.S. Data, *Journal of Financial Stability, Elsevier*, 32(C), pp. 124–141.

Hicks, John, (1937), Mr. Keynes and the 'Classics': A Suggested Interpretation, *Econometrica*, 5(2), pp. 147–159.

Hirose, Y., Kurozumi, T., Van Zandweghe, W. (2018), *Monetary Policy and Macroeconomic Stability Revisited*, 2018 Meeting Papers 219, Society for Economic Dynamics.

Hodrick, R. J., Prescott, E. C., (1997), Postwar U.S. Business Cycles: An Empirical Investigation, *Journal of Money, Credit and Banking*, 29(1), pp. 1–16, Published by: Blackwell Publishing.

Hodrick, R., Prescott, E. C., (1997), Postwar U.S. Business Cycles: An Empirical Investigation, *Journal of Money, Credit and Banking*, 29(1), pp. 1–16.

Holmes, A., (1969), Operational Constraints on the Stabilization of Money Supply Growth. Federal Reserve Bank of Boston, Controlling monetary aggregates: proceedings of the [1st] Monetary Conference, held at on Nantucket Island, June 8–10, 1969, 1.—Boston, Mass.: Federal Reserve Bank of Boston. - 1969, pp. 65–77

Huerta de Soto, J., (2006), Translated from Spanish by Melinda A. Stroup First English, *Money, Bank Credit and Economic Cycles*, Ludwig von Mises Institute, 518 West Magnolia Avenue, Auburn, Alabama 63832–4528.

IMF (2003), Financial Soundness Indicators—Background Paper, Prepared by the Staff of the Monetary and Financial Systems and Statistics Departments, Approved by Carol S. Carson and Stefan Ingves.

IMF (2006), World Economic Outlook, Globalization and Inflation, Chapter IV. Awash With Cash: Why are Corporate Savings So High?

Isarescu, M. C., (2006), *Reflectii Economice* (In English: *Economic Reflections*), Vol. II, Romanian Academy.

Isarescu, M.C. (2012), Politica monetara postcriza: Reconfigurarea obiectivelor si a instrumentelor, Disertatie cu ocazia decernarii titlului de Doctor Honoris Causa al Universitatii "Andrei Saguna".

Kahn, J. A., (2008), Durable Goods Inventories and the Great Moderation, Staff Reports 325, Federal Reserve Bank of New York.

Kapinos, P., Musatov, A., (2018), Smaller Banks Less Able to Withstand Flattening Yield Curve, *Economic Letter, Federal Reserve Bank of Dallas*, 13(8), pp. 1–4.

Karunaratne, N. D., (2002), Predicting Australian Growth and Recession Via the Yield Curve, *Economic Analysis and Policy*, 32(2), pp. 233–250.

Kawamoto, T., Ozaki, T., Kato, N., Maehashi, K. (2017), *Methodology for Estimating Output Gap and Potential Growth Rate: An Update*, Bank of Japan Research Papers 17-05-31, Bank of Japan.

Keen, S., (2011), A Monetary Minsky Model of the Great Moderation and the Great Recession, *Journal of Economic Behavior & Organization*, doi:10.1016/j.jebo.2011.01.010, p. 15.

Keynes, J. M., (1937), Alternative Theories of the Rate of Interest, *Economic Journal*, 47, pp. 241–252.

Kindleberger, C., Aliber, R., (2005), *Manias, Panics and Crashes: A History of Financial Crises*. Palgrave Macmillan, London.

Kisinbay, T., Baba, C., (2011), Predicting Recessions; A New Approach for Identifying Leading Indicators and Forecast Combinations, *IMF Working Papers 11/235*, International Monetary Fund.

Kregel, J., (2012), Minsky and the Narrow Banking Proposal: No Solution for Financial Reform, *Economics Public Policy Brief Archive No. 125, Levy Economics Institute.*

Krugman, P. R., (1998), It's Baaack: Japan's Slump and the Return of the Liquidity Trap, *Brookings Papers on Economic Activity, Economic Studies Program*, The Brookings Institution, 29(2), pp. 137–206.

Krugman, P., (2009), *The Return of Depression Economics and the Crisis of 2008*, W. W. Norton & Company, Inc. 500 Fifth Avenue, New York, N.Y. 10110.

Krugman, P., R., Eggertsson, G. B., (2011), Debt, Deleveraging and the Liquidity Trap, *Meeting Papers 1166, Society for Economic Dynamics.*

Kumhof, M., Benes, J., (2012), The Chicago Plan Revisited, *IMF Working Papers 12/202*, International Monetary Fund.

Kumhof, M., Ranciere, R., Throckmorton, N. A., Lebarz, C., Richter, A. W., (2012), Income Inequality and Current Account Imbalances, IMF Working Papers 12/8, International Monetary Fund.

Kumhof, M., Ranciere, R., Winant, P., (2013), Inequality, Leverage and Crises; The Case of Endogenous Default, *IMF Working Papers 13/249*, International Monetary Fund.

Kydland, F. E., Prescott, E. C., (1990), Business Cycles: Real Facts and a Monetary Myth, *Quarterly Review, Federal Reserve Bank of Minneapolis*, 14, pp. 3–18.

Leijonhufvud, A., (1973), Effective Demand Failures, *The Swedish Journal of Economics*, 75(1), pp. 27–48.

Loisel, O., *Course on Monetary Economics*, ENSAE Paris, Chapter 7: Quantitative vs. credit easing, 2019, available online at: http://olivierloisel.com/monetary_economics/Chapter%207.pdf [Accessed 05 June 2020].

Lown, C. S., Morgan., D. P., Rohatgi, S., (2000), Listening to Loan Officers: The Impact of Commercial Credit Standards on Lending and Output, *Economic Policy Review*, Federal Reserve Bank of New York, pp. 1–16.

Mackay, C., (1841), Memoirs of Extraordinary Popular Delusions and the Madness of Crowds, *London: Richard Bentley.*

McConnell, J., Buser, S., (2011), The Origins and Evolution of the Market for Mortgage-Backed, *Annual Review of Financial Economics*, 3, pp. 173–192.

McFadden, D., (1977), Quantitative Methods for Analyzing Travel Behaviour of Individuals: Some Recent Developments, *Cowles Foundation for Research in Economics*, Cowles Foundation Discussion Papers 474, Yale University.

Meng, H., Zhou, W.-X., Sornette, D., (2014), *Symmetric Thermal Optimal Path and Time-Dependent Lead-Lag Relationship: Novel Statistical Tests and Application to UK and US Real-Estate and Monetary Policies*, Swiss Finance Institute Research Paper Series 14–57, Swiss Finance Institute, revised Nov 2014.

Minsky, H. P., (1980), Ph. D. – *Finance and Profits: The Changing Nature of American Business Cycles*, Hyman P. Minsky Archive 258, available online at: https://digitalcommons.bard.edu/hm_archive/258 [Accessed 20 January 2020].

Minsky, H. P., (1982), *Can "it" Happen Again?: Essays on Instability and Finance*, M.E. Sharpe, Armonk, N.Y.

Minsky, H. P., (1993), On the Non-Neutrality of Money, *FRBNY Quarterly Review (Spring)*, 18, pp. 77–82.

Minsky, H. P., (2011), *Cum stabilizăm o economieinstabilă*, Bucureşti, Editura Publica.

Minsky, H. P., (2016), *Can It Happen Again?: Essays on Instability and Finance*, Routledge.

Mishkin, F., (2018), *Financial Markets and Institutions*, 9th Edition, Columbia University. Stanley Eakins, East Carolina University.

Mishkin, F., (2019), *Economics of Money, Banking and Financial Markets*, 12th Edition, The Pearson Series in Economics, Columbia University.

Moisa, A., Necula, C., Bobeica, G., (2010), Estimating Potential GDP for the Romanian Economy. An Eclectic Approach, *Journal for Economic Forecasting*, Institute for Economic Forecasting, 0(3), pp. 5–25.

Navajas, M. C., Thegeya, A., (2013), Financial Soundness Indicators and Banking Crises, *IMF Working Paper*, WP/13/263.

Obstfeld, M., (2019), Worrying Implications of "Libra" for the International Monetary System, *Conference on "The Future of the international Monetary System"*, Banque Centrale du Luxembourg.

Obstfeld, M., Taylor, A. M., (2003), Globalization and Capital Markets, in Michael Bordo, Alan M. Taylor and Jeffrey Williamson, eds., *Globalization in Historical Perspective*, Chicago, University of Chicago Press, pp. 121–190.

Officer, Lawrence H., (2008), What Was the Interest Rate Then? A Data Study. MeasuringWorth.com, 109 pp. URL: http://www.measuringworth.org/interestrates/intstudy.pdf [Accessed March 23 2020].

Piketty, T., (2014), *Capital in the Twenty-First Century*, translated by Arthur Goldhammer, The Belknap Press of Harvard University Press Cambridge, Massachusetts London, England.

Potter, C. W., (2001), A History of Influenza, *Journal of Applied Microbiology*, 91, pp. 572–579.

Pozsar, Z., Tobias, A., Ashcraft, A. B., Boesky, H., (2010), Shadow banking, *Staff Reports 458*, Federal Reserve Bank of New York.

Rajan, Raghuram G., Zingales, L., (2001), The Influence of the Financial Revolution on the Nature of Firms, NBER Working Papers 8177, National Bureau of Economic Research, Inc.

Ravn, M. O., Uhlig, H., (2002), On Adjusting the Hodrick-Prescott Filter for the Frequency of Observations, *The Review of Economics and Statistics*, MIT Press, 84(2), pp. 371–375.

Ravn, M. O., Uhlig, H., (2002), On Adjusting the Hodrick-Prescott Filter for the Frequency of Observations, *MIT Press Journals, Review of Economics and Statistics*, 84(2), pp. 371–376.

Reinhart, C. M., Rogoff, K. S., (2009), *This Time is Different: Eight Centuries of Financial Folly*. Princeton University Press, Princeton.

Ryan-Collins, J., Werner, R. A., Castle, J., (2016), A Half-Century Diversion of Monetary Policy? An Empirical Horse-Race to Identify the UK Variable most Likely to Deliver the Desired Nominal GDP Growth Rate, *Journal of International Financial Markets, Institutions and Money*, 43(C), 158–176.

Schularick, M., Taylor, A. M., (2009), Credit Booms Gone Bust: Monetary Policy, Leverage Cycles and Financial Crises, *1870–2008 Working Paper 15512*, available online at: http://www.nber.org/papers/w15512 [Accessed 2 April 2020], National Bureau of Economic Research, 1050 Massachusetts Avenue Cambridge, MA 02138.

Sigurjónsson, F. (2015), *Monetary Reform – A Better Monetary System for Iceland*, available at: https://www.stjornarradid.is/media/forsaetisraduneyti-media/media/skyrslur/monetary-reform.pdf [Accessed 5 May 2020].

Sims, C. A. (1972), Money, Income, and Causality, *The American Economic Review*, 62(4), 540–552.

Sims, C. A. (1980a), Comparison of Interwar and Postwar Business Cycles: Monetarism Reconsidered, *American Economic Review*, 70, 250–57.

Sims, C. A. (1980b), Macroeconomics and Reality, *Econometrica*, 48, 1–48.

Sims, C. A., (2009), Inflation Expectations, Uncertainty and Monetary Policy, *BIS Working Papers No 275,* Monetary and Economic Department.

Solow, R. M., (1957), Technical Change and the Aggregate Production Function, *The Review of Economics and Statistics*, 39(3), pp. 312–320.

Spitznagel, M., (2012), How the Fed Favors The 1%, *The Wall Street Journal of Editorial*, available online at: https://www.wsj.com/articles/SB10001424052702304356604577343430113336486 [Accessed 1 August 2020].

Stadler, G. W., (1994), Real Business Cycles, *Journal of Economic Literature, American Economic Association*, 32(4), pp. 1750–1783.

Stevanović, S., Milenković, I., (2020), Comparative Analysis of the Implementation of the Inflation Targeting Monetary Strategy in Canada and New Zealand. *Economic Themes*, 58(3), 401–414.

Stock, J. H., Watson, M. W., (2007), Why Has U.S. Inflation Become Harder to Forecast?, *Journal of Money, Credit and Banking*, 39(S1), pp. 4–33.

Summers, L., (2013), IMF Fourteenth Annual Research Conference in Honor of Stanley Fischer, Washington, DC, available online at: http://larrysummers.com/imf-fourteenth-annual-research-conference-in-honor-of-stanley-fischer/ [Accessed 25 July 2020].

Sungki, H., (2019), Do Yield Curve Inversions Predict Recessions in Other Countries?, *Federal Reserve Bank of St. Louis*, available online at: https://www.stlouisfed.org/on-the-economy/2019/august/yield-curve-inversions-predict-recessions-other-countries [Accessed 30 July 2020].

Taleb, N. N., (2015), How to (Not) Estimate Gini Coefficients for Fat Tailed Variables, *Tail Risk Working Paper Series*, available online at: https://arxiv.org/pdf/1510.04841.pdf [Accessed 20 June 2020].

Taleb, N. N., Blyth, M., (2011), The Black Swan of Cairo: How Suppressing Volatility Makes the World Less Predictable and More Dangerous, *Foreign Affairs*, 90(3), pp. 33–39.

Taylor, J. B., (2009), The Financial Crisis and the Policy Responses: An Empirical Analysis of What Went Wrong, *NBER Working Papers 14631, National Bureau of Economic Research, Inc., A Journal of Politics and Society*, 21(2–3), pp. 1–30.

Tănăsescu, C., Bucur, A., Oprean-Stan, C., (2016), An Approach on the Modelling of Long Economic Cycles in the Context of Sustainable Development. *Revista Economica*, 68(4), pp. 177–190.

Tănăsescu, C. R., Oprean, C., (2016), Designing Fiscal Policy during Turbulent Times: From Proximate Genus to Specific Differencia. In *Managing Innovation and Diversity in Knowledge Society Through Turbulent Time: Proceedings of the MakeLearn and TIIM Joint International Conference 2016* (pp. 695–695). ToKnowPress.

Testimony of Chairman Alan Greenspan, (2005), Federal Reserve Board's Semiannual Monetary Policy Report to the Congress, Before the Committee on Banking, Housing and Urban Affairs, U.S. Senate, available at: https://www.federalreserve.gov/boarddocs/hh/2005/february/testimony.htm.

The Great Lockdown, International Monetary Fund, (April 2020), World Economic Outlook.

Tibshirani, R., (1996), Regression Shrinkage and Selection via the Lasso, *Journal of the Royal Statistical Society, Series B (Methodological)*, pp. 267–288.

Triffin, R., (1959), Statement in Employment, Growth and Price Levels, *Hearings before the Joint Economic Committee, Congress of the United States, 86th Congress, First Session, Part 9A*, pp. 2905–2954.

Turner, A. (2014), *Wealth, Debt, Inequality and Low Interest Rates: Four Big Trends and Some Implications*, Institute for Economic Thinking, Cass Business School

Unger, R., (2016), Traditional Banks, Shadow Banks and the US Credit Boom: Credit Origination versus Financing, *Discussion Papers 11/2016, Deutsche Bundesbank.*

Veblen, T., (1909), The Limitations of Marginal Utility, *Journal of Political Economy*, 17, pp. 620–636.

Vodă, A. D., Dobrotă, G., Cristea, L. A., (2020), Procyclical, Countercyclical and Acyclical Fiscal Policies. *Annals Economic Sciences Series*, XX(2), 1101.

Werner, R. A., (1997), Towards a New Monetary Paradigm: A Quantity Theorem of Disaggregated Credit, with Evidence from Japan, *Kredit und Kapital, Duncker and Humblot*, Berlin, 30(2), pp. 276–309.

Werner, R. A., (2016), A Lost Century in Economics: Three Theories of Banking and the Conclusive Evidence, *International Review of Financial Analysis, Elsevier*, 46(C), pp. 361–379.

Werner, R. A., Voutsinas, K., (2011), Credit Supply and Corporate Capital Structure: Evidence from Japan, *International Review of Financial Analysis*, 20(5), pp. 320–334.

Wessel, D., (2018), Alternatives to the Fed's 2 Percent Inflation Target, Rethinking the Fed's 2 Percent Inflation Target, *A Report from Hutchins Center on Fiscal & Monetary Policy at Brookings.*

## Electronic Sources

1. http://data.worldbank.org/indicator
2. http://www.econ.yale.edu/~shiller/data.htm
3. http://www.eviews.com/help/helpintro.html#page/content/Regress2-Stepwise_Least_Squares_Regression.html
4. http://www.imf.org/external/np/exr/facts/sdr.htm
5. https://apps.bea.gov/iTable/iTable.cfm?reqid=19&step=2#reqid=19&step=2&isuri=1&1921=survey
6. https://data.nber.org/databases/macrohistory/contents/
7. https://fred.stlouisfed.org/
8. https://www.businesscycle.com/ecri-business-cycles/international-business-cycle-dates-chronologies
9. https://www.federalreservehistory.org/essays/great_moderation#defining, accessed 14 September 2019
10. https://www.imf.org/external/datamapper/datasets/GDD
11. https://www.nber.org/cycles.html
12. https://www.quandl.com/
13. https://www.quandl.com/

# Appendixes

Date: 06/29/19 Time: 11:56
Sample: 1959Q1 2019Q1
Included observations: 241
Correlations are asymptotically consistent approximations

| CYCLE_M0,CYCLE_RGDP(-i) | CYCLE_M0,CYCLE_RGDP(+i) | i | lag | lead |
|---|---|---|---|---|
| | | 0 | -0.2099 | -0.2099 |
| | | 1 | -0.2062 | -0.1572 |
| | | 2 | -0.1745 | -0.0721 |
| | | 3 | -0.1406 | 0.0070 |
| | | 4 | -0.0937 | 0.0608 |
| | | 5 | -0.0412 | 0.0774 |
| | | 6 | -0.0051 | 0.0824 |

**Appendix 1.** M0 and Real GDP

Source: Authors' computations.

Date: 06/29/19 Time: 11:59
Sample: 1959Q1 2019Q1
Included observations: 241
Correlations are asymptotically consistent approximations

| CYCLE_M1,CYCLE_RGDP(-i) | CYCLE_M1,CYCLE_RGDP(+i) | i | lag | lead |
|---|---|---|---|---|
| | | 0 | 0.0482 | 0.0482 |
| | | 1 | -0.0223 | 0.1201 |
| | | 2 | -0.0771 | 0.1675 |
| | | 3 | -0.1113 | 0.1807 |
| | | 4 | -0.1261 | 0.1880 |
| | | 5 | -0.1354 | 0.1695 |
| | | 6 | -0.1558 | 0.1537 |

**Appendix 2.** M1 and Real GDP

Source: Authors' computations.

Date: 06/29/19 Time: 12:00
Sample: 1959Q1 2019Q1
Included observations: 241
Correlations are asymptotically consistent approximations

| CYCLE_M2,CYCLE_RGDP(-i) | CYCLE_M2,CYCLE_RGDP(+i) | i | lag | lead |
|---|---|---|---|---|
| | | 0 | 0.2069 | 0.2069 |
| | | 1 | 0.0842 | 0.3164 |
| | | 2 | -0.0059 | 0.3684 |
| | | 3 | -0.0741 | 0.3651 |
| | | 4 | -0.1390 | 0.3290 |
| | | 5 | -0.1784 | 0.2602 |
| | | 6 | -0.1995 | 0.1887 |

**Appendix 3.** M2 and Real GDP

Source: Authors' computations.

Date: 06/29/19 Time: 12:05
Sample: 1959Q1 2019Q1
Included observations: 241
Correlations are asymptotically consistent approximations

| CYCLE_M2_M1,CYCLE_RGDP(-i) | CYCLE_M2_M1,CYCLE_RGDP(+i) | i | lag | lead |
|---|---|---|---|---|
| | | 0 | 0.1641 | 0.1641 |
| | | 1 | 0.0724 | 0.2465 |
| | | 2 | 0.0057 | 0.2863 |
| | | 3 | -0.0468 | 0.2879 |
| | | 4 | -0.1024 | 0.2585 |
| | | 5 | -0.1356 | 0.2071 |
| | | 6 | -0.1453 | 0.1481 |

**Appendix 4.** M2-M1 and Real GDP

Source: Authors' computations.

VAR Lag Order Selection Criteria
Endogenous variables: DL_M0 DL_M2_CURRENCY DL_M2_M1
Exogenous variables: C
Date: 06/29/19 Time: 18:09
Sample: 1959M01 2019M05
Included observations: 688

| Lag | LogL | LR | FPE | AIC | SC | HQ |
|---|---|---|---|---|---|---|
| 0 | 7172.023 | NA | 1.79e-13 | -20.84018 | -20.82041 | -20.83253 |
| 1 | 7373.120 | 399.8548 | 1.02e-13 | -21.39860 | -21.31953 | -21.36801 |
| 2 | 7452.378 | 156.9047 | 8.33e-14 | -21.60284 | -21.46446 | -21.54931 |
| 3 | 7505.440 | 104.5815 | 7.33e-14 | -21.73093 | -21.53324 | -21.65445 |
| 4 | 7514.097 | 16.98707 | 7.33e-14 | -21.72993 | -21.47293 | -21.63051 |
| 5 | 7539.535 | 49.69246 | 6.99e-14 | -21.77772 | -21.46141 | -21.65535 |
| 6 | 7548.504 | 17.44259 | 6.99e-14 | -21.77763 | -21.40201 | -21.63231 |
| 7 | 7585.048 | 70.74992 | 6.46e-14 | -21.85770 | -21.42277 | -21.68944 |
| 8 | 7614.771 | 57.28621 | 6.08e-14 | -21.91794 | -21.42370 | -21.72673 |
| 9 | 7646.200 | 60.29953 | 5.69e-14 | -21.98314 | -21.42959 | -21.76899 |
| 10 | 7667.056 | 39.83397 | 5.50e-14 | -22.01761 | -21.40475 | -21.78051 |
| 11 | 7714.174 | 89.57855 | 4.93e-14 | -22.12841 | -21.45625 | -21.86838 |
| 12 | 8051.240 | 637.8772 | 1.90e-14 | -23.08209 | -22.35062 | -22.79911 |
| 13 | 8094.832 | 82.11522 | 1.72e-14 | -23.18265 | -22.39187* | -22.87673* |
| 14 | 8111.533 | 31.31508 | 1.68e-14 | -23.20504 | -22.35495 | -22.87617 |
| 15 | 8123.143 | 21.66768 | 1.67e-14 | -23.21263 | -22.30323 | -22.86081 |
| 16 | 8136.982 | 25.70629 | 1.64e-14 | -23.22669 | -22.25799 | -22.85193 |
| 17 | 8145.163 | 15.12565 | 1.65e-14 | -23.22431 | -22.19630 | -22.82661 |
| 18 | 8152.400 | 13.31651 | 1.66e-14 | -23.21919 | -22.13187 | -22.79854 |
| 19 | 8159.493 | 12.99034 | 1.67e-14 | -23.21364 | -22.06702 | -22.77005 |
| 20 | 8165.744 | 11.39246 | 1.68e-14 | -23.20565 | -21.99972 | -22.73911 |
| 21 | 8181.007 | 27.68614 | 1.65e-14 | -23.22386 | -21.95861 | -22.73438 |
| 22 | 8189.195 | 14.78296 | 1.65e-14 | -23.22150 | -21.89695 | -22.70907 |
| 23 | 8200.911 | 21.04661 | 1.64e-14 | -23.22939 | -21.84553 | -22.69402 |
| 24 | 8233.683 | 58.59016 | 1.53e-14 | -23.29850 | -21.85533 | -22.74018 |
| 25 | 8243.793 | 17.98599 | 1.53e-14 | -23.30172 | -21.79925 | -22.72046 |
| 26 | 8264.163 | 36.06277 | 1.48e-14 | -23.33478 | -21.77299 | -22.73057 |
| 27 | 8275.267 | 19.56128 | 1.47e-14 | -23.34089 | -21.71980 | -22.71375 |
| 28 | 8277.394 | 3.727950 | 1.50e-14 | -23.32091 | -21.64051 | -22.67082 |
| 29 | 8291.190 | 24.06291 | 1.48e-14 | -23.33486 | -21.59515 | -22.66182 |
| 30 | 8298.065 | 11.93152 | 1.49e-14 | -23.32868 | -21.52966 | -22.63270 |
| 31 | 8312.844 | 25.51823 | 1.47e-14 | -23.34548 | -21.48715 | -22.62655 |
| 32 | 8319.431 | 11.31805 | 1.48e-14 | -23.33846 | -21.42083 | -22.59659 |
| 33 | 8325.073 | 9.643868 | 1.49e-14 | -23.32870 | -21.35176 | -22.56389 |
| 34 | 8332.750 | 13.05449 | 1.50e-14 | -23.32485 | -21.28860 | -22.53710 |
| 35 | 8340.399 | 12.94152 | 1.51e-14 | -23.32093 | -21.22537 | -22.51022 |
| 36 | 8382.463 | 70.79949* | 1.37e-14* | -23.41704* | -21.26218 | -22.58340 |

* indicates lag order selected by the criterion
LR: sequential modified LR test statistic (each test at 5% level)
FPE: Final prediction error
AIC: Akaike information criterion
SC: Schwarz information criterion
HQ: Hannan-Quinn information criterion

**Appendix 5.** Lag Order Selection

Source: Authors' computations.

VAR Lag Order Selection Criteria
Endogenous variables: DL_M2_CURRENCY DL_BANK_CREDIT DL_LENDABLE_RESERVES
Exogenous variables: C
Date: 06/29/19 Time: 17:26
Sample: 1959M01 2019M05
Included observations: 688

| Lag | LogL | LR | FPE | AIC | SC | HQ |
|---|---|---|---|---|---|---|
| 0 | 5763.067 | NA | 1.07e-11 | -16.74438 | -16.72461 | -16.73673 |
| 1 | 5864.589 | 201.8626 | 8.20e-12 | -17.01334 | -16.93426 | -16.98275 |
| 2 | 5894.695 | 59.59945 | 7.71e-12 | -17.07469 | -16.93631 | -17.02116 |
| 3 | 5985.590 | 179.1490 | 6.08e-12 | -17.31276 | -17.11507 | -17.23628 |
| 4 | 6003.757 | 35.64657 | 5.92e-12 | -17.33941 | -17.08241 | -17.23998 |
| 5 | 6033.679 | 58.45276 | 5.57e-12 | -17.40023 | -17.08392 | -17.27786 |
| 6 | 6059.078 | 49.39432 | 5.31e-12 | -17.44790 | -17.07228 | -17.30259 |
| 7 | 6075.414 | 31.62851 | 5.20e-12 | -17.46923 | -17.03430 | -17.30097 |
| 8 | 6103.101 | 53.36121 | 4.92e-12 | -17.52355 | -17.02931 | -17.33235 |
| 9 | 6133.488 | 58.30137 | 4.63e-12 | -17.58572 | -17.03218 | -17.37157 |
| 10 | 6154.436 | 40.00840 | 4.47e-12 | -17.62045 | -17.00760 | -17.38336 |
| 11 | 6165.564 | 21.15541 | 4.44e-12 | -17.62664 | -16.95448 | -17.36660 |
| 12 | 6331.499 | 314.0232 | 2.81e-12 | -18.08285 | -17.35138 | -17.79987 |
| 13 | 6389.357 | 108.9884 | 2.44e-12 | -18.22488 | -17.43410* | -17.91895* |
| 14 | 6400.485 | 20.86367 | 2.43e-12 | -18.23106 | -17.38097 | -17.90219 |
| 15 | 6408.662 | 15.26047 | 2.43e-12 | -18.22867 | -17.31927 | -17.87685 |
| 16 | 6424.732 | 29.85180 | 2.38e-12 | -18.24922 | -17.28052 | -17.87446 |
| 17 | 6451.049 | 48.65648 | 2.27e-12 | -18.29956 | -17.27155 | -17.90186 |
| 18 | 6468.510 | 32.12983 | 2.21e-12 | -18.32416 | -17.23684 | -17.90351 |
| 19 | 6474.383 | 10.75522 | 2.23e-12 | -18.31507 | -17.16844 | -17.87147 |
| 20 | 6492.136 | 32.35890 | 2.18e-12 | -18.34051 | -17.13458 | -17.87398 |
| 21 | 6496.284 | 7.522678 | 2.21e-12 | -18.32641 | -17.06116 | -17.83692 |
| 22 | 6500.527 | 7.660506 | 2.24e-12 | -18.31258 | -16.98803 | -17.80015 |
| 23 | 6511.647 | 19.97660 | 2.23e-12 | -18.31874 | -16.93488 | -17.78337 |
| 24 | 6531.872 | 36.15781 | 2.16e-12 | -18.35137 | -16.90820 | -17.79306 |
| 25 | 6549.390 | 31.16577 | 2.10e-12* | -18.37613* | -16.87366 | -17.79487 |
| 26 | 6553.055 | 6.488580 | 2.14e-12 | -18.36062 | -16.79884 | -17.75642 |
| 27 | 6556.627 | 6.293717 | 2.17e-12 | -18.34485 | -16.72375 | -17.71770 |
| 28 | 6563.158 | 11.44684 | 2.19e-12 | -18.33767 | -16.65727 | -17.68758 |
| 29 | 6571.624 | 14.76728 | 2.19e-12 | -18.33612 | -16.59641 | -17.66308 |
| 30 | 6574.960 | 5.790026 | 2.23e-12 | -18.31965 | -16.52063 | -17.62367 |
| 31 | 6581.422 | 11.15731 | 2.25e-12 | -18.31227 | -16.45395 | -17.59335 |
| 32 | 6590.984 | 16.42864 | 2.25e-12 | -18.31391 | -16.39627 | -17.57204 |
| 33 | 6596.413 | 9.278250 | 2.27e-12 | -18.30352 | -16.32658 | -17.53871 |
| 34 | 6608.826 | 21.11068 | 2.25e-12 | -18.31345 | -16.27720 | -17.52569 |
| 35 | 6612.595 | 6.376467 | 2.29e-12 | -18.29824 | -16.20268 | -17.48754 |
| 36 | 6634.672 | 37.15799* | 2.20e-12 | -18.33626 | -16.18139 | -17.50261 |

* indicates lag order selected by the criterion
LR: sequential modified LR test statistic (each test at 5% level)
FPE: Final prediction error
AIC: Akaike information criterion
SC: Schwarz information criterion
HQ: Hannan-Quinn information criterion

**Appendix 6.** Criteria for VAR Lag Order

Source: Authors' computations.

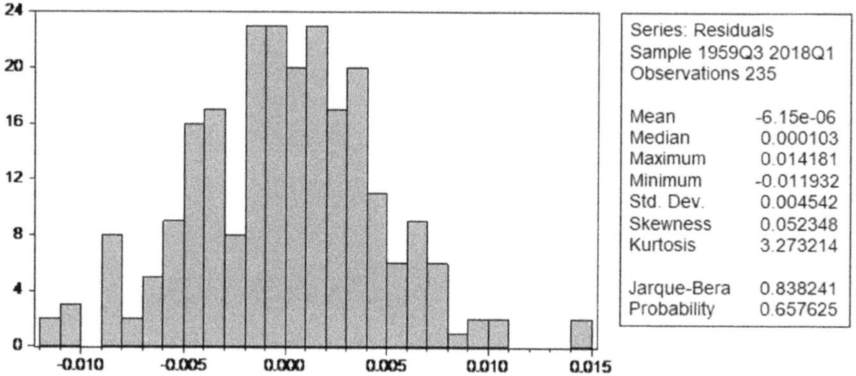


**Appendix 7.** Jarque–Bera Test

Source: Authors' computations.

Date: 08/14/21 Time: 14:32
Sample: 1959Q1 2019Q1
Included observations: 236

| Autocorrelation | Partial Correlation | | AC | PAC | Q-Stat | Prob |
|---|---|---|---|---|---|---|
| | | 1 | 0.316 | 0.316 | 23.825 | 0.000 |
| | | 2 | 0.247 | 0.163 | 38.414 | 0.000 |
| | | 3 | 0.122 | 0.006 | 42.002 | 0.000 |
| | | 4 | 0.101 | 0.031 | 44.493 | 0.000 |
| | | 5 | -0.022 | -0.088 | 44.610 | 0.000 |
| | | 6 | -0.004 | -0.001 | 44.614 | 0.000 |
| | | 7 | -0.043 | -0.028 | 45.062 | 0.000 |
| | | 8 | -0.039 | -0.017 | 45.441 | 0.000 |
| | | 9 | 0.050 | 0.100 | 46.065 | 0.000 |
| | | 10 | 0.056 | 0.036 | 46.849 | 0.000 |
| | | 11 | 0.023 | -0.023 | 46.985 | 0.000 |
| | | 12 | -0.084 | -0.130 | 48.772 | 0.000 |
| | | 13 | -0.052 | -0.025 | 49.442 | 0.000 |
| | | 14 | -0.043 | 0.018 | 49.913 | 0.000 |
| | | 15 | -0.074 | -0.042 | 51.323 | 0.000 |
| | | 16 | 0.072 | 0.159 | 52.660 | 0.000 |

**Appendix 8.** Autocorrelation of Real GDP (logarithm and first difference applied)

Source: Authors' computations.

| Private depository credit for GDP circulation | Unique Identifier | Seasonally Adjusted |
|---|---|---|
| Private depository institutions; open market paper; asset | Z1/Z1/FL703069175.Q | No, it has values of 0 |
| Private depository institutions; Treasury securities; asset | Z1/Z1/FL703061105.Q | TRAMO-Seats |
| Private depository institutions; agency- and GSE-backed securities; asset | Z1/Z1/FL703061705.Q | TRAMO-Seats |
| Private depository institutions; municipal securities; asset | Z1/Z1/FL703062005.Q | TRAMO-Seats |
| Private depository institutions; depository institution loans n.e.c.; asset | Z1/Z1/FL703068005.Q | TRAMO-Seats |
| Private depository institutions; other loans and advances; asset | Z1/Z1/FL703069005.Q | TRAMO-Seats |
| Private depository institutions; consumer credit; asset | Z1/Z1/FL703066005.Q | TRAMO-Seats |

**Appendix 9.** Private depository credit for GDP circulation components

Source: FRB–Z.1

| Domestic credit to NF sector GNE velocity | Unique Identifier | Seasonally Adjusted |
|---|---|---|
| Nonfinancial business; debt securities and loans; liability | Z1/Z1/LA144104005.Q | Yes |
| State and local governments, excluding employee retirement funds; debt securities | Z1/Z1/LA154104005.Q | Yes |
| Federal government; debt securities and loans; liability | Z1/Z1/LA314104005.Q | Yes |
| Consumer Credit | Z1/Z1/FL703066005.Q | TRAMO-Seats |

**Appendix 10.** Domestic nonfinancial sectors GDP circulation velocity components

Source: FRB–Z.1.

Date: 09/08/19 Time: 15:36
Sample: 1959Q1 2019Q1
Included observations: 240

Autocorrelation | Partial Correlation

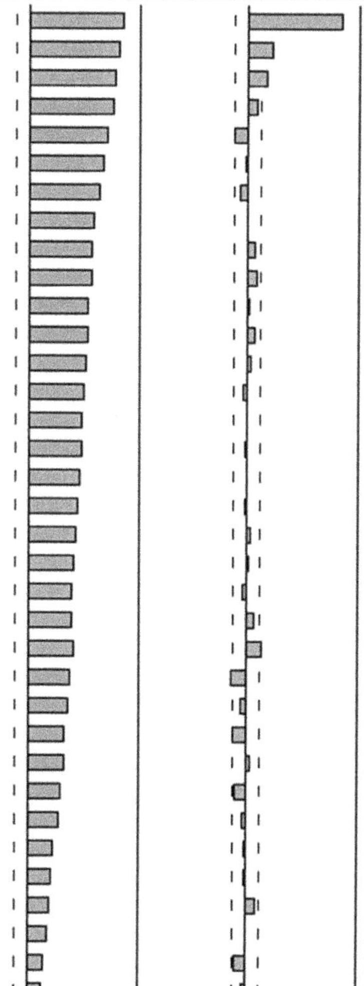

| | AC | PAC | Q-Stat | Prob |
|---|---|---|---|---|
| 1 | 0.889 | 0.889 | 192.18 | 0.000 |
| 2 | 0.842 | 0.243 | 365.03 | 0.000 |
| 3 | 0.818 | 0.181 | 529.09 | 0.000 |
| 4 | 0.795 | 0.091 | 684.60 | 0.000 |
| 5 | 0.739 | -0.122 | 819.60 | 0.000 |
| 6 | 0.702 | -0.009 | 941.96 | 0.000 |
| 7 | 0.657 | -0.078 | 1049.5 | 0.000 |
| 8 | 0.622 | 0.007 | 1146.5 | 0.000 |
| 9 | 0.599 | 0.077 | 1236.7 | 0.000 |
| 10 | 0.584 | 0.086 | 1322.9 | 0.000 |
| 11 | 0.558 | 0.019 | 1402.0 | 0.000 |
| 12 | 0.550 | 0.075 | 1479.1 | 0.000 |
| 13 | 0.542 | 0.031 | 1554.4 | 0.000 |
| 14 | 0.524 | -0.041 | 1625.0 | 0.000 |
| 15 | 0.510 | -0.005 | 1692.2 | 0.000 |
| 16 | 0.498 | -0.021 | 1756.5 | 0.000 |
| 17 | 0.485 | 0.006 | 1817.8 | 0.000 |
| 18 | 0.466 | -0.017 | 1874.6 | 0.000 |
| 19 | 0.456 | 0.034 | 1929.1 | 0.000 |
| 20 | 0.441 | 0.011 | 1980.5 | 0.000 |
| 21 | 0.419 | -0.033 | 2027.1 | 0.000 |
| 22 | 0.418 | 0.080 | 2073.7 | 0.000 |
| 23 | 0.433 | 0.132 | 2124.0 | 0.000 |
| 24 | 0.400 | -0.144 | 2167.1 | 0.000 |
| 25 | 0.378 | -0.061 | 2205.7 | 0.000 |
| 26 | 0.351 | -0.134 | 2239.1 | 0.000 |
| 27 | 0.348 | 0.040 | 2272.1 | 0.000 |
| 28 | 0.307 | -0.109 | 2298.0 | 0.000 |
| 29 | 0.279 | -0.025 | 2319.4 | 0.000 |
| 30 | 0.244 | -0.024 | 2335.9 | 0.000 |
| 31 | 0.216 | -0.012 | 2348.9 | 0.000 |
| 32 | 0.203 | 0.088 | 2360.4 | 0.000 |
| 33 | 0.187 | 0.005 | 2370.2 | 0.000 |
| 34 | 0.145 | -0.108 | 2376.2 | 0.000 |
| 35 | 0.126 | -0.038 | 2380.7 | 0.000 |

**Appendix 11.** GDP Deflator Autocorrelation

Source: Authors' computations.

Date: 08/15/20 Time: 20:41
Sample: 1949Q1 2019Q3
Included observations: 283

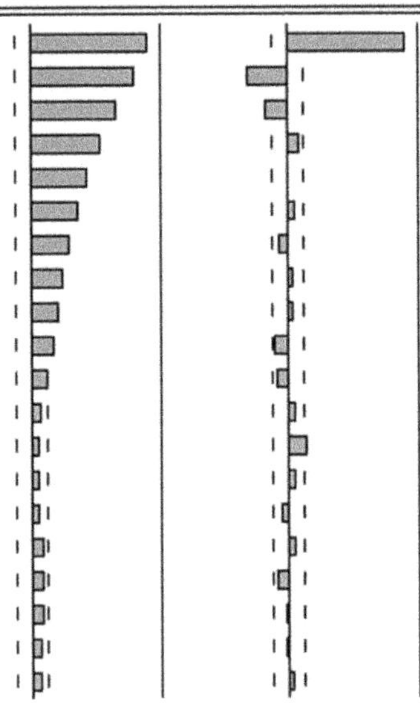


| | AC | PAC | Q-Stat | Prob |
|---|---|---|---|---|
| 1 | 0.931 | 0.931 | 247.67 | 0.000 |
| 2 | 0.821 | -0.335 | 441.17 | 0.000 |
| 3 | 0.688 | -0.172 | 577.44 | 0.000 |
| 4 | 0.565 | 0.086 | 669.74 | 0.000 |
| 5 | 0.457 | 0.007 | 730.43 | 0.000 |
| 6 | 0.377 | 0.065 | 771.72 | 0.000 |
| 7 | 0.307 | -0.074 | 799.25 | 0.000 |
| 8 | 0.255 | 0.036 | 818.25 | 0.000 |
| 9 | 0.215 | 0.031 | 831.81 | 0.000 |
| 10 | 0.174 | -0.101 | 840.78 | 0.000 |
| 11 | 0.126 | -0.083 | 845.47 | 0.000 |
| 12 | 0.081 | 0.046 | 847.42 | 0.000 |
| 13 | 0.056 | 0.154 | 848.35 | 0.000 |
| 14 | 0.053 | 0.061 | 849.20 | 0.000 |
| 15 | 0.063 | -0.053 | 850.40 | 0.000 |
| 16 | 0.084 | 0.046 | 852.51 | 0.000 |
| 17 | 0.092 | -0.093 | 855.09 | 0.000 |
| 18 | 0.093 | -0.011 | 857.69 | 0.000 |
| 19 | 0.081 | -0.025 | 859.71 | 0.000 |
| 20 | 0.067 | 0.033 | 861.10 | 0.000 |

**Appendix 12.** Autocorrelation of Output Gap/Real Potential GDP

Source: Authors' computations.

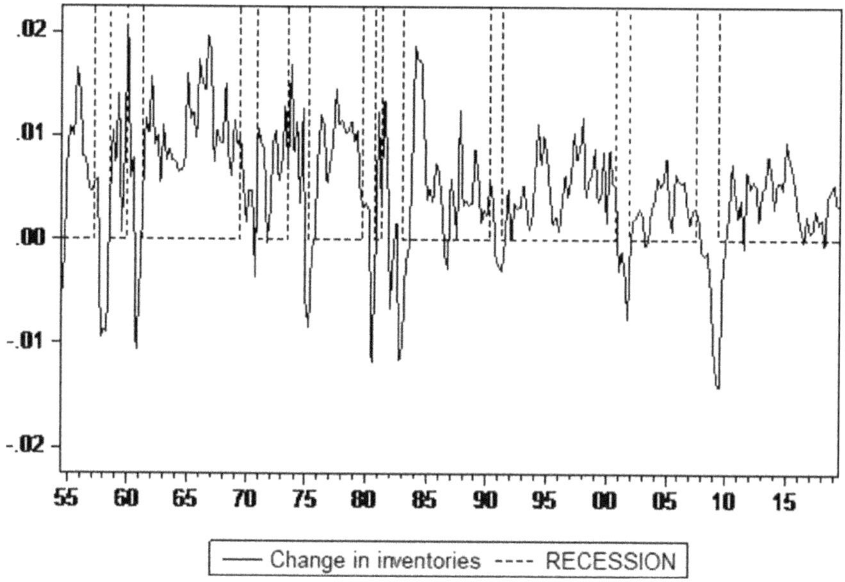


**Appendix 13.** Negative changes in Inventories and recessions
Source: Authors' computations; data from St. Louis Fed.

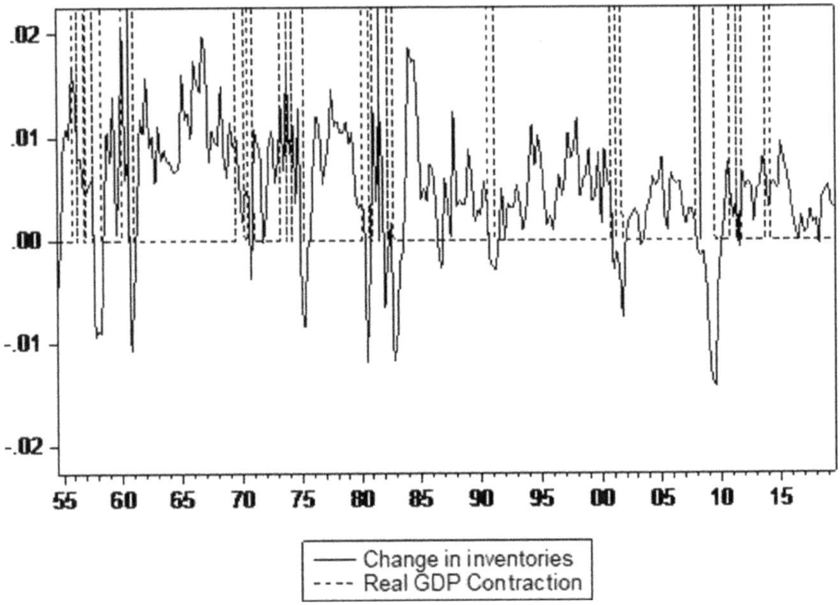


**Appendix 14.** Negative changes in Inventories and Real GDP contractions

Source: Authors' computations, data from St. Louis Fed.

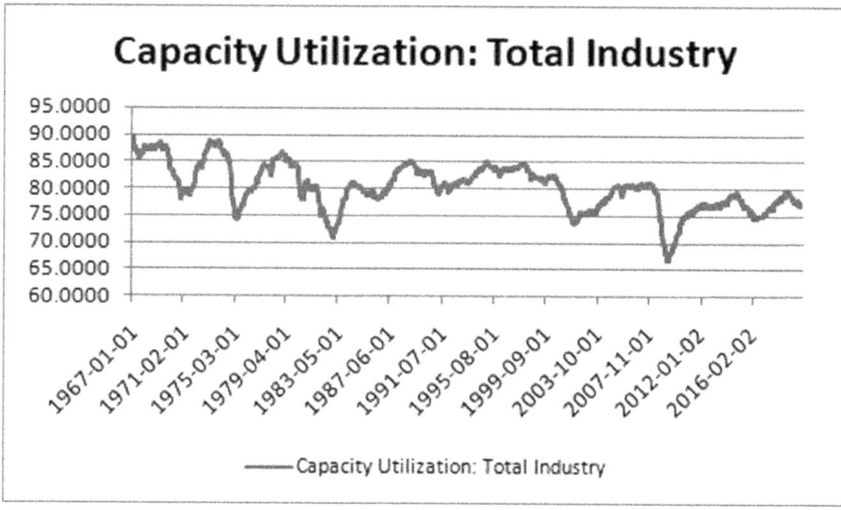


**Appendix 15.** Capacity Utilization: Total Industry, Percentage of Capacity, Monthly, Seasonally Adjusted

Source: St. Louis Fed.

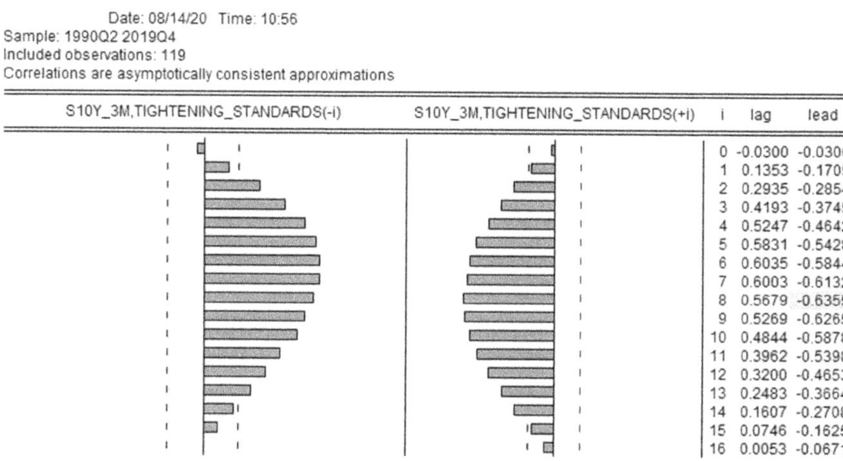

Date: 08/14/20 Time: 10:56
Sample: 1990Q2 2019Q4
Included observations: 119
Correlations are asymptotically consistent approximations

| S10Y_3M,TIGHTENING_STANDARDS(-i) | S10Y_3M,TIGHTENING_STANDARDS(+i) | i | lag | lead |
|---|---|---|---|---|
| | | 0 | -0.0300 | -0.0300 |
| | | 1 | 0.1353 | -0.1705 |
| | | 2 | 0.2935 | -0.2854 |
| | | 3 | 0.4193 | -0.3745 |
| | | 4 | 0.5247 | -0.4642 |
| | | 5 | 0.5831 | -0.5428 |
| | | 6 | 0.6035 | -0.5844 |
| | | 7 | 0.6003 | -0.6132 |
| | | 8 | 0.5679 | -0.6355 |
| | | 9 | 0.5269 | -0.6265 |
| | | 10 | 0.4844 | -0.5878 |
| | | 11 | 0.3962 | -0.5398 |
| | | 12 | 0.3200 | -0.4653 |
| | | 13 | 0.2483 | -0.3664 |
| | | 14 | 0.1607 | -0.2708 |
| | | 15 | 0.0746 | -0.1625 |
| | | 16 | 0.0053 | -0.0671 |

**Appendix 16.** Cross-correlation between Yield spread (10 Years –3 Month Treasury Yield –[Bond Equivalent Basis]) and Net Percentage of Domestic Banks Tightening Standards

Source: Authors' computations; data from St. Louis Fed.

Dependent Variable: RECESSION(2)
Method: ML - Binary Probit (Quadratic hill climbing)
Date: 12/30/19 Time: 14:53
Sample (adjusted): 1961M01 2019M08
Included observations: 704 after adjustments
Convergence achieved after 5 iterations
Covariance matrix computed using second derivatives

| Variable | Coefficient | Std. Error | z-Statistic | Prob. |
|---|---|---|---|---|
| C | -1.426217 | 0.080674 | -17.67884 | 0.0000 |
| PERMITS | -6.544504 | 0.570562 | -11.47027 | 0.0000 |

| | | | |
|---|---|---|---|
| McFadden R-squared | 0.319628 | Mean dependent var | 0.127841 |
| S.D. dependent var | 0.334150 | S.E. of regression | 0.260012 |
| Akaike info criterion | 0.525842 | Sum squared resid | 47.45953 |
| Schwarz criterion | 0.538787 | Log likelihood | -183.0963 |
| Hannan-Quinn criter. | 0.530845 | Deviance | 366.1926 |
| Restr. deviance | 538.2244 | Restr. log likelihood | -269.1122 |
| LR statistic | 172.0318 | Avg. log likelihood | -0.260080 |
| Prob(LR statistic) | 0.000000 | | |

| | | | |
|---|---|---|---|
| Obs with Dep=0 | 614 | Total obs | 704 |
| Obs with Dep=1 | 90 | | |

**Appendix 17.** New Private Housing Units Authorized by Building Permits and Recessions

Source: Authors' computations; data from St. Louis Fed.

Dependent Variable: RECESSION(2)
Method: ML - Binary Probit (Quadratic hill climbing)
Date: 12/30/19 Time: 11:40
Sample (adjusted): 1959M12 2019M08
Included observations: 717 after adjustments
Convergence achieved after 5 iterations
Covariance matrix computed using second derivatives

| Variable | Coefficient | Std. Error | z-Statistic | Prob. |
|---|---|---|---|---|
| C | -1.399169 | 0.079046 | -17.70067 | 0.0000 |
| HOUSING_STARTS | -9.833907 | 0.872058 | -11.27667 | 0.0000 |

| | | | |
|---|---|---|---|
| McFadden R-squared | 0.296113 | Mean dependent var | 0.140865 |
| S.D. dependent var | 0.348125 | S.E. of regression | 0.283742 |
| Akaike info criterion | 0.577881 | Sum squared resid | 57.56414 |
| Schwarz criterion | 0.590643 | Log likelihood | -205.1703 |
| Hannan-Quinn criter. | 0.582809 | Deviance | 410.3407 |
| Restr. deviance | 582.9642 | Restr. log likelihood | -291.4821 |
| LR statistic | 172.6235 | Avg. log likelihood | -0.286151 |
| Prob(LR statistic) | 0.000000 | | |
| Obs with Dep=0 | 616 | Total obs | 717 |
| Obs with Dep=1 | 101 | | |

**Appendix 18.** Privately Owned Housing Starts: 1-Unit Structures and Recessions
Source: Authors' computations; data from St. Louis Fed.

Dependent Variable: RECESSION(2)
Method: ML - Binary Probit (Quadratic hill climbing)
Date: 12/29/19 Time: 01:15
Sample (adjusted): 1963M01 2019M08
Included observations: 680 after adjustments
Convergence achieved after 5 iterations
Covariance matrix computed using second derivatives

| Variable | Coefficient | Std. Error | z-Statistic | Prob. |
|---|---|---|---|---|
| C | -4.475755 | 0.309864 | -14.44424 | 0.0000 |
| MONTHLY_SUPPLY_H | 50.28789 | 4.365247 | 11.52006 | 0.0000 |

| | | | |
|---|---|---|---|
| McFadden R-squared | 0.329889 | Mean dependent var | 0.132353 |
| S.D. dependent var | 0.339124 | S.E. of regression | 0.256185 |
| Akaike info criterion | 0.529688 | Sum squared resid | 44.49781 |
| Schwarz criterion | 0.542988 | Log likelihood | -178.0940 |
| Hannan-Quinn criter. | 0.534836 | Deviance | 356.1879 |
| Restr. deviance | 531.5359 | Restr. log likelihood | -265.7679 |
| LR statistic | 175.3480 | Avg. log likelihood | -0.261903 |
| Prob(LR statistic) | 0.000000 | | |
| Obs with Dep=0 | 590 | Total obs | 680 |
| Obs with Dep=1 | 90 | | |

**Appendix 19.** Monthly supply of houses and Recessions

Source: Authors' computations; data from St. Louis Fed.

Dependent Variable: RECESSION
Method: ML - Binary Probit (Quadratic hill climbing)
Date: 12/29/19 Time: 00:56
Sample: 1968M01 2019M10
Included observations: 622
Convergence achieved after 5 iterations
Covariance matrix computed using second derivatives

| Variable | Coefficient | Std. Error | z-Statistic | Prob. |
|---|---|---|---|---|
| C | -2.057874 | 0.164228 | -12.53058 | 0.0000 |
| INITIAL_CLAIMS | 15.71607 | 1.425203 | 11.02725 | 0.0000 |

| | | | |
|---|---|---|---|
| McFadden R-squared | 0.665066 | Mean dependent var | 0.144695 |
| S.D. dependent var | 0.352076 | S.E. of regression | 0.202779 |
| Akaike info criterion | 0.283351 | Sum squared resid | 25.49402 |
| Schwarz criterion | 0.297605 | Log likelihood | -86.12221 |
| Hannan-Quinn criter. | 0.288891 | Deviance | 172.2444 |
| Restr. deviance | 514.2631 | Restr. log likelihood | -257.1315 |
| LR statistic | 342.0187 | Avg. log likelihood | -0.138460 |
| Prob(LR statistic) | 0.000000 | | |

| | | | |
|---|---|---|---|
| Obs with Dep=0 | 532 | Total obs | 622 |
| Obs with Dep=1 | 90 | | |

**Appendix 20.** Initial claims and Recessions

Source: Authors' computations; data from St. Louis Fed.

Dependent Variable: RECESSION
Method: ML - Binary Probit (Quadratic hill climbing)
Date: 12/31/19 Time: 15:11
Sample (adjusted): 1960M03 2019M10
Included observations: 716 after adjustments
Convergence achieved after 5 iterations
Covariance matrix computed using second derivatives

| Variable | Coefficient | Std. Error | z-Statistic | Prob. |
|---|---|---|---|---|
| C | -2.292446 | 0.165418 | -13.85851 | 0.0000 |
| ADS | -259.5083 | 22.53279 | -11.51692 | 0.0000 |

| | | | |
|---|---|---|---|
| McFadden R-squared | 0.696648 | Mean dependent var | 0.141061 |
| S.D. dependent var | 0.348328 | S.E. of regression | 0.172280 |
| Akaike info criterion | 0.252446 | Sum squared resid | 21.19182 |
| Schwarz criterion | 0.265221 | Log likelihood | -88.37554 |
| Hannan-Quinn criter. | 0.257379 | Deviance | 176.7511 |
| Restr. deviance | 582.6603 | Restr. log likelihood | -291.3301 |
| LR statistic | 405.9092 | Avg. log likelihood | -0.123430 |
| Prob(LR statistic) | 0.000000 | | |

| | | | |
|---|---|---|---|
| Obs with Dep=0 | 615 | Total obs | 716 |
| Obs with Dep=1 | 101 | | |

**Appendix 21.** ADS Index and Recessions

Source: Authors' computations; data from St. Louis Fed.

Dependent Variable: RECESSION
Method: ML - Binary Probit (Quadratic hill climbing)
Date: 02/16/20 Time: 10:49
Sample: 1967M03 2019M10
Included observations: 632
Convergence achieved after 5 iterations
Covariance matrix computed using second derivatives

| Variable | Coefficient | Std. Error | z-Statistic | Prob. |
|---|---|---|---|---|
| CHICAGO_FED_NAT | -153.1680 | 13.91584 | -11.00674 | 0.0000 |
| C | -1.698296 | 0.112391 | -15.11063 | 0.0000 |

| | | | |
|---|---|---|---|
| McFadden R-squared | 0.506831 | Mean dependent var | 0.142405 |
| S.D. dependent var | 0.349742 | S.E. of regression | 0.227914 |
| Akaike info criterion | 0.410043 | Sum squared resid | 32.72524 |
| Schwarz criterion | 0.424121 | Log likelihood | -127.5735 |
| Hannan-Quinn criter. | 0.415510 | Deviance | 255.1470 |
| Restr. deviance | 517.3621 | Restr. log likelihood | -258.6811 |
| LR statistic | 262.2151 | Avg. log likelihood | -0.201857 |
| Prob(LR statistic) | 0.000000 | | |

| | | | |
|---|---|---|---|
| Obs with Dep=0 | 542 | Total obs | 632 |
| Obs with Dep=1 | 90 | | |

**Appendix 22.** CFNAI

Source: Authors' computations, data from St. Louis Fed.

Dependent Variable: RECESSION(1)
Method: ML - Binary Probit (Quadratic hill climbing)
Date: 01/09/20 Time: 13:48
Sample: 1871 1971
Included observations: 101
Convergence achieved after 3 iterations
Covariance matrix computed using second derivatives

| Variable | Coefficient | Std. Error | z-Statistic | Prob. |
|---|---|---|---|---|
| C | 0.067620 | 0.135524 | 0.498953 | 0.6178 |
| LONG_TERM_CPAPER | -46.16408 | 11.45879 | -4.028705 | 0.0001 |

| | | | |
|---|---|---|---|
| McFadden R-squared | 0.137133 | Mean dependent var | 0.574257 |
| S.D. dependent var | 0.496921 | S.E. of regression | 0.455671 |
| Akaike info criterion | 1.216688 | Sum squared resid | 20.55601 |
| Schwarz criterion | 1.268473 | Log likelihood | -59.44277 |
| Hannan-Quinn criter. | 1.237652 | Deviance | 118.8855 |
| Restr. deviance | 137.7797 | Restr. log likelihood | -68.88987 |
| LR statistic | 18.89421 | Avg. log likelihood | -0.588542 |
| Prob(LR statistic) | 0.000014 | | |

| | | | |
|---|---|---|---|
| Obs with Dep=0 | 43 | Total obs | 101 |
| Obs with Dep=1 | 58 | | |

**Appendix 23.** Yield spread, Long-term minus commercial paper

Source: Authors' computations; data from St. Louis Fed and updated time series from Chapter 26 from Shiller, Robert, Market Volatility, 1989.

Dependent Variable: RECESSION(1)
Method: ML - Binary Probit (Quadratic hill climbing)
Date: 02/02/20 Time: 00:48
Sample (adjusted): 1871 2010
Included observations: 140 after adjustments
Convergence achieved after 3 iterations
Covariance matrix computed using second derivatives

| Variable | Coefficient | Std. Error | z-Statistic | Prob. |
|---|---|---|---|---|
| C | -0.039229 | 0.116501 | -0.336731 | 0.7363 |
| LONG_TERM_ONE_YEAR | -51.50669 | 9.475426 | -5.435817 | 0.0000 |

| | | | |
|---|---|---|---|
| McFadden R-squared | 0.197219 | Mean dependent var | 0.500000 |
| S.D. dependent var | 0.501795 | S.E. of regression | 0.438851 |
| Akaike info criterion | 1.141462 | Sum squared resid | 26.57747 |
| Schwarz criterion | 1.183486 | Log likelihood | -77.90236 |
| Hannan-Quinn criter. | 1.158539 | Deviance | 155.8047 |
| Restr. deviance | 194.0812 | Restr. log likelihood | -97.04061 |
| LR statistic | 38.27649 | Avg. log likelihood | -0.556445 |
| Prob(LR statistic) | 0.000000 | | |
| Obs with Dep=0 | 70 | Total obs | 140 |
| Obs with Dep=1 | 70 | | |

**Appendix 24.** Yield spread, long-term minus One year

Source: Authors' computations; data from updated time series from Chapter 26 from Shiller, Robert, *Market Volatility*, 1989.

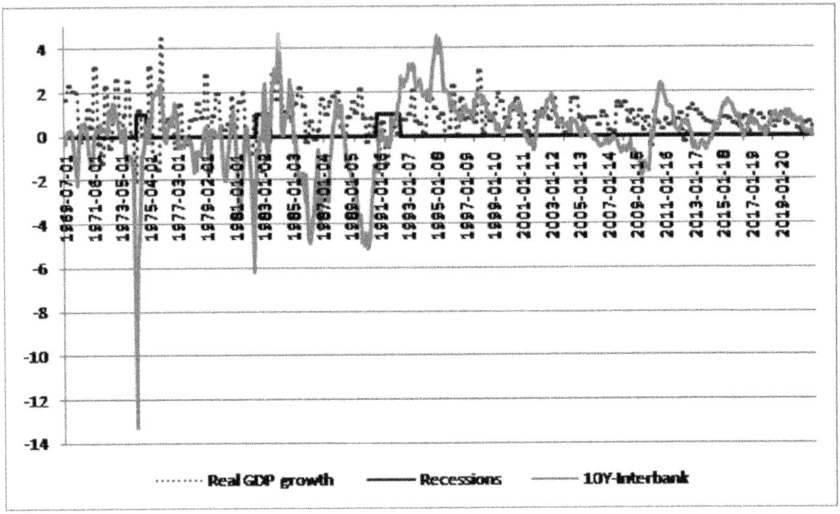


**Appendix 25.** Australia's Real GDP growth (seasonally adjusted, previous quarter), recessions and yield spread (%)

Source: Authors' computations; economic growth, 10-year-long government bond (10Y) and interbank data from OECD and recessions from ECRI.

Dependent Variable: RECESSION(3)
Method: ML - Binary Probit (Quadratic hill climbing)
Date: 06/27/20 Time: 13:09
Sample (adjusted): 1970M01 2019M07
Included observations: 595 after adjustments
Convergence achieved after 5 iterations
Covariance matrix computed using second derivatives

| Variable | Coefficient | Std. Error | z-Statistic | Prob. |
|---|---|---|---|---|
| C | -2.139356 | 0.133149 | -16.06734 | 0.0000 |
| COMMERCIAL_BILL | 197.5484 | 18.98478 | 10.40562 | 0.0000 |

| | | | |
|---|---|---|---|
| McFadden R-squared | 0.315345 | Mean dependent var | 0.144538 |
| S.D. dependent var | 0.351930 | S.E. of regression | 0.287531 |
| Akaike info criterion | 0.572407 | Sum squared resid | 49.02580 |
| Schwarz criterion | 0.587158 | Log likelihood | -168.2911 |
| Hannan-Quinn criter. | 0.578152 | Deviance | 336.5821 |
| Restr. deviance | 491.6083 | Restr. log likelihood | -245.8041 |
| LR statistic | 155.0261 | Avg. log likelihood | -0.282842 |
| Prob(LR statistic) | 0.000000 | | |

| | | | |
|---|---|---|---|
| Obs with Dep=0 | 509 | Total obs | 595 |
| Obs with Dep=1 | 86 | | |

**Appendix 26.** Recession and commercial – bill rates spread (1970M01–2019M10)

Source: Authors' computations; data from St. Louis Fed.

Dependent Variable: RECESSION(3)
Method: ML - Binary Probit (Quadratic hill climbing)
Date: 06/27/20 Time: 13:14
Sample (adjusted): 1976M06 2019M07
Included observations: 518 after adjustments
Convergence achieved after 5 iterations
Covariance matrix computed using second derivatives

| Variable | Coefficient | Std. Error | z-Statistic | Prob. |
|---|---|---|---|---|
| COMMERCIAL_BILL | 174.0272 | 21.63311 | 8.044481 | 0.0000 |
| C | -2.008440 | 0.137592 | -14.59712 | 0.0000 |

| | | | |
|---|---|---|---|
| McFadden R-squared | 0.195773 | Mean dependent var | 0.117761 |
| S.D. dependent var | 0.322636 | S.E. of regression | 0.293205 |
| Akaike info criterion | 0.590689 | Sum squared resid | 44.36016 |
| Schwarz criterion | 0.607098 | Log likelihood | -150.9884 |
| Hannan-Quinn criter. | 0.597118 | Deviance | 301.9768 |
| Restr. deviance | 375.4871 | Restr. log likelihood | -187.7436 |
| LR statistic | 73.51036 | Avg. log likelihood | -0.291483 |
| Prob(LR statistic) | 0.000000 | | |

| | | | |
|---|---|---|---|
| Obs with Dep=0 | 457 | Total obs | 518 |
| Obs with Dep=1 | 61 | | |

**Appendix 27.** Recession and commercial – bill rates spread (1976M06–2019M10)

Source: Authors' computations; data from St. Louis Fed.

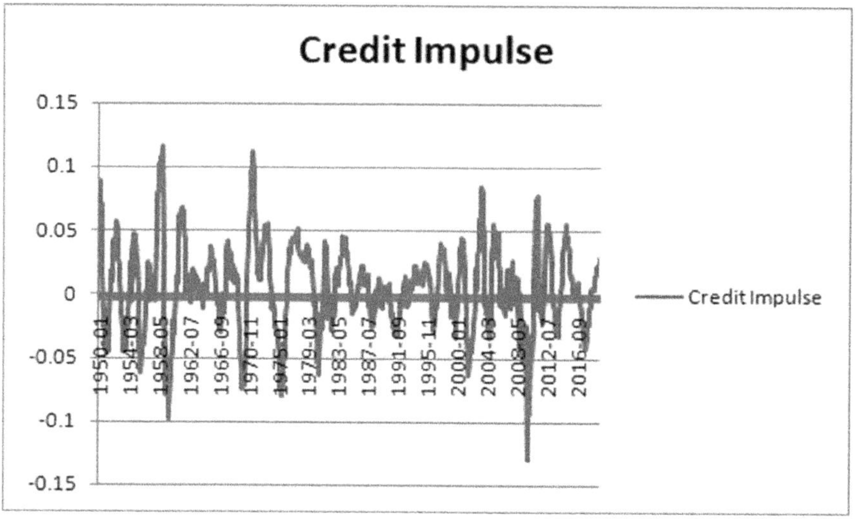


**Appendix 28.** Credit Impulse

Source: Authors' computations; data from FRB H8.

Dependent Variable: RECESSION(1)
Method: ML - Binary Probit (Quadratic hill climbing)
Date: 12/30/19 Time: 04:54
Sample (adjusted): 1954M07 2019M09
Included observations: 783 after adjustments
Convergence achieved after 5 iterations
Covariance matrix computed using second derivatives

| Variable | Coefficient | Std. Error | z-Statistic | Prob. |
|---|---|---|---|---|
| C | -1.090035 | 0.058532 | -18.62301 | 0.0000 |
| CREDIT_IMPULSE | -11.61383 | 1.770431 | -6.559890 | 0.0000 |

| | | | |
|---|---|---|---|
| McFadden R-squared | 0.072490 | Mean dependent var | 0.140485 |
| S.D. dependent var | 0.347712 | S.E. of regression | 0.338736 |
| Akaike info criterion | 0.757957 | Sum squared resid | 89.61371 |
| Schwarz criterion | 0.769868 | Log likelihood | -294.7400 |
| Hannan-Quinn criter. | 0.762537 | Deviance | 589.4801 |
| Restr. deviance | 635.5509 | Restr. log likelihood | -317.7755 |
| LR statistic | 46.07084 | Avg. log likelihood | -0.376424 |
| Prob(LR statistic) | 0.000000 | | |

| | | | |
|---|---|---|---|
| Obs with Dep=0 | 673 | Total obs | 783 |
| Obs with Dep=1 | 110 | | |

**Appendix 29.** Credit Impulse – recession predictor

Source: Authors' computations.

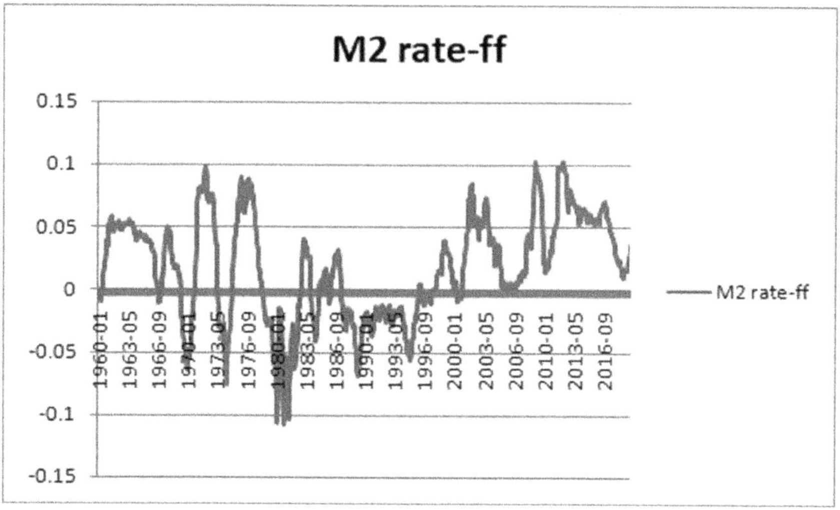


**Appendix 30.** M2-FF

Source: Authors' computations; data from St. Louis Fed.

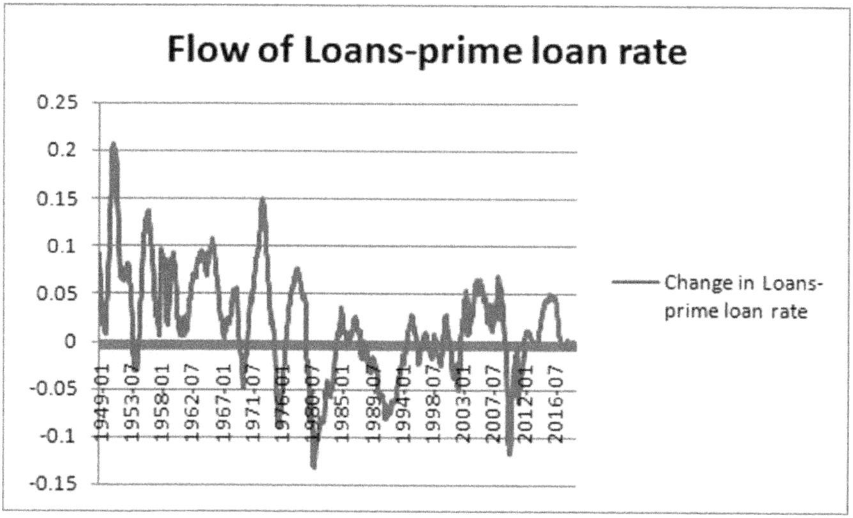


**Appendix 31.** Flow of loans – prime loan rate

Source: Authors' computations; data from St. Louis Fed.

Sample: 1947Q1 2019Q4
Included observations: 291

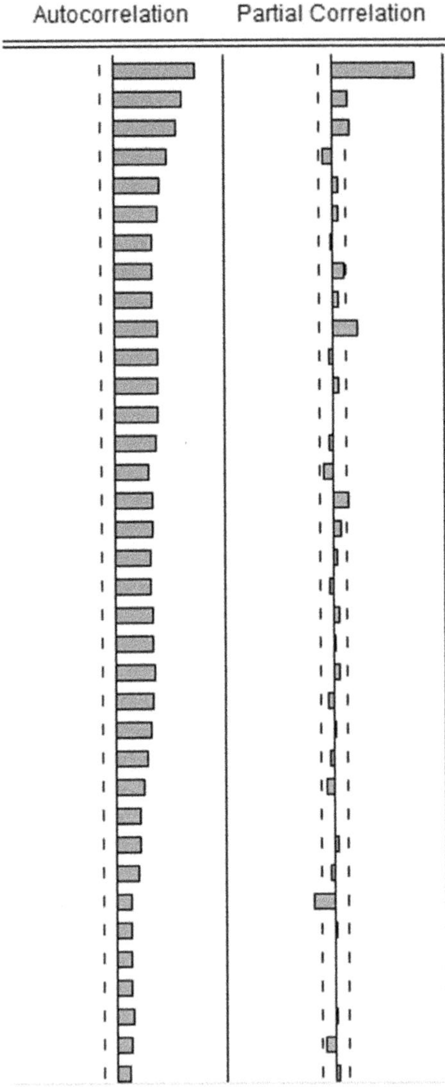


| | AC | PAC | Q-Stat | Prob |
|---|---|---|---|---|
| 1 | 0.771 | 0.771 | 174.64 | 0.000 |
| 2 | 0.652 | 0.143 | 300.13 | 0.000 |
| 3 | 0.605 | 0.162 | 408.67 | 0.000 |
| 4 | 0.496 | -0.098 | 481.89 | 0.000 |
| 5 | 0.437 | 0.046 | 538.83 | 0.000 |
| 6 | 0.412 | 0.061 | 589.64 | 0.000 |
| 7 | 0.354 | -0.022 | 627.23 | 0.000 |
| 8 | 0.353 | 0.108 | 664.77 | 0.000 |
| 9 | 0.358 | 0.057 | 703.55 | 0.000 |
| 10 | 0.421 | 0.242 | 757.22 | 0.000 |
| 11 | 0.423 | -0.026 | 811.62 | 0.000 |
| 12 | 0.422 | 0.046 | 865.97 | 0.000 |
| 13 | 0.425 | -0.000 | 921.45 | 0.000 |
| 14 | 0.393 | -0.025 | 969.09 | 0.000 |
| 15 | 0.334 | -0.084 | 1003.5 | 0.000 |
| 16 | 0.363 | 0.148 | 1044.2 | 0.000 |
| 17 | 0.361 | 0.072 | 1084.9 | 0.000 |
| 18 | 0.349 | 0.041 | 1123.0 | 0.000 |
| 19 | 0.338 | -0.031 | 1158.7 | 0.000 |
| 20 | 0.356 | 0.064 | 1198.6 | 0.000 |
| 21 | 0.356 | 0.013 | 1238.5 | 0.000 |
| 22 | 0.378 | 0.052 | 1283.9 | 0.000 |
| 23 | 0.365 | -0.052 | 1326.2 | 0.000 |
| 24 | 0.350 | 0.010 | 1365.4 | 0.000 |
| 25 | 0.309 | -0.036 | 1395.9 | 0.000 |
| 26 | 0.265 | -0.082 | 1418.4 | 0.000 |
| 27 | 0.241 | -0.000 | 1437.2 | 0.000 |
| 28 | 0.237 | 0.031 | 1455.3 | 0.000 |
| 29 | 0.206 | -0.029 | 1469.1 | 0.000 |
| 30 | 0.150 | -0.190 | 1476.5 | 0.000 |
| 31 | 0.132 | 0.019 | 1482.2 | 0.000 |
| 32 | 0.138 | 0.007 | 1488.4 | 0.000 |
| 33 | 0.131 | 0.000 | 1494.2 | 0.000 |
| 34 | 0.159 | 0.014 | 1502.6 | 0.000 |
| 35 | 0.133 | -0.086 | 1508.5 | 0.000 |
| 36 | 0.122 | 0.027 | 1513.5 | 0.000 |

**Appendix 32.** PCE Inflation Rate, Quarterly, Seasonally Adjusted

Source: Authors' computations; data from St. Louis Fed.

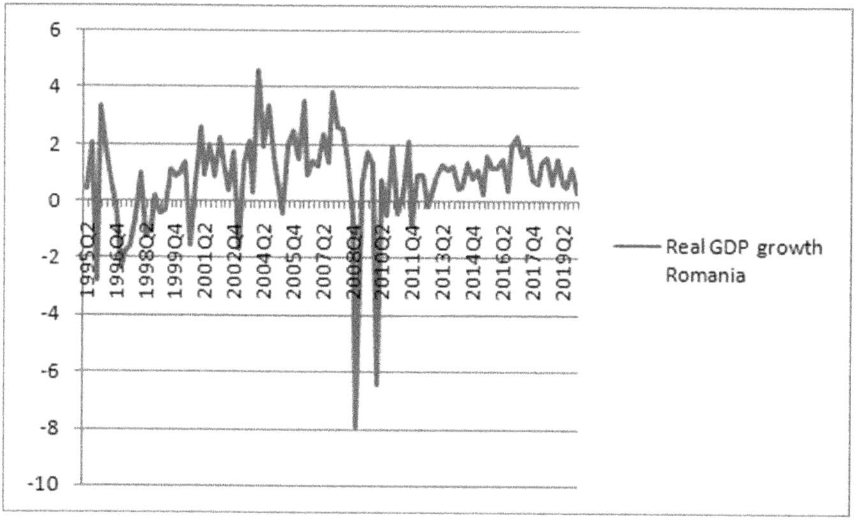


**Appendix 33.** Real GDP growth Romania

Source: Authors' computations; data from INSSE.

Null Hypothesis: REAL_INTEREST_RATE has a unit root
Exogenous: Constant
Lag Length: 13 (Automatic - based on SIC, maxlag=19)

| | | t-Statistic | Prob.* |
|---|---|---|---|
| Augmented Dickey-Fuller test statistic | | -2.316200 | 0.1671 |
| Test critical values: | 1% level | -3.439205 | |
| | 5% level | -2.865338 | |
| | 10% level | -2.568849 | |

*MacKinnon (1996) one-sided p-values.

**Appendix 34.** Real interest rate stationarity

Source: Authors' computations; data from St. Louis Fed.

Date: 06/17/20 Time: 11:10
Sample: 1959Q2 2019Q3
Included observations: 242
Correlations are asymptotically consistent approximations

| FED_FUNDS,NOMINAL_GDP(-i) | FED_FUNDS,NOMINAL_GDP(+i) | i | lag | lead |
|---|---|---|---|---|

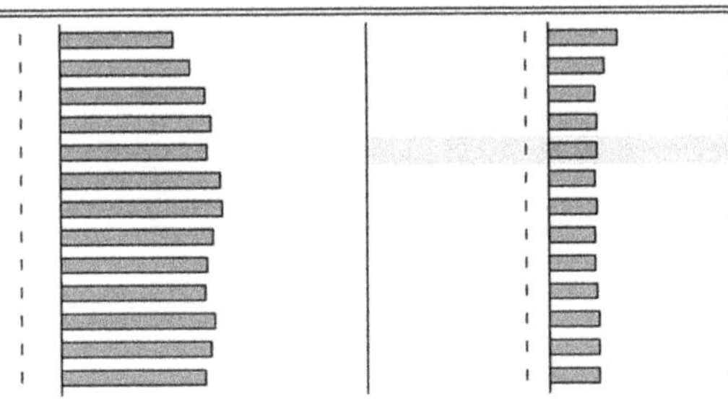

| i | lag | lead |
|---|---|---|
| 0 | 0.3858 | 0.3858 |
| 1 | 0.4497 | 0.3081 |
| 2 | 0.4929 | 0.2550 |
| 3 | 0.5107 | 0.2700 |
| 4 | 0.5071 | 0.2653 |
| 5 | 0.5420 | 0.2607 |
| 6 | 0.5535 | 0.2633 |
| 7 | 0.5242 | 0.2550 |
| 8 | 0.5017 | 0.2579 |
| 9 | 0.4942 | 0.2677 |
| 10 | 0.5267 | 0.2749 |
| 11 | 0.5111 | 0.2828 |
| 12 | 0.4921 | 0.2772 |

**Appendix 35.** Cross-correlations, Nominal GDP, and Federal Funds rate
Source: Authors' computations; data from BEA and St. Louis Fed

Date: 06/17/20 Time: 11:12
Sample: 1959Q2 2019Q3
Included observations: 242
Correlations are asymptotically consistent approximations

| PCE_CORE_INFLATION,FED_FUNDS(-i) | PCE_CORE_INFLATION,FED_FUNDS(+i) | i | lag | lead |
|---|---|---|---|---|

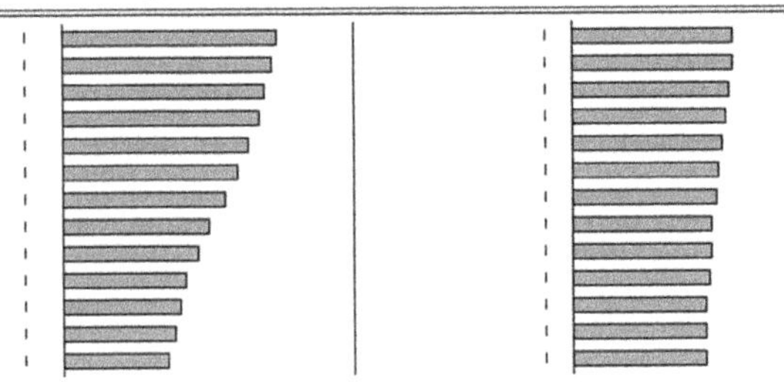

| i | lag | lead |
|---|---|---|
| 0 | 0.7671 | 0.7671 |
| 1 | 0.7493 | 0.7638 |
| 2 | 0.7272 | 0.7504 |
| 3 | 0.7017 | 0.7360 |
| 4 | 0.6684 | 0.7208 |
| 5 | 0.6278 | 0.7038 |
| 6 | 0.5823 | 0.6966 |
| 7 | 0.5308 | 0.6712 |
| 8 | 0.4878 | 0.6589 |
| 9 | 0.4479 | 0.6491 |
| 10 | 0.4195 | 0.6373 |
| 11 | 0.4089 | 0.6382 |
| 12 | 0.3818 | 0.6382 |

**Appendix 36.** Cross-correlations, PCE core inflation, and Federal Funds rate
Source: Authors' computations; data from BEA and St. Louis Fed

## Appendix 37. Colored figures

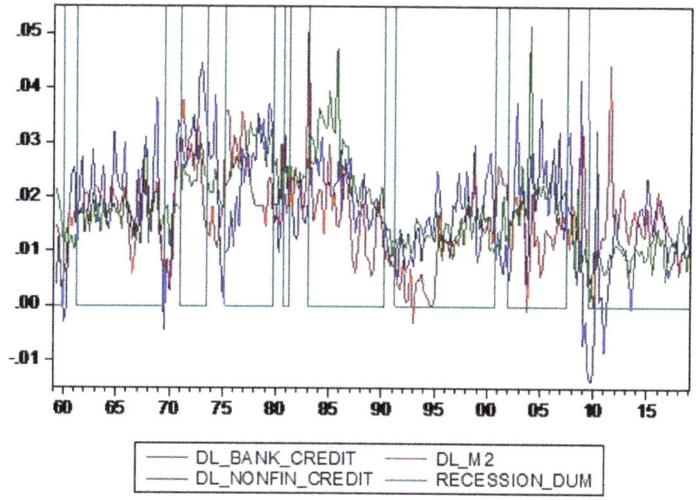


**Figure 13.** Bank Credit, Nonfinancial Credit, Money and Recessions

Source: Authors' computations, M2 from H3, Bank credit from H8 and Nonfinancial credit from Federal Reserve database, all data is seasonally adjusted, quarterly frequency

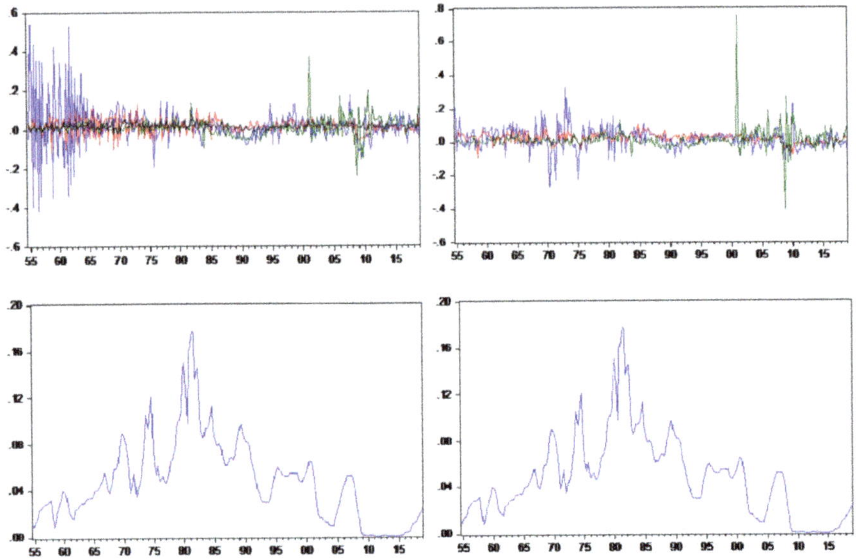


**Figure 17.** Evolution of financial credit

Source: Authors' computations

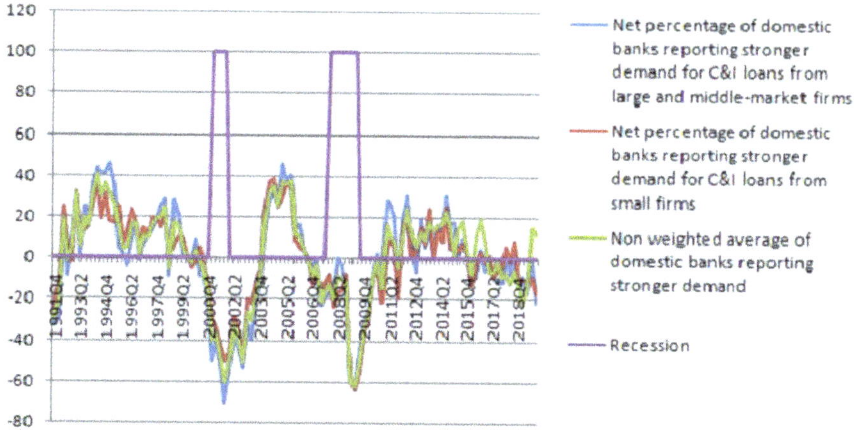


**Figure 38.** Recessions and demand for loans

Source: Authors' computations, data from FRB, Senior Loan Officer Opinion Survey on Bank Lending Practices

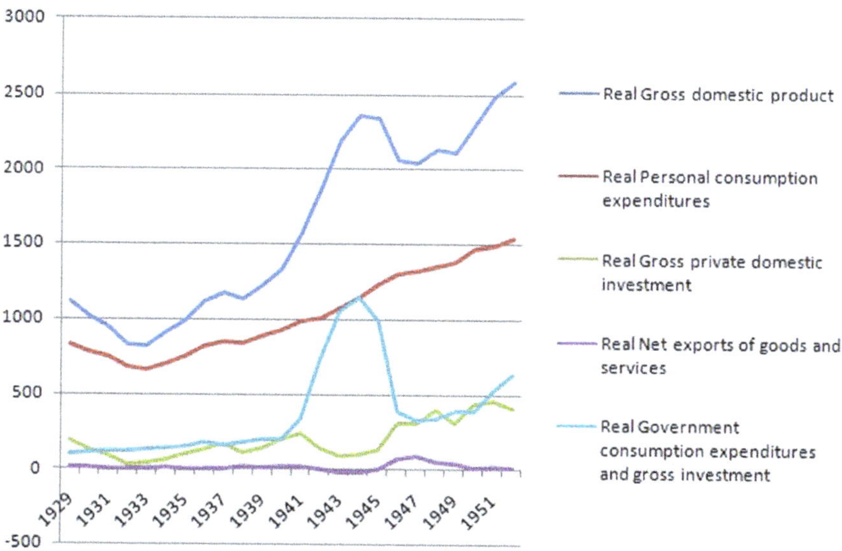


**Figure 66.** Real GDP and its components

Source: Authors' computations, data from BEA

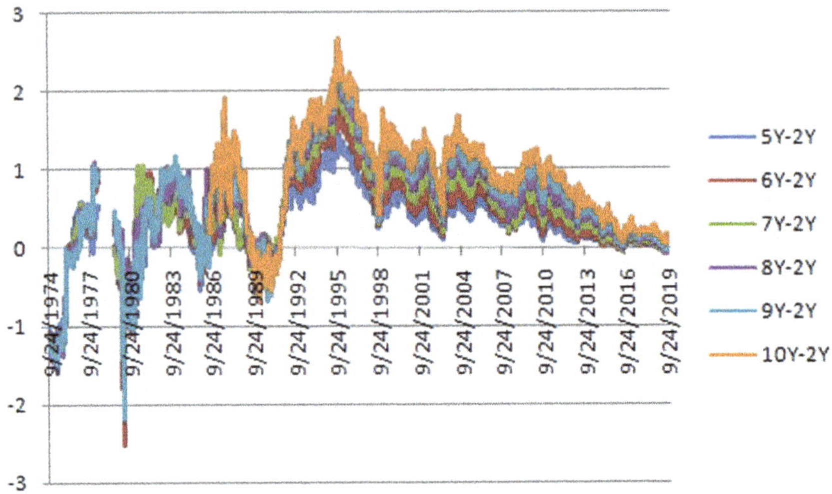


**Figure 68.** Yield Spreads, Japan

Source: Authors' computations, data from Finance Ministry, Japan

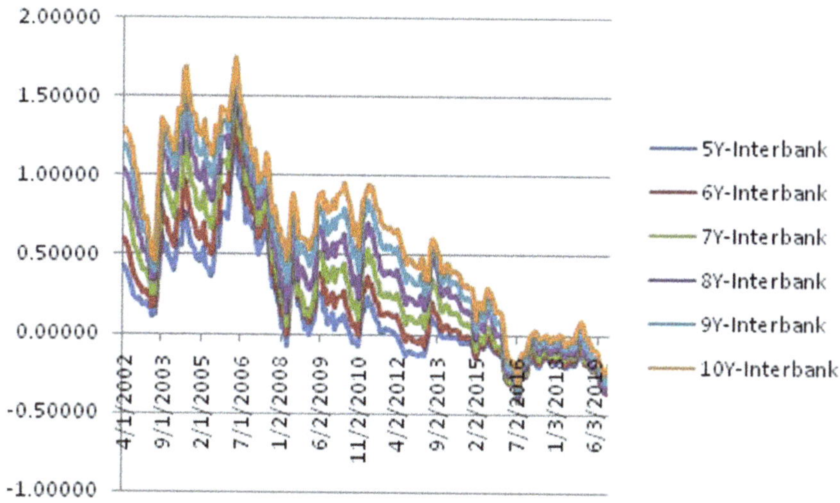


**Figure 69.** Yield Spreads for Japan with the short end of the yield spread being the Interbank Rate

Source: Authors' computations, data from Finance Ministry, Japan and OECD, 3-Month or 90-day Rates and Yields: Interbank Rates for Japan [IR3TIB01JPM156N] from FRED

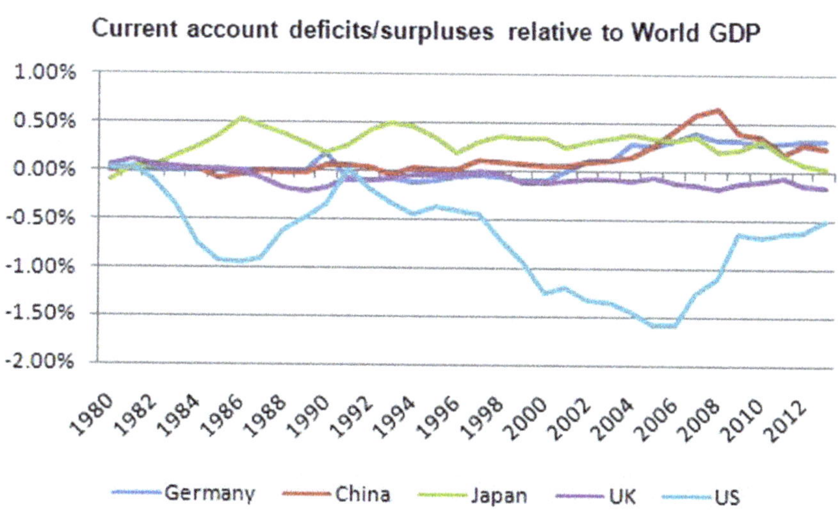


**Figure 111.** Current Account deficit of US

Source: Dragoe (2016)

# List of Appendixes

# List of Figures

# List of Tables

www.ingramcontent.com/pod-product-compliance
Ingram Content Group UK Ltd.
Pitfield, Milton Keynes, MK11 3LW, UK
UKHW020710041026
15590UKWH00002B/590

9 783631 876947